DEBATING RELIGIOUS LIBERTY
AND DISCRIMINATION

Debating Religious Liberty and Discrimination

JOHN CORVINO
RYAN T. ANDERSON
SHERIF GIRGIS

OXFORD
UNIVERSITY PRESS

OXFORD
UNIVERSITY PRESS

Oxford University Press is a department of the University of Oxford. It furthers the University's objective of excellence in research, scholarship, and education by publishing worldwide. Oxford is a registered trade mark of Oxford University Press in the UK and certain other countries.

Published in the United States of America by Oxford University Press
198 Madison Avenue, New York, NY 10016, United States of America.

CIP data is on file at the Library of Congress
ISBN 978–0–19–060306–9 (hardcover)
ISBN 978–0–19–060307–6 (paperback)

3 5 7 9 8 6 4 2

Paperback printed by Sheridan Books, Inc., United States of America
Hardback printed by Bridgeport National Bindery, Inc., United States of America

For Robert P. George
—Ryan T. Anderson and Sherif Girgis

For my nieces and nephew: Tess, Hadley, Preston,
Devyn, and Layla
—John Corvino

CONTENTS

1

Introduction

New Challenges, Old Questions

RYAN T. ANDERSON, JOHN CORVINO,
AND SHERIF GIRGIS

■■■

IT MIGHT SEEM PUZZLING THAT the three of us have joined to produce a point-counterpoint book on "religious liberty and discrimination." Isn't everyone in favor of religious liberty, and everyone against discrimination?

Well, yes and yes, sort of. Certainly, all three of us endorse religious liberty, and all three of us oppose unjust discrimination. We are all protolerance and antibigotry. But the devil is in the details, and these topics are rich with controversial details. So although we divide the book into two sides—with Anderson and Girgis coauthoring in one voice, opposite Corvino—these issues allow myriad positions. Of course, the same is true of other controversial issues: the existence of God, say, or affirmative action, or immigration. But the debate over religious liberty and discrimination is especially difficult to frame in pro-versus-con, or conservative-versus-liberal format.

We say this even apart from our shared distaste for the typical "with us or against us" polarization that plagues most public debate today. One reason is that our topic covers a variety of difficult and to some extent independent questions: about the place of religion in a free society, the role of government, the public/private distinction, the limits of tolerance, the nature of bigotry, and so on. It also depends more than usual on hard-to-answer empirical and prudential questions, and insights from a range of disciplines (law, philosophy, and history, among others). Moreover, the conflicts suggest numerous remedies, both legal and social: Sometimes they call for passing or changing laws, or granting exemptions from existing laws; sometimes they call for social pressure of various sorts. And they pose questions for actors at multiple levels: government leaders, business owners, employees, customers, voters, and so on.

The three of us came to know one another in the context of the same-sex marriage debate, in which we have been active participants: Corvino, a same-sex-marriage advocate, was the counterpoint-author with Maggie Gallagher of the book *Debating Same-Sex Marriage*; and Anderson and Girgis, advocates of a traditional understanding of marriage, were the coauthors with Robert P. George of the book *What Is Marriage? Man and Woman: A Defense*. All three of us wrote articles, gave talks, attended conferences, and participated in debates—sometimes with each other. Through that process, we came to know and respect one another, even as we sharply disagreed.

Then, on June 26, 2015, the U.S. Supreme Court rendered its same-sex marriage decision in *Obergefell v. Hodges*. Proponents cheered what they viewed as a victory for equality in all fifty states.[1] Opponents decried what they viewed as an unlawful judicial redefinition of marriage.[2] The marriage debate, which had already begun to shift, now shifted more dramatically. The most pressing question became not "Should government recognize same-sex marriage?" but instead "Now that same-sex couples are marrying, while a significant portion of the country remains opposed, how can we all peacefully coexist?"

In particular, conflicts arose when those with religious objections to same-sex marriages were asked to recognize, facilitate, or otherwise lend support to them: when county clerks were asked to issue marriage licenses to same-sex couples, for example; or when photographers, bakers, florists, and other business owners were asked to provide services for same-sex weddings. Although such conflicts were not directly a function of *Obergefell*—they had arisen beforehand, and they typically have more to do with antidiscrimination law than with marriage law—they quickly became the new frontier in the ongoing "culture wars." Hence our dual focus on "religious liberty" and "discrimination."

Of course such conflicts are not limited to same-sex marriage or to LGBT (lesbian, gay, bisexual, and transgender) issues: They arise whenever people have conscientious objections to laws and policies that bind them. They have a longstanding history, reaching back in the United States to colonial times, when pacifist Quakers sought exemptions from serving in the militia. In the last century, they arose when Amish citizens fought successfully to be exempt from mandatory schooling past eighth grade and unsuccessfully to be exempt from paying Social Security taxes. More recently, they have arisen with respect to abortion, contraception, sex or gender reassignment therapies, and other medical services—not only for doctors and other healthcare workers who object to participating in them but also for large corporations whose owners object to providing employees with health insurance that covers them. They arise when Muslim prisoners seek to wear beards that exceed permitted lengths, or when Sikhs seek exemptions from helmet laws so that they may wear their turbans or from weapons regulations so that they may carry their kirpans (ceremonial daggers). In an increasingly diverse, interconnected, and legally complex society, they seem to be arising more frequently.

4 | DEBATING RELIGIOUS LIBERTY AND DISCRIMINATION

In this book we explore such conflicts. In point-counterpoint format, we debate various questions concerning religious liberty, tolerance, and discrimination. Although we focus largely on the United States, each side aims to articulate principles with broader resonance. And although many of the conflicts have legal implications, this book is not only about the law or the Constitution: It's also about how everyday citizens should approach religious and moral diversity. Many who have written previously about these issues are lawyers and legal scholars (as is one of us). In what follows, however, we are as concerned with philosophical questions as with legal ones. Indeed, a big part of what interests us about this topic is how it lies at the intersection of morality, law, and public policy.

Among the specific questions we will explore are the following: When, if ever, should citizens receive exemptions from neutral, generally applicable laws? Do religion and conscience require separate protection under their own civil liberty, and if so, why? Should we give religious conscience greater weight than nonreligious conscience when contemplating exemptions and accommodations? How should we think about the federal Religious Freedom Restoration Act (RFRA, pronounced "riff-ra"), which was passed by Congress in 1993 and has since inspired similar laws at the state level? What are the benefits and hazards of moral and religious pluralism, and how should we manage them? What is discrimination? What makes it invidious or unjust, and when should it be illegal? What kinds of material, social, and dignitary harms should we use the law to fight? Should antidiscrimination laws cover sexual orientation and gender identity (SOGI)? How should the government treat hospitals, schools, adoption agencies, and other institutions whose religious commitments conflict with antidiscrimination laws, healthcare mandates, or other legal regulations? Beyond the law, what is the appropriate role of social pressure with respect to these various questions? How should we treat religious beliefs and practices with which we strongly differ: Should we celebrate them, tolerate them, or actively discourage them?

The two sides in this book differ sharply on many of these questions, although there are interesting points of agreement as well. The point-counterpoint format allows us to engage each other rigorously, clarifying and refining our respective positions. Overall, our hope is to contribute constructively to an ongoing public conversation. With that in mind, we have attempted to frame things in a manner that is accessible enough for wide audiences—voters, politicians, students, and ordinary citizens of various stripes—but also detailed enough to be of interest to opinion leaders and academic specialists. And we touch on policy questions as much as ongoing academic debates. The notes provide references and occasionally additional commentary or suggestions for further reading.

The book is organized as follows. Each side begins with an opening essay. Corvino's essay explores the worry that religious liberty is today morphing into religious privilege, favoring not only religious citizens over their secular counterparts but also certain kinds of (usually conservative Christian) religion over others. He sees this trend as a repeat of the Puritan mistake, in which religious liberty means liberty to do things according to the dictates of preferred religious traditions. After determining that the best reason for religious accommodations and exemptions is religion's historical tendency to be a site of conflict, he argues that religious liberty should not be used as a license to discriminate. He also raises a number of questions about the moral and legal consistency of current approaches, and he explores the meaning and rhetorical function of accusations of bigotry.

Anderson and Girgis's essay argues that it is progressives who commit the Puritan mistake today, by seeking not simply to ensure access to same-sex marriage or services like abortion but to press private parties into service in an illiberal attempt to stifle dissent. Offering theoretical accounts of the values served by religious liberty and antidiscrimination, and general frameworks for analyzing particular claims based on each, they argue that we can achieve "win-win" outcomes by respecting the moral and religious liberty claims in this debate without undoing anyone's legitimate policy goals. They also suggest that those who deny this tend to overlook the ways in which respect for people's conscience and religion makes structurally different demands—and thus require a different form of protection—from respect for other interests; the benefits religious liberty offers believers and nonbelievers alike; and the role it plays in preserving other civil liberties and valuable forms of pluralism. After these essays, each side offers a critical reply to the other.

As noted, all three of us aim to formulate moral principles with broad, crosscultural relevance. That said, the book was inspired by conflicts arising in the United States, and we think it is important to situate these conflicts in their historical setting. Therefore, in the remainder of this Introduction, we quickly review some of the relevant U.S. history, up to and including RFRA. Our essays and replies will take for granted familiarity with some of this information—especially with RFRA and the Supreme Court cases that preceded it.

1.1 RELIGIOUS FREEDOM IN THE UNITED STATES: A BRIEF HISTORY

Most American schoolchildren are taught that the Pilgrims came over on the *Mayflower* in search of religious liberty. That is half true. The Pilgrims, and later the Puritans, came to this land to escape religious persecution—only to then turn around and practice their own brand of religious persecution. The result was a messy and sometimes bloody history of intolerance in the name of God's will.

The colonists' intolerance extended not only to the Native "heathens" but also to those who practiced Christianity in the "wrong" way. The Pilgrims persecuted other Protestants in Plymouth County. So did the leaders of the Massachusetts Bay Colony, the City on a Hill. Under Governor John Winthrop it sent Roger Williams into exile, where he then established Rhode Island as a religiously tolerant place. Over time, however, Rhode Island went on to forbid Jews to vote.

It was worse for the Quakers. In 1656, Massachusetts Bay Colony forbade Quakers from coming in, with flogging as a punishment. When the Quakers persisted, the Colony upped the penalties—for men, losing one ear for a first offense and the other for a second; for women, whipping for first and second offenses; and for both, boring through the tongue for a third offense. Several Quakers lost ears. But that didn't stop them. The colony upped the penalty to death for a fourth offense. Two Quakers were hanged in the fall of 1659. And on June 1, 1660, Mary Dyer was hanged in Boston Common. This captured the attention of the king, who promptly put an end to the practice.

Quakers and Jews weren't the only ones persecuted; so were Catholics. Maryland was established by the Catholic George Calvert. Calvert, a personal friend of King Charles (who himself was married to a Catholic, Henrietta Maria), used that connection to obtain a charter for a colony where Catholics could practice their faith openly. They named it Maryland—for the Blessed Virgin Mary and Queen Henrietta Maria. In the 1630s it thrived. But by 1690, the Church of England was the established church in Maryland and Catholics couldn't worship publicly.

In short, when it comes to colonial America, religious persecution—in the sense of persecution both *based in* religion and *aimed at* religion—was as American as apple pie.

Against this checkered backdrop, the U.S. Constitution stands as a remarkable achievement. Discussions of religious liberty and the Constitution usually focus on the First Amendment, about which we'll say more. But it's important to recognize that the Constitution's protections for religious liberty go farther and deeper. One of the first things the founders did was to ensure that there would be no religious test for office. They thus opened the way for full political participation for Catholics and Jews, at least at the federal level. (Unfortunately, well into the 1800s some states had laws banning Jews and Catholics from public office.) Likewise, the Constitution allowed for an alternative to oath-taking, thus allowing Quakers to be full participants; this rule applied to the states as well.

But perhaps the most important way the Constitution protects religious freedom is in the general way it aims to protect all freedom: through federalism and the separation of powers. The founders sought to protect everyone against government's excesses by limiting the federal government's power and by curtailing the power of any one faction to overtake the system.

This close connection between civil liberties, religious liberties, and limits on government power is reflected in the combination of rights reinforced by the First Amendment, passed by the first Congress and ratified soon thereafter. Its text reads as follows: "Congress shall make no law respecting an establishment of religion, or prohibiting the free exercise thereof; or abridging the freedom of speech, or of the press; or the right of the people peaceably to assemble, and to petition the Government for a redress of grievances." The first two clauses—the establishment clause and the free exercise clause—quite obviously protect religious liberty, but so do the clauses guaranteeing freedom of speech, freedom of the press, the right to assemble, and the right to petition government. These freedoms work together.

Of course, there are controversies over what precisely these guarantees entail—controversies that have occupied the courts for generations and that persist through many of the arguments of this book. Take, for example, the establishment clause.

Everyone understands that clause to prohibit the government from making laws that specifically prohibit or mandate religious acts; theological correctness is never enough to justify law. The founders wanted not only to protect people's freedom to practice religion (or not) as they saw fit but also to protect religion from what they viewed as the corrupting influence of government. The establishment clause thus precludes the government from either forcing people to go to church or preventing them from going to church. It precludes the government from telling a synagogue whom it should or shouldn't appoint as rabbi—or from forcing anyone to fund the synagogue or the rabbi. It also precludes the government from favoring certain religions over others—by giving tax breaks only to Christian churches, for example.

But does the establishment clause preclude the government from giving *any* aid to religion—say, by giving tax breaks to religious congregations on a neutral basis, or by funding faith-based programs? That question is a matter of some controversy.

Next, consider the free exercise clause, which is at the root of many of the conflicts covered in this book. The clause states that the government may make no law "prohibiting the free exercise of" religion. The government cannot, for example, do what the Massachusetts Bay Colony did to the Quakers. It cannot outlaw any religion or interfere with religious practice per se.

Yet there are limits on the constitutional guarantee. The Aztecs once exercised religion by ripping out people's hearts in human sacrifice, but don't try this today. Sometimes religious exercise conflicts with important governmental interests, and when it does, the law may restrict it. In order to be constitutionally permissible under current Supreme Court precedents, such restrictions must stem from otherwise *neutral, generally applicable* laws. Laws against killing are neutral with respect to religion: They weren't passed to target the Aztecs or any other religious sect. By contrast, France's law banning facial covering was expressly designed to prohibit the burka or the niqab (veils worn by Muslim women); such a law is not neutral in its intent, even though it is worded neutrally.[3] Relatedly, a hypothetical law that stated "No Muslims may wear facial coverings" would not be *generally applicable.*

Or consider the case of *Church of the Lukumi Babalu Aye v. City of Hialeah* (1993).[4] After a Santerían Church announced its intention to locate in Hialeah, Florida, the city council passed an ordinance prohibiting the slaughter of animals "in a public or private ritual or ceremony not for the primary purpose of food consumption." The ordinance clearly targeted the Santeríans, who occasionally practice animal sacrifice. The U.S. Supreme Court unanimously struck down the ordinance as an unconstitutional violation of the free exercise clause.[5]

It's not just Santeríans who have been targeted by laws that are neutral on their face but discriminatory in their underlying intent. In November 1922, Oregon voters passed an initiative requiring all students to attend public schools, with the ostensible rationale of promoting shared American values. The real target, however, was parochial schools: Oregonians wanted to limit the influence of recent Catholic immigrants. The initiative was part of a second (or third, depending on how you count) wave of American anti-Catholicism, fueled largely by the Ku Klux Klan.

A Catholic school in Oregon challenged the law all the way up to the U.S. Supreme Court. In what became an iconic decision, *Pierce v. Society of Sisters* (1925), the Court unanimously struck down the Oregon initiative as a violation of parents' liberty to decide what sort of education was best for their children.[6]

Even genuinely neutral laws may sometimes give way to religious exercise. Indeed, some such accommodations even predate the Constitution. Few things are more important to a fledgling nation than national defense and military service, yet religious pacifists have been accommodated ever since colonial times. On July 18, 1775, during the height of the War for Independence, the Continental Congress declared: "As there are some people, who, from religious principles, cannot bear arms in any case, this Congress intend no violence to their consciences, but earnestly recommend it to them, to contribute liberally in this time of universal calamity, to the relief of their distressed brethren in the several colonies, and to do all other services to their oppressed Country, which they can consistently with their religious principles."[7] A century and a half later, when conscription was first instituted as a result of World War I, the Selective Draft Act of 1917 specifically exempted "any well-recognized religious sect or organization at present organized and existing whose creed or principles forbid its members to participate in war in any form."[8] In 1940, Congress broadened these protections to include anyone "who, by reason of religious training and belief, is conscientiously opposed to participation to war in any form."[9]

Conscription in war may be a unique case (for reasons Corvino discusses in his main essay). At other times, however, the government has been less accommodating of religious conviction. Consider *Reynolds v. United States* (1878), a case involving a Mormon in the Utah territory convicted of bigamy.[10] George Reynolds believed that it was his religious duty to take multiple wives, circumstances permitting; that this duty was enjoined by God and revealed in the Bible; and that failure to perform it would result in his eternal damnation.[11] Nevertheless, the U.S. Supreme Court unanimously upheld his conviction.

Writing for the Court, Chief Justice Morrison Waite distinguished between religious belief, which is beyond the reach of the law, and religious practices, which are not necessarily so: "Can a man excuse his [illegal] practices . . . because of his religious belief? To permit this would be to make the professed doctrines of religious belief superior to the law of the land, and in effect to permit every citizen to become a law unto himself."[12]

The belief/practice distinction in *Reynolds* is somewhat puzzling. If the free exercise of religion merely involved freedom of belief, how could the law ever prevent it? After all, laws only regulate behavior. The question posed by *Reynolds*—and indeed, much free exercise clause jurisprudence—is about the extent to which religious practice may excuse some individuals from laws that validly restrict the conduct of others. It's also worth noting that *Reynolds* was decided during, and was doubtless colored by, a strong wave of anti-Mormon sentiment.

The high-water mark of free exercise jurisprudence is widely identified with two decisions: *Sherbert v. Verner* (1963)[13] and *Yoder v. Wisconsin* (1972).[14] Adell Sherbert worked for a textile mill that switched from a five- to a six-day work week and thus required Saturday work, which violated her beliefs as a Seventh-Day Adventist. The South Carolina Employment Commission denied Sherbert unemployment benefits, on the grounds that she had "failed, without good cause . . . to accept available suitable work when offered."[15] But the U.S. Supreme Court reversed their denial, finding that the law unconstitutionally burdened her free exercise of religion. Writing for the majority, Justice William Brennan opined that "[South Carolina's] ruling forces her to choose between following the precepts of her religion and forfeiting benefits, on the one hand, and abandoning one of the precepts of her religion in order to accept work, on the other hand. Governmental imposition of such a choice puts the same kind of burden upon the free exercise of religion as would a fine imposed against appellant for her Saturday worship."[16] Note that South Carolina explicitly exempted Sunday worshippers from being denied benefits for refusing Sunday work.

The Court's ruling gave rise to what eventually came to be known as the *Sherbert* test. According to this test, the government violates people's First Amendment rights whenever it substantially burdens their sincere religious beliefs, unless the burden is necessary for achieving a "compelling" state interest. This standard, closely related to what is elsewhere known as "strict scrutiny," imposes a high constitutional bar for applying restrictions that burden certain fundamental legal rights.

Nine years later, the Court decided *Wisconsin v. Yoder* (1972). At issue was a Wisconsin law that required all students to attend school until age sixteen. Amish parents believed that education beyond the eighth grade was a threat to their agrarian way of life and a danger to their children's eternal salvation (by exposing them to worldly influences), and they challenged the law. They won: All nine justices held that the additional required years substantially burdened the Amish people's sincere religious beliefs without adequate justification. (Justice Douglas filed a partial dissent, noting that the Amish children's interests deserved more attention in the case.) *Yoder* exempts the Amish, and only the Amish, from compulsory education past the eighth grade.

Sherbert and *Yoder* stand out in part because they are among the rare instances when the Court ruled in favor of challengers in free exercise cases during that period. The Court considered various other religious liberty cases between 1960 and 1990, and in the vast majority, it denied the requested exemptions: The government, after all, can successfully justify certain burdens on the free exercise of religion. In the "Blue Laws Cases"—*Gallagher v. Crown Kosher Market, McGowan v. Maryland,* and *Braunfeld v. Brown* (all 1961)—the Court ruled that laws requiring businesses to close on Sunday were constitutional, even though they financially disadvantaged business owners who observed a Saturday sabbath. In *United States v. Lee* (1982), the Court held that even Amish employers must pay Social Security taxes, underscoring the point that "the state may justify a limitation on religious liberty by showing that it is essential to accomplish an overriding governmental interest" (the *Sherbert* test).[17] With the exception of *Yoder*, a few unemployment cases like *Sherbert*, and a case striking down a Tennessee law that prohibited ministers or priests from holding public office,[18] the Court generally deferred to state legislatures' judgment.

The next big moment in Supreme Court free exercise jurisprudence is *Employment Division v. Smith* (1990), the infamous "peyote case."[19] Alfred Smith and his coworker Galen Black were Oregon alcohol counselors who tested positive for drugs as a result of ingesting peyote, a plant-based hallucinogen, for Native American sacramental purposes. They were subsequently denied unemployment benefits on the grounds of "misconduct": Peyote, which contains mescaline, was illegal in Oregon at the time.

Their case garnered considerable public sympathy. The two were drug counselors, not drug addicts. Peyote is not a "gateway drug." Its use had long been a ritual practice of the Native American Church, a peaceful minority religion. Moreover, the United States has a history of granting exemptions for intoxicating substances used for sacramental purposes: During the Prohibition era, for example, communion wine was permitted. Smith, the lead figure in the case, had a compelling personal story.[20] It thus shocked and angered many observers when the U.S. Supreme Court ruled against Smith and Black.

It is worth pausing to note that the role of the Court is not to determine whether a law is good and wise, but whether it is constitutional. Of course, sometimes these questions can't be completely teased apart. That said, there are times when the Court essentially declares: We grant that this law may be unnecessary or even silly, but it's not unconstitutional, and so we're going to uphold it. And that is what the Court did in *Smith*.

Writing for the majority, Justice Antonin Scalia acknowledges that it is "not surprising that a number of States have made an exception to their drug laws for sacramental peyote use."[21] But to say that such exceptions are permitted or desirable is not the same as saying that they're constitutionally required. Oregon's peyote prohibition was part of a neutral, generally applicable law; it was not created to target the Native American Church. (Contrast that with Oregon's education law of the 1920s and how it targeted Catholics.)

Scalia struggles somewhat in his opinion to reconcile *Smith* with *Sherbert* and *Yoder*. He argues, convincingly enough, that Sherbert involved a "context that lent itself to individualized governmental assessment of the reasons for the relevant conduct"—namely, the context of employment compensation. That's quite different from asking the Court to grant exemptions from an across-the-board criminal prohibition. He treats *Yoder* as a unique case, involving a "hybrid right" of religious and parental liberty. But in Smith's case, he concludes that the controlling principle should be the one the Court invoked way back in the *Reynolds* polygamy case, when it warned against allowing the religious citizen to become a "law unto himself": "To make an individual's obligation to obey such a law contingent upon the law's coincidence with his religious beliefs, except where the State's interest is 'compelling'—permitting him, by virtue of his beliefs, 'to become a law unto himself'—contradicts both constitutional tradition and common sense."[22]

Notwithstanding these efforts to distinguish *Sherbert* and *Yoder*, most observers think *Smith* overruled them in all but name. The decision prompted immediate and widespread criticism. One interesting thing to note is that while religious liberty today is often associated with the "right wing" of the culture wars, the *Smith* majority consisted mostly of justices (such as Scalia) identified as conservative, whereas the *Sherbert* majority consisted of justices identified as liberal, including the decision's author, Justice Brennan, and Chief Justice Earl Warren.

It was the backlash against *Smith* that prompted passage of RFRA. The idea behind RFRA was to "restore," and perhaps even expand, the *Sherbert* test. The Act states that "Government shall not substantially burden a person's exercise of religion even if the burden results from a rule of general applicability," unless the government "demonstrates that application of the burden to the person—(1) is in furtherance of a compelling governmental interest; and (2) is the least restrictive means of furthering that compelling governmental interest." There is some debate, as we shall show, about whether RFRA's test is more stringent than the *Sherbert*-era test.

In 1993, RFRA passed with unanimous support in the House and ninety-seven votes in the Senate. It was endorsed by dozens of organizations across the political spectrum, from the American Civil Liberties Union and Americans United for Separation of Church and State to the Traditional Values Coalition and the National Association of Evangelicals. Observing the act's diverse legislative cosponsors—including Senators Ted Kennedy, Democrat of Massachusetts, and Orrin Hatch, Republican of Utah—President Bill Clinton quipped: "The power of God is such that even in the legislative process miracles can happen."[23] Upon signing it, he declared: "This act reverses the Supreme Court's decision Employment Division against Smith and reestablishes a standard that better protects all Americans of all faiths in the exercise of their religion in a way that I am convinced is far more consistent with the intent of the Founders of this Nation than the Supreme Court decision."[24]

The Act was originally written in such a way as to apply to state and local governments as well as the federal government. However, four years later, in *City of Boerne v. Flores*,[25] the Supreme Court struck down RFRA as applied to state and local governments, holding that such application exceeded Congress's constitutional powers.

The Act remains applicable to the federal government, having been applied in U.S. Supreme Court cases such as the 2006 case *Gonzales v. O Centro Espirita Beneficente União do Vegetal* (granting an exemption from federal drug laws for ayahuasca, a hallucinogenic sacramental tea) and the 2014 case *Burwell v. Hobby Lobby Stores, Inc.* (granting an exemption from the Affordable Care Act's contraception mandate). Congress later passed the Religious Land Use and Institutionalized Persons Act (RLUIPA, pronounced "R-loopa" or "ruh-loopa"), to safeguard prisoners' religious liberty rights and protect houses of worship from burdensome zoning regulations. Although RLUIPA is a federal law, it applies to any state or local government entity that accepts federal funding, as most do. This Act also clarifies that "exercise of religion" refers to any exercise of religion, "whether or not compelled by, or central to, a system of religious belief."

Both RFRA and RLUIPA have been successfully invoked by a wide variety of believers, including, in recent years, Apache Indians told not to wear headdresses with eagle feathers, Sikhs told not to carry kirpans to their government jobs, inner-city black churches facing discriminatory zoning regulations, Muslim prisoners forbidden to grow beards, a New Mexico church forbidden to import a hallucinogenic sacramental tea, and Jewish inmates denied kosher meals. Meanwhile, dozens of states have passed their own state-level RFRAs, and others have contemplated them—sometimes prompting considerable controversy.

Take Indiana. In March 2015 Indiana's governor, Mike Pence, signed into law a state bill that in most ways mirrored the federal RFRA. There were some potential differences: The law explicitly applied to corporations, including for-profit corporations, and explicitly allowed people to invoke it as a defense in disputes to which the government was not a party. On both points, however, most courts have interpreted the federal RFRA the same way.[26] Indiana simply made explicit in its own RFRA what may have already been implicit in the federal RFRA.

Nevertheless, these two points proved a political flashpoint, because they meant that a private for-profit business could invoke Indiana's RFRA if sued for refusing to provide services for a same-sex wedding, in violation of local antidiscrimination ordinances. (Indiana lacks statewide antidiscrimination ordinances that cover sexual orientation or gender identity, although some Indiana cities have them.) Whether such invocations would be successful is a separate question: At the time of the Indiana RFRA debate (March 2015) there hadn't been a single case where a RFRA had been successfully invoked for an exemption from an antidiscrimination ordinance.[27] And we don't know of any since then.

Ultimately, the most significant difference between the 2015 Indiana RFRA and the 1993 federal RFRA was political timing: Indiana's appeared a year after a federal district court struck down the state's law defining civil marriage as the union of husband and wife, and just months before the U.S. Supreme Court's *Obergefell* decision. Same-sex marriage supporters thus saw the law as a "license to discriminate."

The ensuing backlash was widespread and swift. The National Collegiate Athletic Association, National Basketball Association, Women's National Basketball Association, and National Football League issued criticisms and threatened to move future sporting events elsewhere. Musicians canceled shows. Several governors and mayors banned state- and city-funded travel to Indiana. Angie's List announced that it would halt a $40 million expansion of its Indianapolis headquarters, and numerous business leaders publicly denounced the law, including Apple CEO Tim Cook, Yelp CEO Jeremy Stoppelman, PayPal CEO Max Levchin, and Berkshire Hathaway CEO Warren Buffett.

In response, Indiana's General Assembly quickly passed an amendment, which Governor Pence signed, ensuring that the law could not be used "to refuse to offer or provide services, facilities, use of public accommodations, goods, employment, or housing to any member or members of the general public." This modification pleased critics but frustrated defenders: After all, the law was largely motivated by the desire to allow those with sincere religious objections to decline to provide same-sex wedding services, and the amendment nullified that purpose. On the other hand, given that most Indiana jurisdictions did not prohibit sexual-orientation discrimination, such service refusals were already legal throughout most of the state anyway. And again, it is not clear that any RFRA would allow an exemption to antidiscrimination law, in jurisdictions that have such laws. It depends on whether denying the exemption is the least restrictive means for achieving a compelling governmental interest.

How did religious freedom become such a cultural flashpoint? And is it possible to find common ground on these issues? We turn now to some of the current controversies.

2

Religious Liberty, Not Religious Privilege

JOHN CORVINO

■ ■ ■

BY ALL ACCOUNTS, GEORGE REYNOLDS was a decent, God-fearing man.[1] He was also a polygamist, having taken a second wife out of a professed sense of religious duty. A member of the Church of Jesus Christ of Latter-day Saints, better known as the Mormons, the thirty-two-year-old Reynolds lived in what was then known as the Utah Territory, working as a bookkeeper and private secretary to Mormon Church presidents.[2] In 1874 he was charged with bigamy, in a "test case" in which Mormon leaders hoped to overturn antipolygamy laws.

Reynolds argued that he was morally obliged to take multiple wives, circumstances permitting; that this obligation was enjoined by God, revealed in the Bible, and protected by the First Amendment; and that his disobedience would result in his eternal damnation.[3] By all accounts he believed these things sincerely. Nevertheless, in 1878, the U.S. Supreme Court unanimously upheld his conviction. In a now-famous passage, Chief Justice Morrison Waite asked: "Can a man excuse his [illegal] practices ... because of his religious belief? To permit this would be to make the professed doctrines of religious belief superior to the law of the land, and in effect to permit every citizen to become a law unto himself."[4] Notwithstanding his religious convictions, George Reynolds had to play by the same rules as everyone else.

We should here distinguish two questions that tend to get jumbled together: first, whether a particular law is justified, and second, whether certain citizens should be exempt from it. One might argue that antipolygamy laws shouldn't exist in the first place, especially in their nineteenth-century form. Such laws did not merely prevent people from seeking multiple marriage *licenses*; they prohibited them from cohabiting with multiple romantic partners, whether legally registered or not.[5] The latter prohibition may seem quaint today, when people may cohabit with as many partners as they please, as long as they don't create safety hazards by overcrowding.

Let's assume, however, that the law that Reynolds flouted was justified. It's the second question that concerns us: Should Reynolds have been exempt from the law, given his sincere religious convictions?

Or consider a more recent controversy. Kim Davis is a Kentucky county clerk. After the U.S. Supreme Court legalized same-sex marriage,[6] Davis stopped issuing marriage licenses and refused to allow deputy clerks to do so, telling reporters: "I can't put my name on a license that doesn't represent what God ordained marriage to be."[7] She claimed that she was acting "under God's authority."[8] A federal judge ordered her either to perform her duties or resign. She refused, and was briefly jailed for contempt of court. Some commentators excoriated Davis for using her office to discriminate. Others hailed her as a religious martyr. Presidential candidate Mike Huckabee went so far as to claim that her jailing amounted to the "criminalization of Christianity."[9]

We confront the same question for Davis: Does she have to play by the same rules as everyone else, or should her religious convictions exempt her from a legal court order?

This book is about religious liberty, tolerance, and discrimination. In my contribution, I am particularly concerned with whether religious believers should receive special legal treatment, and if so, why. I'm grateful to pursue this question alongside Ryan Anderson and Sherif Girgis, two of the sharpest interlocutors I've ever debated. In our ongoing dialogue they have pushed me to think harder about these issues.

As noted in the introduction, I first came to know Anderson and Girgis through the marriage debate. But this book is notably different from my earlier book *Debating Same-Sex Marriage* (with Maggie Gallagher), and it's worth observing why. That book concerned a single, fairly straightforward question—whether legal marriage should be extended to same-sex couples—and each side had a definitive answer.[10] By contrast, this book is about a multitude of related questions. I agree with my counterpoint authors about some and disagree about many others. For some, I am confident of the right answer; for others, I am still working through what to think and why. Overall, my hope is to provide readers with the same opportunity that Anderson and Girgis have given me: an invitation to think more deeply about the pressing issues at hand.

Returning to those issues: Among various other claims, Davis argued for accommodation under Kentucky's state "Religious Freedom Restoration Act," or RFRA. Such acts provide exemptions from generally applicable rules that burden sincere religious beliefs, unless denying the exemption is the least restrictive means of furthering a compelling governmental interest. For complex legal reasons, Davis's RFRA challenge did not go far in federal court.[11] Nevertheless, Davis would probably have had a good *state court* argument for a RFRA accommodation.[12] But this fact raises the worry that RFRAs and related developments unfairly advantage religious citizens over their secular counterparts.

To see why, imagine a second clerk; call her Ms. Conjugal. Ms. Conjugal, who identifies as agnostic, has just finished reading my counterpoint authors' earlier book *What Is Marriage? Man and Woman: A Defense*, which makes no explicit appeal to religious premises. Convinced by its arguments, she concludes that she can no longer authorize same-sex marriages. As a nonbeliever, however, Ms. Conjugal cannot appeal to Kentucky's RFRA or to "religious liberty" considerations. In that way, the law appears to favor Ms. Davis over Ms. Conjugal.

Such cases raise questions not only about special treatment of religion but also about special treatment of *certain kinds of* religion. Imagine a third clerk, Mr. Burqa. Mr. Burqa is a fundamentalist Muslim who believes that women ought never to expose their faces in public; he objects to granting licenses to women who enter his office without a full-face veil. (This is a minority view among Muslims, vanishingly rare in the United States.) Here's the question: Should Mr. Burqa be accommodated in the same way as Ms. Davis? After all, his claim takes the same form—a request for accommodation based on sincere religious beliefs—and presumably could be accommodated in the same way.

Or imagine a fourth clerk: Ms. Lifelong. She believes that what God has joined together, man shall not put asunder; she refuses to issue marriage licenses to divorced people or to authorize deputy clerks to do so. How many of Kim Davis's defenders would take up Ms. Lifelong's accommodation request?

In the United States, special treatment for certain religious claims includes not only workplace accommodations but also exemptions from otherwise binding statutory law. For example:

- All states require children to attend school or its equivalent until age sixteen. But Amish students are exempted: They only have to attend school through eighth grade.[13]

- All states require that children receive certain vaccinations before entering public school. But children whose parents have religious objections are exempt from this requirement in forty-seven states.[14]
- Federal law requires all employers of a certain size to provide health insurance to their employees, including all approved forms of contraceptive coverage. But the U.S. Supreme Court ruled that "closely held" corporations need not provide such coverage if their owners object for religious reasons.[15]
- Most city zoning ordinances prohibit the placement of homeless shelters and other group homes in single-family residential neighborhoods. But under federal law, churches that operate such shelters are exempt from such regulations if the state or local government imposing them receives federal funding (as most do).[16]
- Every state has laws requiring certain persons to report child abuse under specific circumstances. But more than half exempt clergy from this requirement if the abuse is revealed in pastoral communications.[17]

Religion is not an absolute get-out-of-the-law-free card: You may not slaughter infidels, throw virgins into volcanoes, or withhold life-saving medical treatment from your children, no matter what your religion teaches. And a modern-day George Reynolds would probably still lose in court, at least if he were seeking multiple marriage *licenses*.[18] But U.S. law grants remarkable latitude to people with religious objections. In what follows, I explore whether and when such latitude is justified.

In section 2.1 of this chapter, I provide context for the debate, drawing a contrast between religious liberty, which I support, and religious privilege, which I oppose. In section 2.2, I raise three specific worries about current approaches to religious liberty. In section 2.3, I step back and explore two fundamental questions: First, why should we ever grant exemptions to neutral, generally applicable laws? Second, why (if at all) should we treat religion as special in this regard? My view is that religious-liberty claims deserve heightened attention, but not unique treatment. In section 2.4 I turn to current controversies regarding antidiscrimination law and wedding services. In section 2.5, I explore the nature of bigotry and evaluate analogies between various objects of discrimination: sexual orientation, gender identity, race, and religion. I summarize and conclude in section 2.6. Although the parts are interconnected, most can be read profitably as stand-alone essays—meaning that if you want to jump around a bit, feel free.

2.1 RELIGIOUS LIBERTY AND RELIGIOUS PRIVILEGE: SOME CONTEXT

Recall that the Puritans came to the New World to escape religious persecution—only to turn around and impose their religious beliefs on others. Law professor Douglas Laycock, one of the nation's foremost religious liberty scholars, refers to this general tendency as the Puritan mistake: Religious liberty means the liberty to do things *our way*.[19]

The human tendency to create in-groups and out-groups and to persecute outsiders is familiar. Religion tends to exacerbate it, mainly by giving people the idea that they have divine backing for their all-too-human prejudices: "God said it, we believe it, that settles it."[20] In a more positive vein, religion is central to many people's personal and communal identities. Religious liberty is thus importantly related to autonomy, the freedom to direct one's own life—in preparation, many believe, for another life to come.

2.1.1 The Establishment Clause

The introduction to the book details some of the nation's early experience of religious strife. The Framers fought to guarantee that "Congress shall make no law respecting an establishment of religion, or prohibiting the free exercise thereof." Yet even with such federal constitutional guarantees in place, religious tests for office endured in several states, preventing Jews, Catholics, and atheists from holding certain positions. Such tests were not entirely abolished until 1961, when the U.S. Supreme Court ruled in *Torcaso v. Watkins* that requiring officeholders to make "a declaration of a belief in God," as Maryland's Constitution did, violated the First Amendment.[21] Writing for the Court, Justice Hugo Black recalled *Everson v. Board of Education*, a case upholding a law that reimbursed transportation costs for parents who sent children to parochial schools. *Everson* is worth remembering for its forceful explication of the establishment clause:

> The "establishment of religion" clause of the First Amendment means at least this: Neither a state nor the Federal Government can set up a church. Neither can pass laws which aid one religion, aid all religions or prefer one religion over another. Neither can force nor influence a person to go to or to remain away from church against his will or force him to profess a belief or disbelief in any religion. No person can be punished for entertaining or professing religious beliefs or disbeliefs, for church attendance or non-attendance. No tax in any amount, large or small, can be levied to support any religious activities or institutions, whatever they may be called, or whatever form they may adopt to teach or practice religion. Neither a state nor the Federal Government can, openly or secretly, participate in the affairs of any religious organizations or groups and vice versa. In the words of Jefferson, the clause against establishment of religion by law was intended to erect "a wall of separation between Church and State."[22]

Although *Everson* was decided five-to-four, the dissent endorsed the majority's interpretation of the establishment clause: They argued that the "wall of separation" entailed that the Court should have gone further and struck down the reimbursement program.

Just as religious tests for office violate the establishment clause, so do government actions that privilege certain religions over others. The establishment clause explains why states cannot sponsor official prayers in public schools, as was once common.[23] The establishment clause explains why a federal court ordered Alabama chief justice Roy Moore to remove a monument of the Ten Commandments that he had erected in the Alabama Judicial Building. He refused, and was subsequently removed as chief justice. He has since been reelected to the post and suspended yet again—this time for ordering the state's probate judges to ignore the Supreme Court's same-sex marriage decision.[24]

Establishment clause violations are not always so blatant. Take "blue laws," which prohibit certain activities, such as alcohol sales, on Sunday. At the time of this writing, Sunday alcohol sales are prohibited in parts of twelve states—at least before noon, when Christians would normally attend church.[25] Sunday automobile sales are prohibited or restricted in parts of eighteen states.[26] Bergen County, New Jersey, goes further, also prohibiting Sunday sales of electronics, clothing, and furniture. Its borough of Paramus forbids any "worldly employment or business" on Sundays and allows only a handful of exceptions, such as the sale of "milk, bread, and baked goods," prepared meals, drugs, newspapers, and gasoline.[27]

The legislative history of these laws leaves no doubt about their purpose: encouraging people to keep holy the sabbath day.[28] But this purpose clearly favors religions that observe Sunday sabbath. Modern-day defenders have therefore tried to justify them on secular grounds, arguing that they are

constitutionally legitimate insofar as they satisfy citizens'
desire for a coordinated day of rest, for example, or for reduced
weekend traffic.[29] These are admittedly desirable goals. But
they don't explain laws that single out Sunday *alcohol* sales—
the most common type of blue law. And defenses of them often
strike a false note, like arguing that you ate all the ice cream in
order to make room in the freezer.[30]

2.1.2 The Free Exercise Clause

The free exercise clause states that Congress shall make no law
"prohibiting the free exercise" of religion. The government may
not prevent you from attending the house of worship of your
choosing; or from reading religious texts, or praying, in whatever form you deem appropriate; or from expressing your faith
in word and deed. As already noted, this guarantee is not absolute: You are not permitted to throw a virgin into a volcano no
matter what you think the gods demand. The general rule, at
least until recently, was that the government may restrict religious practices as long as doing so is an incidental effect of an
otherwise neutral, generally applicable law.

Consider again George Reynolds, who argued that antipolygamy laws violated his free exercise rights. The Court conceded that such laws restricted Reynolds's religious practice
but argued that they were nevertheless necessary for protecting
"peace and good order," including the welfare of "pure minded
women . . . and innocent children."[31] To grant an exemption in
such cases, the Court claimed, would be "to permit every citizen to become a law unto himself."[32]

Yet a century later, the Court seemed more open to man-
dating special accommodations for religious citizens. Recall
Sherbert v. Verner (1963): Adell Sherbert was a Seventh-Day
Adventist who left her job after her employer switched from
a five- to a six-day work week, thus requiring her to work on

Saturday, her sabbath.[33] South Carolina subsequently denied her unemployment benefits, on the grounds that she was "unavailable for work" on Saturdays. The Court ruled in her favor.

Writing for the majority, Justice William Brennan opined that "[South Carolina's] ruling forces her to choose between following the precepts of her religion and forfeiting benefits, on the one hand, and abandoning one of the precepts of her religion in order to accept work, on the other hand. Governmental imposition of such a choice puts the same kind of burden upon the free exercise of religion as would a fine imposed against appellant for her Saturday worship."[34]

Justice Brennan's analogy to a "fine" is overstated at best. (My counterpoint authors use a similar analogy.)[35] A fine is a punishment for violating criminal law, something not at issue here. Sherbert was free to do what she liked with her days; she simply could not collect an unemployment check while unavailable for Saturday work.

More important, had Sherbert's unavailability for work been due to a nonreligious reason—even a very important one—the Court would not have mandated benefits. As Justice Potter Stewart points out in a separate opinion, "South Carolina would deny unemployment benefits for a mother unavailable for work on Saturdays because she was unable to get a babysitter. . . . This is not, in short, a scheme which operates so as to discriminate against religion as such."[36]

There is, however, a better argument for compensating Sherbert, one that Justice Brennan mentions only in passing. South Carolina law also decreed that "no employee should be required to work on Sunday" as a condition of receiving unemployment benefits.[37] The law thus favored Sunday worshippers over Saturday worshippers, violating the establishment clause in the same way blue laws do.[38]

Sherbert, in other words, reached the right result for the wrong reason.[39] The problem with South Carolina employment law was not that it burdened religion: It did, although it also *favored* religion by elevating religious reasons over others when determining unemployment benefits. The problem is that it privileged Sunday worship over Saturday worship. That's not religious liberty; it's majority religious privilege.

A more serious outlier among free exercise cases is *Wisconsin v. Yoder* (1972), in which the Court held that Amish children could be exempted from compulsory education past the eighth grade. The reasoning is murky, and it leans not only on free exercise clause principles but also on the Amish people's distinctive heritage, their long history of law-abidingness, and the interest of parents in directing their children's education. Unfortunately, the decision gives shockingly little attention to the interests of those children in being sufficiently prepared to enter mainstream American society, should they choose one day to leave the Amish way of life.

There are tensions between some of the Court's decisions, which did not go unnoticed by observers—including members of the Court. In their separate opinions in *Sherbert*, for example, Justices William Douglas, Potter Stewart, and John Marshall Harlan each observe the majority opinion's inconsistency with the Court's upholding of blue laws, which mandate Sunday store closings: If it's unconstitutional to force a Saturday worshipper like Sherbert to choose between violating her conscience and for-going income, why is it not similarly unconstitutional to force Saturday-worshipping business owners to do the same? After all, the practical effect of blue laws is to require these owners to close their stores for two days, one mandated by law and the other by religious scruples. Justice Stewart notes frankly that the Court has not succeeded in "papering over" such contradictions.[40]

By the time the Court heard *Employment Division v. Smith* (1990),[41] the infamous "peyote case," the contradictions had become impossible to ignore. Recall that peyote, a hallucinogenic, plant-based drug, was illegal in Oregon. Alfred Smith and

Galen Black used it anyway, in rituals of the Native American Church. They lost their jobs after testing positive for mescaline and were subsequently denied unemployment benefits. When the case first arrived at the U.S. Supreme Court, the Court remanded it to the Oregon Supreme Court "for a determination whether sacramental peyote use is proscribed by the State's controlled substance law."[42] Oregon confirmed that the men broke the law, and the *Smith* Court upheld Oregon's judgment.

Writing for the Court, Justice Antonin Scalia famously quotes *Reynolds*'s "law unto himself" line in explaining the decision: "To make an individual's obligation to obey such a law contingent upon the law's coincidence with his religious beliefs, except where the State's interest is 'compelling'—permitting him, by virtue of his beliefs, 'to become a law unto himself'— contradicts both constitutional tradition and common sense."[43] In plain English: Religion is not a get-out-of-the-law-free card.

I think Justice Scalia was correct. Let me be clear: I don't believe that Oregon should have outlawed peyote, for Native Americans *or anyone else*. But given that it did, it ought to apply the law consistently. It should not matter whether Smith and Black were devout adherents of the Native American Church, or casual "Cafeteria"-style adherents, or people who wanted to try the religion on for size, or nonbelievers who were simply curious about peyote. If peyote isn't dangerous, it shouldn't be against the law. If it is dangerous, religious beliefs do not change its potency. To make people's obligation to obey laws depend on whether the law fits their religious beliefs is generally a mistake.

2.1.3 The Religious Freedom Restoration Act

Yet that is precisely what RFRA does. Recall that RFRA was passed to "restore" religious freedom after *Smith*. It prohibits the federal government from substantially burdening a person's exercise of religion, even with a neutral, generally applicable law, unless the government demonstrates that the burden (1) furthers a "compelling governmental interest," and (2) is the "least restrictive means" for doing so. When laws fail to pass this stringent standard, they aren't struck down; instead, they are suspended only for the particular individuals who raise religious objections.

The Religious Freedom Restoration Act has undoubtedly been used in the service of some laudable goals. In some of these cases, however, it is not clear why the exemption should favor the religious. If a prisoner may grow a short beard for religious reasons, why not for reasons of familial tradition or personal conviction? Besides, in most of these cases, the exemption could be achieved legislatively without the use of a "superstatute" such as RFRA.[44] Indeed, that legislative solution is precisely what happened in Oregon, which reacted to *Smith* by immediately amending its drug laws to allow the religious use of peyote.[45]

My own view is that RFRA was an unnecessary overreaction to *Smith*. In what follows, however, I am not going to argue for RFRA's repeal. My aims are both more modest and more general. Regarding RFRA, I want to show that its "least restrictive means" criterion, taken at face value, is too stringent: It should be weakened, so that incidental burdens on religion trigger "intermediate" scrutiny rather than strict scrutiny. (I'll say more about what those legal terms mean in the next section.) Moreover, RFRA's protections should not apply to for-profit corporations, and they should cover secular conscience claims as well as religious beliefs. Interestingly, my counterpoint authors agree with me on the latter point, and they come close to agreeing with me on the former point (intermediate scrutiny) as well.

More generally, I will argue that we should be more cautious about granting religious exemptions to neutral, generally applicable laws, and that we should especially avoid doing so when exemptions create burdens for already vulnerable minorities.

In familiar terms: Religious liberty should not be a license to discriminate.

The "license to discriminate" concern is particularly pressing in the wake of the Supreme Court's *Obergefell* ruling, as several states have rushed to pass state-level RFRAs and so-called First Amendment Defense Acts (FADAs) in an effort to allow citizens to refuse to recognize legally valid same-sex marriages.

Take Mississippi's FADA, HB1523; it was titled the "Protecting Freedom of Conscience from Government Discrimination Act." But the law "protected" three—and only three—religious or moral beliefs:

(1) Marriage is or should be recognized as the union of one man and one woman;

(2) Sexual relations are properly reserved to such a marriage; and

(3) Male (man) or female (woman) refer to an individual's immutable biological sex as objectively determined by anatomy and genetics at time of birth.[46]

The law said that the state would take no "discriminatory action" against those who act in accordance with these beliefs.[47] It defined "discriminatory action" sweepingly to include penalties in taxation, grants, benefits, licenses, employment, and so on. And it covered not only private individuals, but for-profit business and even government workers.

In practice, this meant that anyone acting on these beliefs could deny others legal rights with impunity. Government clerks could cite the law in refusing to issue a marriage license to a same-sex couple. They could refuse to handle same-sex couples' joint tax returns, spousal pension benefits, insurance benefits, survivor benefits, and so on. What's more, by specifying the belief that "sexual relations are properly reserved to [heterosexual] marriage," the law licensed discrimination against unwed parents as well as same-sex couples.

Notice how this FADA gives sweeping protection to those with certain (conservative, Christian) beliefs about marriage and no protection to those with opposing beliefs, in a manner quite contrary to the text and spirit of the First Amendment. Keep in mind that Mississippi offers no state-wide protections for LGBT citizens. Under this law, it would be illegal in Mississippi to take "discriminatory action" against someone (even a clerk) for opposing same-sex marriage, but *not* for supporting same-sex marriage—let alone for being gay.

Not surprisingly, a federal court struck down Mississippi's FADA on both equal protection clause and establishment clause grounds: "The State has put its thumb on the scale to favor some religious beliefs over others," Judge Carlton Reeves wrote. "Showing such favor tells 'nonadherents that they are outsiders, not full members of the political community.' "[48]

A very similar FADA was considered at the federal level in June 2015, on the eve of the *Obergefell* decision.[49] Its effects would have been sweeping. According to the testimony of twenty legal scholars, led by Katherine Franke at Columbia University, the proposed federal FADA would

- Prevent the government from taking enforcement action against an employer that refuses to provide mandated health insurance coverage to the dependents of same-sex or unmarried parents;[50]
- Prevent the government from taking enforcement action against a retirement plan that refuses to provide annuity benefits to same-sex spouses of plan beneficiaries;[51]
- Eliminate the federal government's ability to prohibit discrimination by recipients of federal grants. . . . For instance, a clinic could refuse to provide contraceptives

to unmarried women or men yet remain eligible for a Title X grant to provide family planning services;[52]

- Prevent the federal government's ability to enforce the Patient Protection and Affordable Care Act in cases where a healthcare provider denied coverage for mandated preventative services—such as counseling for sexually transmitted infections, contraception, or domestic violence screening and counseling—to employees who are married to a same-sex partner or who have extramarital relations/sex.[53]

- Prevent the secretary of Housing and Urban Development and/or the U.S. attorney general from enforcing the Fair Housing Act against a landlord that advertises that it will not rent to unmarried parents.[54]

- Prevent the federal government from denying Title X funding to a health clinic that provides family planning care only to those patients who provide a marriage license in order to qualify for such services.[55]

- Prevent the federal government from denying a Violence Against Women Act grant to a domestic violence shelter that requires all residents to attest their opposition to marriage equality and/or extramarital relations/sex before securing housing.[56]

- Require that the federal government provide preferred tax status to nonprofits that discriminate or otherwise violate the tax code. For instance, charitable hospitals could refuse to apply a mandated financial assistance policy to patients who are married to someone of the same sex and still maintain their tax-exempt status.[57]

- Deny some federal courts the capacity to adjudicate lawsuits between private parties, since a court could be interpreted as "imposing a penalty" within the meaning of the bill.[58]

A later, revised FADA exempted publicly traded for-profit entities and specified that healthcare institutions would not be protected if they refused "to provide medical treatment necessary to cure an illness or injury" because of their religious or moral beliefs.[59] However, it would still protect hospitals if they discriminated by refusing to provide financial assistance for such care, or by refusing to provide preventative care. The revision also slightly narrowed the notion of "discriminatory action"— but only by eliminating the absurdly broad phrase "[or] otherwise discriminate against such person." The central problems remained.

Perhaps further revisions would make for a more reasonable version. Many proponents do not seem to want a more reasonable version, however. Consider what happened in July 2016. After Judge Reeves struck down Mississippi's FADA, the proposed federal FADA was modified to avoid the equal protection clause violation: The new version would cover both opponents and supporters of same-sex marriage. Immediately thereafter, the Family Research Council, an influential conservative Christian lobbying organization, withdrew its support.[60] The reason is obvious: Their goal in supporting FADA was not to protect freedom but to signal disapproval of same-sex marriage. It was liberty for me, but not for thee—a repeat of the Puritan mistake.

2.2 THE TROUBLE WITH TODAY'S RELIGIOUS EXEMPTIONS

Hobby Lobby Stores, Inc. is a nationwide chain of over six hundred stores selling arts, crafts, and home decor products; it is included in *Forbes*'s annual list of America's largest private companies, employing roughly twenty-eight thousand people.[61] Founded by David and Barbara Green in the 1970s, it is committed to operating "in a manner consistent with Biblical principles."[62]

In 2010, Congress passed the Patient Protection and Affordable Care Act. This Act is administered by the Department of Health and Human Services (HHS), which among other things requires employer health plans to provide women with preventative care that includes a full range of contraceptive coverage. Hobby Lobby's owners object to some contraceptives, including intrauterine devices (IUDs) and "morning-after pills" such as Plan B, because they believe them to act as abortifacients by preventing implantation of fertilized eggs.

It's worth noting that the mainstream medical community denies that these drugs are abortifacients, in part because it defines pregnancy as beginning after implantation. By contrast, the HHS mandate does not include drugs, such as RU-486, that are specifically designed to end pregnancy.[63] Conflicting definitions of pregnancy aside, there is some dispute over whether the contested contraceptives actually interfere with implantation.[64]

Pregnancy is life-altering for anyone, but for some, it can even be life-threatening.[65] In cases where pregnancy is unintended, undesired, or dangerous, contraceptives such as the morning-after pill provide a safer and less intrusive option than abortion.

In *Burwell v. Hobby Lobby Stores, Inc.*, the Court decided that the HHS mandate violated RFRA by requiring employers with religious objections to cover such contraceptives. Writing for the five-member majority, Justice Alito granted that protecting women's health constituted a compelling governmental interest—a point forcefully underscored in Justice Anthony Kennedy's concurrence. But Justice Alito denied that the HHS mandate was the least restrictive means for achieving that compelling interest. After all, the contraceptives could be paid for directly by the government itself. Or they could be paid for separately by the insurance company, an accommodation that was already in place under the Patient Protection and

Affordable Care Act for religious nonprofit organizations. So the Court granted Hobby Lobby an exemption to the mandate under RFRA.

One could read *Hobby Lobby* as a fairly innocuous decision. If a law substantially burdens religious exercise, and there is a less restrictive means for the federal government to achieve its aims, then RFRA requires the government to use that means. There was such a means here, obviously, because it was already in use for religious nonprofits: Just fill out a form certifying that you object to the contraceptives, send it to the insurance company, and they take over, "exclud[ing] contraceptive coverage from the employer's plan and provid[ing] separate payments for contraceptive services for plan participants without imposing any cost-sharing requirements".[66] So the decision seems a straightforward application of RFRA.

Yet many find *Hobby Lobby* worrisome, not only in how it applies RFRA but also in how it reveals problems with current approaches to religious exemptions more generally. In this section, I will explain some of these worries. The first of these is specific to RFRA; the others apply more broadly: first, that the "least restrictive means" test and other features of RFRA are too demanding as written; second, that today's exemptions place greater third-party burdens than the exemptions of the *Sherbert/Yoder* era; and third, that the activities that are being counted as "religion" for exemption and accommodation purposes are expansive and expanding.

2.2.1 The "Least Restrictive Means" Test

The Religious Freedom Restoration Act requires governmental burdens on religious exercise to serve a "compelling government interest" by the "least restrictive means"—a standard elsewhere known as "strict scrutiny." Strict scrutiny typically applies when laws abridge fundamental constitutional rights (such as freedom of religion or speech) or make use of "suspect classifications" (such as race or national origin). The idea is that burdens on such rights must clear a very high bar—so high, in fact, that the standard has sometimes been called "'strict' in theory, fatal in fact."[67]

Part of that standard is the "compelling interest test." The Court has never precisely defined what qualifies a government interest as compelling, which makes it easy to abuse the notion. Presumably it must be absolutely essential to safety and welfare. But in a highly regulated society, many civic obligations will fall short of this standard. As Justice Scalia explains, the implications are broad:

> Any society adopting such a system would be courting anarchy, but that danger increases in direct proportion to the society's diversity of religious beliefs, and its determination to coerce or suppress none of them. Precisely because "we are a cosmopolitan nation made up of people of almost every conceivable religious preference," and precisely because we value and protect that religious divergence, we cannot afford the luxury of deeming *presumptively invalid*, as applied to the religious objector, every regulation of conduct that does not protect an interest of the highest order.[68]

When we combine compelling interest with the "least restrictive means" condition, the implications are even broader. There is some debate over whether RFRA's "least restrictive means" test is more stringent than the narrow tailoring of the *Sherbert* test.[69] What is clear is that the Court has read it as more restrictive. In *City of Boerne vs. Flores*, which struck down RFRA as applied to the states, the Court stated explicitly that the least restrictive means requirement "was not used in the pre-*Smith* jurisprudence RFRA purported to codify—which also indicates that the legislation is broader than is appropriate if the goal is to prevent and remedy constitutional violations."[70] In

Hobby Lobby the Court reaffirms this point: "By enacting RFRA, Congress went far beyond what this Court has held is constitutionally required."[71]

Applying the "least restrictive means" standard to the case at hand: Justice Alito is absolutely correct that having the government pay for the contraceptive coverage is less restrictive on Hobby Lobby than having the company pay for it. That's because having the government pay for *anything* is less restrictive on Hobby Lobby than having the company pay for it: It's a no-brainer. But this move presents two serious problems—one obvious, one less so.

The obvious problem is that the argument proves too much. For any mandate at all, shifting the financial burden to the government will be less restrictive on the employer than requiring the employer to pay.[72] Suppose Hobby Lobby's owners believe that migraines are a punishment from God and they refuse to pay for migraine medication. Or suppose they believe that childhood birth defects reflect "spiritual" defects, and they refuse to pay for corrective surgery. In light of the Court's decision in *Hobby Lobby*, RFRA would appear to license both of those refusals.

Such cases are not far-fetched. Jehovah's Witnesses believe that blood is sacred and must not be transfused, even in an emergency. (Doctors may legally override this belief in the case of minors, over the Church's strenuous objections.) After *Hobby Lobby*, Jehovah's Witness business owners could invoke RFRA to refuse to purchase insurance that covers blood transfusions, even in emergencies. Similarly, those with religious objections to HPV vaccines or to drugs such as Truvada (which prevents HIV transmission) could refuse to pay for those, claiming that they promote promiscuity.

The second, less obvious problem is this: Just because less restrictive means are possible, it does not follow that they are politically or financially feasible, much less that they end up being utilized.[73] Indeed, for years after the Tenth Circuit issued the injunction in this case (ultimately affirmed by the Supreme Court), Hobby Lobby's employees did not receive the alternative provision for coverage—mainly for partisan political reasons.[74] While Justice Alito's opinion for the Court emphasized that "the effect of the HHS-created accommodation on the women employed by Hobby Lobby and the other companies involved in these cases would be precisely zero," that was not how things played out.[75] Remember: RFRA only requires that there is a less restrictive alternative *possible*, not that it actually be offered.

There are other significant problems. The Court correctly notes the owners' sincere religious belief that providing the insurance coverage would make them complicit in wrongdoing; it then concludes that the mandate substantially burdens that belief because of the fines levied for noncompliance. But as Justice Ruth Bader Ginsburg points out, there's a difference between the factual claim that a plaintiff's religious beliefs are sincere, which the Court must generally accept at face value, and the legal claim that they are substantially burdened, which requires judicial inquiry.[76]

How burdensome is the mandate? It's not as if the owners are being required to use the contraceptives, or even to pay for them directly. They are being required to contribute to an undifferentiated insurance fund that covers a broad range of healthcare services, from which their employees *might* choose contraceptives. The burden on the owners' religious beliefs seems rather distant and attenuated.

But the problems don't end there. Just three days after issuing its decision, the Court granted an injunction in a case in which Wheaton College, an evangelical school in Illinois, objected to the very alternative that the Court had touted as a less restrictive means in *Hobby Lobby*: signing an opt-out form that transfers responsibility for contraceptive coverage to the insurance company.[77] Wheaton argued that because the opt-out form "triggered" the insurance company's legal obligation to provide the contraceptives, filling it out still made the college complicit.

In a dissent joined by all the female justices, Justice Sonia Sotomayor wrote: "Those who are bound by our decisions usually believe they can take us at our word. Not so today. After expressly relying on the availability of the religious-nonprofit accommodation to hold that the contraceptive coverage requirement violates RFRA as applied to closely held for-profit corporations, the Court now, as the dissent in *Hobby Lobby* feared it might, retreats from that position."[78] The Wheaton case has been combined with various others under *Zubik v. Burwell*, popularly known as the "Little Sisters of the Poor" case—the outcome of which is uncertain at the time of this writing. It appears that objectors will not be satisfied unless the women are required to obtain separate policies with separate insurance cards, which might also require separate doctors—at a significant burden to female employees. Linda Greenhouse is probably right when she observes that "the organizations don't want to pay for birth control and they don't want anyone else to pay for it either."[79]

Hobby Lobby is also the first case ever to treat a for-profit corporation as a person capable of practicing religion. Of course it has long been common to treat corporations as persons as a legal fiction, and that may be the correct thing to do here as a matter of law. But as a matter of policy, it seems odd to treat Hobby Lobby as capable of practicing religion in the sense intended by RFRA or the free exercise clause. Hobby Lobby sells craft products.[80] It employs roughly twenty-eight thousand people of diverse religious perspectives. As Justice Ginsburg notes in her dissent, it would be illegal for the company to impose religious criteria on its employees—for example, by hiring only Christians.[81] Yet the decision allows the owners to impose their faith on employees indirectly, by denying them insurance coverage that is otherwise legally mandated.

2.2.2 Nonminimal Burdens on Third Parties

Law professors Andrew Koppelman and Frederick Gedicks have noted that "one of the principal attractions of the idea of religious liberty has always been that the exercise of one person's religion doesn't hurt anyone else. In Thomas Jefferson's classic formulation: 'it does me no injury for my neighbour to say there are twenty gods, or no god. It neither picks my pocket nor breaks my leg.' "[82] Many familiar religious-liberty claims from Jefferson's time through the *Sherbert-Yoder* era fit this description: Whether people are baptized in infancy or adulthood; whether they pray in English or some other tongue; whether they observe the sabbath on Saturday or Sunday—or at all—has little effect on their neighbors. Live and let live.

Some of the claims in the news today are similar. Whether a woman wears a bikini or a "burkini" (a modest form of swimwear favored by Muslims but now banned in France) should be no one's business but the woman's.[83]

But other claims are different. As Douglas NeJaime and Reva Siegel have argued, current U.S. controversies are often "complicity-based," implicating not only the claimant's choices but also those of parties who do not share the claimant's faith.[84] When employers refuse to provide legally mandated insurance coverage that employees may use for contraception (or even to sign a form declining to do so), when hospital workers are forbidden to provide information that might be relevant to an abortion decision, when ultra-Orthodox Jewish men delay a flight because they refuse to be seated near women, or when county clerks refuse to issue marriage licenses to same-sex couples, they are not simply affecting their own lives; they are creating burdens for others.

On this point, it's worth noting the contrast between the Court's decision in *Hobby Lobby* and its 1982 decision in *United States v. Lee*. That case involved an Amish employer who had religious objections to paying Social Security taxes. Writing for an eight-member majority (with a ninth justice, Stevens, concurring in the judgment), Chief Justice Warren Burger acknowledged that the law burdened Amish employers' sincere religious beliefs. But he nevertheless upheld the law, drawing a sharp distinction between the religious faith of employers and that of the people with whom they interact upon entering the commercial sphere: "When followers of a particular sect enter into commercial activity as a matter of choice, the limits they accept on their own conduct as a matter of conscience and faith are not to be superimposed on the statutory schemes which are binding on others in that activity. Granting an exemption from Social Security taxes to an employer operates to impose the employer's religious faith on the employees."[85] Of course, *Lee* was decided before RFRA was passed, providing further evidence that RFRA, far from "restoring" the *Sherbert* test, goes beyond it in ways previously rejected by the Court.

Another example of third-party burdens is the case of Kentucky county clerk Kim Davis. Claiming that she was acting "under God's authority," Davis refused to obey a court order to issue marriage licenses to same-sex couples or to allow her deputy clerks to do so. Her position changed over time: Sometimes she said that she didn't want her office to issue same-sex marriage licenses at all, suggesting that couples needing them could simply drive to another county. At other times she said that she simply wanted her name removed. At one point she even publicly suggested that licenses issued without her name—per court order—were legally invalid.[86]

Some (including my counterpoint author Ryan Anderson) have argued that by recognizing marriage rights for same-sex couples, the U.S. Supreme Court "redefined Kim Davis's job."[87] This is simply false. The county clerk's job is to ensure that people meet the *legal requirements* for a license, not their eligibility for a sacrament. Such requirements change all the time: Legislatures enact, repeal, and modify laws, and sometimes (as in this case) courts overrule them. Davis knew all of this when she accepted her government position.

By analogy, consider a different case. Suppose Kentucky changed the age of eligibility for a driver's license from seventeen to sixteen. Now imagine a clerk—call her Ms. Majority—whose religion teaches that people don't become full adults until age seventeen; only then can they be trusted with responsibilities such as driving. (Perhaps they mark the birthday with some religious rite of passage, like a bar mitzvah.) If Ms. Majority refused to issue driver's licenses to eligible sixteen-year-olds, we would not excuse her on the grounds that Kentucky "redefined" her job. Her job was, and still is, to determine whether people meet the legal requirements for a license—just like Kim Davis.

In substituting her religious beliefs for the law, Kim Davis placed burdens on third parties who did not share those beliefs. Such actions look less like religious liberty than religious discrimination.

2.2.3 The Diversity and Pervasiveness of Religion

Hobby Lobby's stretching of the meaning of religious exercise does not stand alone. To borrow Chief Justice Burger's words in *Bowen v. Roy* (1986), the alleged injuries to religious liberty have become "far removed from the historical instances of religious persecution and intolerance that gave concern to those who drafted the Free Exercise Clause of the First Amendment."[88] (*Bowen* involved Native American parents who objected to the government's requirement that their daughter be assigned a Social Security number in order to receive welfare benefits, claiming that it would "rob her spirit." The Court rejected their claim.)

Perhaps this drift is inevitable in an increasingly complex society. It should nevertheless give one pause. In the United States alone, there are thousands of different religious sects; within these there is often wide diversity of belief. Religion may range from how, where, and when one worships to matters of dress and grooming, the use or avoidance of technology (automobiles, medical interventions, photographs, and more), the insurance policies one is willing to provide, even the cakes one is willing to bake. There is scarcely any facet of life untouched by religion thus understood.

Some view this pervasiveness as an argument for why RFRA is necessary. Consider the following passage from Douglas Laycock:

> It is important to understand that every religion is at risk. Every church offends some interest group, and many churches offend numerous interest groups. No church is big enough or tough enough to fight them all off, over and over, at every level of government. The situation is even more hopeless for individual believers with special needs not shared by their whole denomination. Consider the case of Frances Quaring, a Pentecostal Christian who studied the Bible on her own and understood the commandment against graven images with unusual strictness. Mrs. Quaring would not allow a photograph in her house. She would not allow a television in her house. She removed the labels from her groceries or obliterated the pictures with black markers. For Mrs. Quaring, it was plainly forbidden to carry a photograph on her driver's license, and when the legislature required photographs, she could not get a driver's license.

It would be nearly impossible for any legislature to know in advance about a believer like Mrs. Quaring and to enact an exemption for her. The Mrs. Quarings of the world cannot hire lobbyists to monitor the legislature and protect their religious liberty from any bill that might interfere with their little known beliefs. The only way to provide for such unforeseeable religious claims is with a general provision guaranteeing free exercise of religion. The Free Exercise Clause was once such a provision, but *Smith* says that it is not such a provision anymore. RFRA would restore such a provision to the United States Code.[89]

I have just the opposite reaction. Whereas Laycock takes the wide diversity and peculiarity of religious beliefs as a good reason *for* having a widespread exemption regime, I think it's an excellent reason *against* doing so. Whether or not it would be "courting anarchy," to borrow Justice Scalia's colorful phrase, it would condition the legitimacy of laws on a potentially endless variety of religious scruples.

Religion's expanding reach can be seen in the employment arena as well. Title VII of the 1964 Civil Rights Act prohibits employment discrimination on the basis of religion, among other factors, and requires religious accommodation whenever it can be granted without undue hardship. The Equal Employment Opportunity Commission (EEOC), which enforces Title VII, offers the following guidelines at its website:

> Title VII protects all aspects of religious observance and practice as well as belief and defines religion very broadly for purposes of determining what the law covers. For purposes of Title VII, religion includes not only traditional, organized religions such as Christianity, Judaism, Islam, Hinduism, and Buddhism, but also religious beliefs that are new, uncommon, not part of a formal church or sect, only subscribed to by a small number of people, or that seem illogical or unreasonable to others. An

employee's belief or practice can be "religious" under Title VII even if the employee is affiliated with a religious group that does not espouse or recognize that individual's belief or practice, or if few—or no—other people adhere to it.[90]

Now imagine an employee who, like Mrs. Quaring, is an unusually strict reader of the Bible. Instead of the passages on graven images, however, this employee—we'll call her Ms. Clock—is obsessed with those regarding time. She opens her Bible and quickly comes upon this passage: "And God saw that the light was good; and God separated the light from the darkness. God called the light Day, and the darkness he called Night. And there was evening and there was morning, the first day" (Genesis 1:4–5 NRSV). On the basis of his reading of the passage, Ms. Clock decides that Daylight Saving Time violates God's Word. (I'm inclined to agree, but only in the sense that it sometimes requires me to get up at ungodly hours.)

What should Ms. Clock's employer do when she shows up an hour late for work on a Monday morning in mid-March? Remember that, according to EEOC guidelines, "religion includes . . . beliefs that are new, uncommon, not part of a formal church or sect, only subscribed to by a small number of people, or that seem illogical or unreasonable to others." According to EEOC guidelines, if employers can accommodate Ms. Clock without undue hardship, they are legally obligated to do so.

One might object to this case by balking at its implausibility. I have two responses. The first is to note that from most people's perspectives, the hypothetical Ms. Clock's beliefs are no more implausible than the real-life Mrs. Quaring's. Virtually all religions include tenets that look bizarre from the perspective of others. Whereas the Mormon belief that God rules the universe from the vicinity of the planet Kolob sounds strange to the average Catholic, the Catholic belief that bread and wine *literally* (and not merely symbolically) become Jesus's flesh and blood sounds equally strange to the average Mormon—and all of the above sounds strange to the atheist.[91]

My second response is to note that Ms. Clock's case is not entirely hypothetical. There is in fact a long history of religious objections to time standardization. When U.S. time zones were adopted in 1883, the mayor of Bangor, Maine, denounced them as an "attempt to change the immutable laws of God Almighty."[92] As Tufts University professor Michael Downing explains, "the idea [was] that we were fooling around with God's time and this was the mechanized world's way of some-how taking over God's world."[93]

In his provocative book *Why Tolerate Religion?* Brian Leiter observes that one defining characteristic of religion is that it includes at least some beliefs that are "insulated from ordinary standards of evidence and rational justification"; he argues that this insulation is one reason to be wary of giving religious conscience special protection.[94] The legal theorist Michael McConnell has criticized Leiter for "stack[ing] the deck by assuming that religious belief 'always' is to some degree 'false, or at least unwarranted.'"[95] "Religious believers do not think they are 'insulating' themselves from all the relevant 'evidence,'" McConnell writes. "They think they are considering evidence of a different, nonmaterial sort, *in addition to* the evidence of science, history, and the senses."[96]

McConnell's rejoinder misses the force of Leiter's concern. Even if one grants "evidence of a different, non-material sort," such evidence is often private in a way that renders it effectively useless for the purpose of resolving interpersonal disputes. Accordingly, the law avoids inquiring into the plausibility of religious claims: It acknowledges that they are generally accepted "on faith." If Mrs. Quaring believes that God forbids her from having her photograph taken, it is not for the government to persuade her otherwise.

McConnell concedes that "we might be justified in dismissing the idiosyncratic beliefs of small numbers of persons, especially when these people do not appear rational in other respects." But he then pivots to a more general point, arguing that "religious belief has been attested to by millions of seemingly intelligent and rational people over long periods of time, who report that they have experienced, in some way, transcendent reality."

Unfortunately for McConnell, debates about religious exemptions and accommodations arise not from generalities about "transcendent reality" but from very specific and often idiosyncratic claims about what God requires in particular circumstances. Their peculiarity is to be expected: As Laycock observes, religious believers frequently "draw their morality from ancient books written in a radically different culture that lived with radically different technology and had a radically different understanding of the world"; they see themselves as obeying a "God whose commands may be beyond human understanding."[97]

It's precisely by being "beyond human understanding" that religious beliefs are "insulated from evidence" in Leiter's sense, and precisely for that reason that Justice Scalia opined that, in a religiously diverse nation, any system requiring strict scrutiny for laws burdening religious beliefs is "courting anarchy."[98]

2.2.4 Is Strict Scrutiny the Appropriate Standard?

As already noted, strict scrutiny is typically invoked when laws substantially abridge fundamental constitutional rights. It's important to distinguish, however, between laws that directly infringe upon such rights and those that do so only incidentally. While strict scrutiny seems the right standard for laws that directly target religion, it is too strong for neutral laws of general applicability.

An analogy to free speech may be helpful. Laws that target particular speech *content* are rarely constitutional. It is unconstitutional, for example, to prohibit people from criticizing the government, or to require them to recite the Pledge of Allegiance.[99] But some laws only incidentally restrict speech. For example, a law prohibiting construction in an environmentally sensitive zone restricts speech by preventing billboards from being erected there. Such a law would not need to pass a strict scrutiny standard, however; the speech restriction is too indirect and attenuated. Nor would a law that prohibits, say, rallies after midnight. "Content neutral" restrictions on speech are instead usually subjected to something called "intermediate scrutiny": They must involve an *important government interest* and be *substantially related* to promoting it.

When it comes to the free exercise of religion, cases like *Hobby Lobby* seem much closer to the "billboard" case than to the "criticizing the government" case: The laws in question don't directly target fundamental freedoms; instead, they incidentally burden them in pursuit of other, constitutionally legitimate aims.

Thus RFRA elevates freedom of religion higher than freedom of speech, giving religion—including religious practice, very broadly defined—greater protection. If anything, this elevation seems backward: Speech is typically necessary for exercising religion, but not vice versa. My own view is that RFRA ought to be modified to require an "intermediate scrutiny" standard for incidental burdens. That would bring it in line with how we treat other fundamental freedoms, and also with how it has often been applied in practice (a point to which I'll return in my Reply).

2.3 WHY RELIGIOUS EXEMPTIONS?

I have argued that the current approach to religious exemptions is problematic for several reasons. I now want to step back and ask whether religious exemptions are justified at all, and if so, why. I will do so by exploring two questions: First, why *exemptions*? And second, why *religious*? In other words, I want to address the general worry that religious exemptions give "special rights" to some citizens, in violation of our commitment to equality under the law.

2.3.1 Why Exemptions?

When I was first learning to drive, my parents occasionally had to remind me that "stop signs are not mere suggestions." They were right. As Christopher Eisgruber and Lawrence Sager explain, "our laws do not descend arbitrarily from an alien entity called 'government.' They are the product of legislative and administrative concerns, enacted by our representatives in service of what those representatives deem good and sufficient reasons."[100] If personal interests could regularly overrule them, one might wonder whether they are justified in the first place. On this point "law and order" types find common cause with civil libertarians from across the political spectrum: Laws restrict liberty, and the government needs very good reasons for restricting liberty. Frequent exemptions could undermine not only those reasons but also respect for the law more generally, resulting in a kind of "Swiss cheese" law. Moreover, if exemptions are handed out selectively—to the religious, say, or to the well-connected—one begins to worry that the law is playing favorites.

These considerations add up to what we might call a global antiexemption argument: Generally speaking, laws ought to be applied consistently.

Nevertheless, virtually everyone agrees that there are at least some cases where exemptions are warranted. The most familiar example is conscientious objection to military service. This is a unique case, however. First, conscientious objector status is usually invoked during *conscription*, when the government requires a citizen to drop everything and take up arms. It is not like saying *"If* you want to open a business, *then* you must do such-and-such": It's an absolute intrusion; it forecloses all alternatives. Second, wartime conscription involves life-or-death matters. Third, and perhaps most significantly: People are conscripted *to fight*, and pacifists by definition decline to fight; conscripting pacifists to fight thus seems to undermine the very purpose of the law in question.

Each of these three factors—absolute intrusion on liberty, life-or-death matters, and the self-defeating nature of enforcing the law—gives weight to the case for exemption; when combined, they create an exceptional situation.

Another case when exemptions seem reasonable is when enforcing an otherwise good law would lead to serious harm. The law requires vaccinations to promote community health and safety, and not just the health of the individual vaccinated. But if a prospective recipient is deathly allergic to a particular vaccine, an exemption is warranted.[101] There are laws against breaking and entering, but one may kick down a door to save someone from a burning building (the "necessity defense"). And surely a world that prohibits breaking and entering but exempts emergency rescuers would be preferable to one that either lacks the prohibition or lacks the exemption. Even though these laws are generally justified, greater goods are at stake in certain cases.

Exemptions are also more easily justified when the law addresses an aggregate harm: Emissions standards can help protect the environment even if the state exempts classic cars, of which there are relatively few. Historic-zoning regulations can preserve the character of a neighborhood even if the historic commission occasionally suspends the rules for safety, cost, or aesthetic reasons. By contrast, when there's an individualized harm—as in cases of theft, assault, or murder—exemptions make less sense. So too when the risks are immediate, rather than distant. To borrow an example from law professor Marci Hamilton, "if a driver is stopped for speeding, the fact that she is a believer or that she is late for church does not relieve her of the obligation to abide by speed limits."[102]

One might also think that exemptions are also justified whenever majority-made policies disproportionately burden minorities.[103] Adell Sherbert's case is like this: South Carolina's employment-compensation policies placed burdens on her that it explicitly declined to place on Sunday-sabbath observers. But we must be careful: Virtually all laws burden citizens unequally. Laws against polygamy disproportionately burden fundamentalist Mormons, among others. Laws against assault disproportionately burden people with violent tendencies—including religious believers who feel duty-bound to inflict corporal punishment on sinners. In arguing for an exemption, it is not enough to show that a law treats citizens unequally: One must show that it does so *without good reason.* There is no good reason for the law to treat Saturday worshippers differently from Sunday worshippers; there is a good reason for it to treat the violent differently from the peaceful.

The upshot is that exemptions are sometimes warranted, but only under certain conditions. One must consider various questions:[104] What is the justification for the law in question? What are the various goods at stake? Does the law needlessly impose unequal burdens, particularly on those already burdened? Perhaps most important, would enforcing the law in this case cause more harm than good—even when taking into account the importance of legal consistency?

Is there any reason to think religion is specially situated with respect to these questions? We turn now to this inquiry.

2.3.2 Why Religion?

Head coverings are legally forbidden in driver's license photos unless they have religious significance. Consider the Sikh man, who wears his turban as a sign of devotion. The turban's significance is so strong that Sikh soldiers in World Wars I and II refused to wear helmets. And Sikhs recently lost a challenge in a Canadian court over their refusal to wear motorcycle helmets.[105]

Motorcycle helmets save lives, but what about driver's license photos? The presence or absence of a turban seems a trivial issue. Indeed, if the Sikh man consistently wears his head covering in public, it would seem helpful for identification purposes for him to wear it in his license photo.

But now consider a character we'll call Mr. Promise. Mr. Promise is an agnostic who rejects Sikh theology. Nevertheless, he wears a turban and does so consistently because he promised his father he would. Under most state laws, "Mr. Sikh" gets an exemption for driver's license photos, but Mr. Promise does not.

Or consider Mr. Tradition, who made no such promise to his father but wears the turban because his father wore one and it feels personally significant to him. Or how about Mr. Combover, who consistently wears a turban because he is deeply sensitive about his balding but cannot afford a convincing toupee?

Mr. Promise, Mr. Tradition, and Mr. Combover may all have very strong feelings about wearing their turbans. Mr. Promise even feels morally bound to do so. But under current law, only Mr. Sikh gets a legal exemption, because only he offers a religious reason. Such privileging of religious citizens seems arbitrary. Some satirical "Pastafarians" of the "Church of the Flying Spaghetti Monster" highlight this arbitrariness by wearing spaghetti strainers on their heads in driver's license photos; because the claim is religious, they are granted the exemption.

Why privilege religious reasons in this way? Some answer that, in the United States, religion gets special treatment because the First Amendment says so. But this answer is not helpful here. For one thing, it is by no means clear that the free exercise clause should be interpreted as granting religious exemptions from otherwise neutral laws, rather than merely as prohibiting Congress from passing laws aimed directly at suppressing religious practice or particular varieties thereof. As we have seen, in cases ranging from *Reynolds* (polygamy) to *Smith* (peyote) to *Lukumi* (animal sacrifice), the U.S. Supreme Court has adopted the second interpretation.

But the main problem is that this answer misses the point of our inquiry, which is less about what the law *does* require than about what it *should* require. Should it single out religion for special accommodation, and if so, why? In what follows I explore four possible answers to this question.

(1) *Religion is a proxy for deep, important commitments.* One plausible reason for singling out religion is that it provides evidence for deep and important commitments. Consider employment accommodations for sabbatarians. Most people would prefer not to work on weekends, but some have deeper reasons than others. Because it would be difficult to weigh each reason individually, the state must instead use rough categories. "Religious reasons" are such a category. Adell Sherbert, for example, could point to her membership in a larger community, with a shared religious tradition of treating the Saturday sabbath as morally binding.

A major problem with this answer is that neither the courts nor regulatory agencies require a shared communal tradition in order to establish a religious claim. As the EEOC guidelines now put it, "an employee's belief or practice can be "religious" under Title VII even if the employee is affiliated with a religious group that does not espouse or recognize that individual's belief or practice, or if few—or no—other people adhere to it."[106]

Of course, the ability to point to a larger tradition may be useful in establishing a religious claim's *sincerity*, which is indeed a relevant requirement. Suppose a professor at a midwestern university tells his dean that during the holy month he is religiously bound to make a pilgrimage to the Holy Land, and thus must receive an accommodation—he must teach his classes remotely, via Skype, during that time. Oh, and by the way: The holy month is February, and the Holy Land is Puerto Vallarta. Most deans would balk at such a request (as did mine) because they would suspect that it had nothing to do with religion at all: The combination of self-interested motive and the lack of any recognizable religious tradition makes the insincerity apparent.

Other cases are more difficult, however. Keep in mind that every religion was new at some point. Mormonism is only two hundred years old. Scientology is less than seventy-five years old. The founders of both were regarded as charlatans by many of their contemporaries, not to mention ours. How long a tradition is necessary, and how many followers are required, to provide the requisite evidence of sincerity?

A second and related problem is that religion is both over- and underinclusive as a proxy for deep and important commitments. In other words, not every religious claim is deep and important, and not every deep and important claim is religious.

Under the Religious Land Use and Institutionalized Persons Act (RLUIPA), churches, synagogues, mosques, and other houses of worship are exempt from many zoning regulations. No one doubts that relocating a growing congregation is inconvenient. So is relocating a growing shoe store, supermarket, or household. But it doesn't follow that a pastor's desire for a bigger building should outweigh the community's desire for modestly sized structures and limited traffic. A Baptist church in New Hampshire is currently pursuing a RLUIPA claim so that it may post an electronic billboard created by "Signs for Jesus" in a neighborhood that prohibits electronic signs; its need for a flashy sign hardly seems deep or important.[107]

Nor is every deep and important claim religious. Recall Justice Stewart's observation in *Sherbert* that "South Carolina would deny unemployment benefits to a mother unavailable for work on Saturdays because she was unable to get a babysitter."[108] Surely a mother's obligation to care for her child is deep and important, regardless of whether it's informed by religious faith.

One might object here that the law is a rough instrument, and that *any* proxy is going to be either over- or underinclusive to some extent.[109] After all, the whole point of considering *proxies* is that direct evidence is either impossible or unfeasible: The state can't examine people's consciences directly, so it relies on a rough external measure instead to determine their level of commitment.

I respond that even as a rough external measure, "religion" as a category falls short. To see why, imagine a young man we'll call Mr. Pacifist. Mr. Pacifist has long been devoted to the cause of nonviolence. Although only twenty, he has participated in antiwar organizations for many years. At his university he is president of "Students Against War." He is not religious.

Compare Mr. Pacifist to another student, Mr. Mission. Mr. Mission is not opposed to war. He is religious, though not especially devout: he attends services occasionally but doesn't feel as though he gets much out of them. But Mr. Mission learns that his church's youth group has a program that sends members to Africa as missionaries for a year, and it piques his interest—living in another country with his friends sounds fun. He worries that his limited participation in church activities thus far might render him ineligible, but church leaders assure him a spot.

Suppose the nation goes to war and tries to conscript both students. Should Mr. Mission be favored for an exemption simply because he has a religious reason, the yearlong mission? Surely not. Not only does Mr. Pacifist have a deeper reason for avoiding conscription, but he also has better tangible evidence of his commitment: years of support for antiwar organizations, as compared to Mr. Mission's record of lax church attendance. What this case shows is that it is longstanding participation in a community of belief, and not religion per se, that provides evidence of deep commitment—and such communities need not be religious.

Note that in the United States, conscientious objector status in wartime is not limited to those with religious reasons: Anyone opposed to all wars (not just the specific war in question) is eligible. What's interesting is that the two cases that extended this option to nonreligious objectors did so simply by stretching the concept of "religious" to cover them. In *United States v. Seeger* (1965), the U.S. Supreme Court held unanimously that the test of religious belief "is whether it is a sincere and meaningful belief occupying in the life of its possessor a place parallel to that filled by the God of those admittedly qualified for the exemption," while adding, somewhat contradictorily, that "the exemption does not cover those who oppose war from a merely personal moral code, nor those who decide that war is wrong on the basis of essentially political, sociological or economic considerations, rather than religious belief." At the time, the relevant statute required the objector's belief in a "Supreme Being." The petitioner, Daniel Seeger, denied such belief, although he did profess "a religious faith in a purely ethical creed."[110]

In *Welsh v. United States*, the Court went even further. The petitioner, Elliot Welsh, explicitly denied that his objection was religious. But a plurality of the Court disregarded Welsh's self-understanding, holding that conscientious objection to war is "religious" as long as it "stems from the registrant's moral, ethical, or religious beliefs about what is right and wrong and these beliefs are held with the strength of traditional religious convictions."[111] Apparently the Court thought that Welsh's objection was sufficiently religious-*ish*. In a separate opinion concurring in *Welsh*'s result, Justice Harlan observed that the Court was distorting the clear meaning of words; he nevertheless sided with Welsh, on the grounds that laws granting conscientious objector status for religious reasons while denying them for nonreligious reasons violated the establishment clause.

(2) *Religious believers experience religious claims as particularly binding.* Another possible justification for privileging religion is the fact that religious believers may experience their dictates of conscience as especially binding. The idea is that religious conscience derives from an external authority, God, who creates the moral law and then holds people accountable, possibly for eternity. Believers thus experience such dictates as "nonoptional" or "volitionally necessary"—they simply *must* comply. This reason seems to motivate the Court's decisions in the conscientious objector cases: When the Court identifies Seeger's and Welsh's claims as "religious," they note that neither man felt his antiwar position as a matter of mere personal preference. On the contrary, each man was willing to go to prison rather than violate his principles.

Once again, the problem with this rationale is that it is both over- and underinclusive. Not all claims that people experience as morally binding are religious—as Seeger's and Welsh's and many other cases demonstrate—and not all religious claims are experienced as morally binding. Not all faiths subscribe to belief in a personal God, much less one who enforces justice. Even religions that do posit such a God contain various "optional" practices, such as whether to wear certain religious garb, or whether to replace a traditional sign on church property with an electronic billboard. Because courts rightly wish to avoid adjudicating "the place of a particular belief in a religion or the plausibility of a religious claim,"[112] they typically defer to believers' self-reporting. But there is no reason to think that believers are more candid or sincere than nonbelievers in reporting whether they experience a claim as morally mandatory.

One can understand the "It's particularly binding" answer to the "Why privilege religion?" question in two distinct ways, and the difference is important. One version states that religious conscience claims *are* more binding than nonreligious conscience claims, because the stakes are higher: They involve eternity. But the state cannot adopt this approach without adopting a particular understanding of God and the afterlife, and thus abandoning religious neutrality.[113]

The other version states that religious conscience claims *are felt as* more binding than nonreligious conscience claims, because (some) religious believers believe that the stakes are higher. I grant that the state may certainly take citizens' beliefs and feelings into account when determining a law's effects. But again, there's no reason to think that the religious/nonreligious distinction does a good job of tracking the distinction between claims felt as binding and those that aren't.[114] And there is a good reason to reject the idea that people should be exempted from laws mainly because they feel particularly strongly about not following them.

One might suggest that the state would be better off asking not "Is the claim *religious*?" but "Is it a matter of *conscience*?"—where *conscience* is understood as a considered judgment regarding one's own moral obligations.[115] Sometimes conscience stems from religious belief, but not always: Atheists submit to moral principles too, and religious believers don't always draw on their faith when forming conscience. Thus conscience is broader than religion. It is also narrower, because religion includes many morally optional rituals and traditions.

Simon Căbulea May has argued that even the category of conscience is problematic for determining a claim's subjective force. He gives the example of a young chess grandmaster—"one of the best chess players in the country"—who wants to avoid two years of mandatory military service so that he can pursue his dream of becoming a chess champion; an interruption now would be fatal to that dream.[116] Like his conscientious objector friends, this young man—we'll call him Mr. Chess[117]—feels his commitment intensely: indeed, May stipulates that he is far less likely to waver in his ambition than his friends are to waver in their moral commitment. Moreover, his "ambition to be world champion is no less central to his self-conception than their moral principles are to theirs."[118] Yet Mr. Chess doesn't feel *morally obligated* to be a chess champion, and most would deny that he has a case for exemption comparable to that of, say, Mr. Pacifist.

May is right to point out that nonmoral claims may be both strongly felt and important to a person's self-conception.[119] It nevertheless strikes me as plausible that the state has good reasons for distinguishing Mr. Chess from Mr. Pacifist in granting exemption from military service. As already noted, war conscription is a very special case, especially because it's counterproductive to conscript pacifists to fight. This reason cuts against Mr. Chess relative to Mr. Pacifist: Unlike his conscientious objector friends, Mr. Chess gives us no reason to think he will defend the nation any less vigorously in war.

In any case, the question at hand is whether we have greater reason for treating religious conscience as binding than nonreligious conscience, and May's "Mr. Chess" case makes no difference to that question: It simply reminds us that nonconscience claims can be felt as binding too.

(3) *Religion is a fundamental good.* Perhaps this last argument points to a better reason for singling out religious exemptions: Just as the state has reason to encourage citizens to live

according to their decisions of conscience, perhaps it also has reasons to encourage them to practice religion. The idea here is that religion—like health, education, family, and so on—is a fundamental good worth promoting. It engages the distinctively human capacity for grappling with basic questions about meaning and existence. It binds people together, often for charitable purposes that promote the general welfare. It provides a way to mark major life events, and it offers solace in times of grief and despair.

There is no doubt that religion does all of these things, and does them well. One could scarcely explain its pervasiveness and endurance otherwise. There is also no doubt that it does great evil. The same fervor that makes some willing to die for their faith makes others willing to kill for it—witness, for example, the 9/11 attacks, Boko Haram suicide bombers, the Salem witch trials, the Crusades, and countless other examples. The Nobel Prize-winning physicist Steven Weinberg has put the point sharply: "With or without [religion], you would have good people doing good things and evil people doing evil things. But for good people to do evil things, that takes religion."[120] The flip side of religion's power at binding people together is that it can encourage dangerous groupthink, leading people to imagine that they have infallible backing for their all-too-fallible prejudices.

Some will object that religion that does evil is not true religion. This objection just ignores the problem by defining it away. It's like arguing that there's no such thing as spousal abuse because anyone who abuses is not a true spouse. In any case, states that adopt principled religious neutrality cannot be in the business of distinguishing between "true" and "false" religion.

That being so, how should we assess the argument that the government ought to promote religion? Perhaps it means not that government should promote "true" religion but that it should support any sincere attempt to grapple with fundamental questions and live according to the dictates of conscience. This seems to be the argument of my counterpoint authors Girgis and Anderson, and I'll address it at greater length in my Reply. For now, I simply note that this argument doesn't answer the question I set out to address in this section: Why treat *religious* conscience differently from other conscience claims, as the law often does? It's called RFRA, not Conscience-FRA.

(4) *Religion is a common site of discrimination and conflict.* A fourth possible reason for treating religious claims as special is that people have historically mistreated one another on account of religion, and exemptions or accommodations function as a corrective measure. Sometimes this mistreatment is blatant, but often it is unintentional. As Martha Nussbaum observes, "laws in democracies are made by the majority. . . . Majority thinking is usually not malevolent, but it is often obtuse, oblivious to the burden [its] rules impose on religious minorities."[121]

I'm reminded here of how my university requires that professors make reasonable accommodations for students who miss exams for religious reasons. Initially I feared that this policy would pose an administrative nightmare: I work at a large, diverse institution, and I often teach large classes; my students observe a plethora of holidays. On the other hand, even though I teach at a state university, my Christian students never have to take an exam on Christmas day. The reason is that official holidays are chosen by the majority, and the majority observes Christmas: a Christian holiday, with elements borrowed from a pagan holiday, which has now become a secular holiday due to Christianity's prevalence. Our university schedule thus places a burden on minority faiths that it does not place on Christians. Realizing that, I came to see the accommodations policy as a reasonable way to restore fairness and promote inclusion.

The point is that majority-made policy often squeezes minorities in ways that even well-meaning people can miss. Perhaps the best reason for considering specifically religious exemptions is that they serve as a useful check on sectarian strife, whether stemming from unintentional privilege or from deliberate persecution.

There is much to be said for this argument, with some important caveats.

The first caveat is that while religion is *special* in this regard, it is not *unique*. It is, rather, one among several factors that have been common grounds for mistreatment—sometimes deliberate, but often unintentional. The design of public facilities often disadvantages people with disabilities, not to mention those at height and weight extremes. Until recently, marriage laws in the United States disadvantaged gay, lesbian, and bisexual persons. Blue laws disadvantage not only Saturday sabbatarians but also the poor: A coordinated, forced day of rest may sound wonderful, unless you're desperate for income. When laws and policies implicate such characteristics, they deserve greater scrutiny.

A second caveat is that greater scrutiny need not result in an exemption. Its doing so should depend not only on whether the rule disadvantages certain citizens but also on what other values are at stake—including the value of legal consistency. My earlier-stated concerns about "Swiss cheese" law still stand.

The value of legal consistency is why I favor extending any RFRA-generated exemptions to comparable secular conscience claims. (My counterpoint authors favor a similar policy, though for different reasons.) Secular citizens do not have as strong an argument for special exemptions as their religious counterparts, because they do not experience sectarian strife in the same way (which is not, of course, to deny that they have been the object of religious persecution). As Laycock observes, "on the whole, nonbelievers take their morality from the same modern milieu that drives democratic decision making and government regulation."[122] That said, if we allow, for example, a prisoner to wear a beard for religious reasons, there are both principled and practical difficulties in forbidding others to do so for comparably serious secular ones.[123]

A third and final caveat—perhaps the most important—is that exemptions should not remove burdens from some minorities only to place burdens on other, possibly even more disfavored, minorities. Otherwise, we undermine the very reason for considering exemptions in the first place—at least, that which we've identified as strongest.

We have already considered some ways in which the current exemption regime not only tolerates but even encourages such burden-shifting, with its stringent "least restrictive means" standard. Hobby Lobby's exemption from certain provisions of the Affordable Care Act was supposed to shift the burden of contraceptive coverage from Hobby Lobby to insurance companies or the government, but instead it shifted it to women—including poor women whose insurance coverage alternatives are limited.[124] Kim Davis's refusal to issue marriage licenses to same-sex couples placed burdens on those couples, who for a time could not receive licenses without driving to another county. Exemptions from antidiscrimination law, if granted, would place burdens on the very minorities whom the law is intended to protect.

Some, including my counterpoint author Ryan Anderson, have argued that there are ways of accommodating people like Davis without generating such burdens: Simply eliminate the legal requirement that the clerk's name appears on marriage licenses, and the conflict disappears.[125] Indeed, that solution has since been provided by Kentucky governor Matt Bevin: Gay couples get their licenses, Davis keeps her job, and no one's conscience is burdened: an apparent "win-win." It seems hard to argue with that.

Hard, but not impossible. While I'm certainly in favor of minimizing conflict, and have no strong view about how important clerks' signatures are for ensuring the integrity of licenses, I worry about the message sent by changing Kentucky law after the fact in response to Davis's requests.

To see why, recall the case of Mr. Burqa, who has the sincere religious belief that women ought never to appear in public with their faces exposed. As county clerk, he objects to granting licenses to any woman who enters his office without a full-face veil. Moreover, he refuses to let his deputy clerks do so as long as his name appears on the licenses, as current law requires.

Should we change our licensing procedures to accommodate Mr. Burqa? I'm inclined to say no. The main reason is that Mr. Burqa's belief that women may not show their faces in public is sexist; it contributes to the subjugation of women. The state should avoid showing it deference.

Or consider another, real world case: In 2009, Keith Bardwell, a Louisiana justice of the peace, refused to officiate at an interracial wedding.[126] Bardwell claimed, and doubtless sincerely believed, that he was not a racist: "I have piles and piles of black friends," he told reporters. "They come to my home, I marry them, they use my bathroom. I treat them just like everyone else."[127] But Bardwell personally objected to interracial marriages, and he refused to sign such licenses or perform such weddings.[128]

When word got out about Bardwell's position, he was pressured to resign—and rightly so. The fact that he was willing to refer interracial couples to another justice of the peace in the parish who would provide such services is irrelevant. Notwithstanding his protestations, Bardwell's moral qualms both reflected and reinforced the racist subjugation of blacks in this country. That he even saw it as a live question whether his "piles and piles of black friends" should be permitted to use his bathroom is evidence of just how deep that racism runs.

I'll further consider analogies between racial and other forms of discrimination in the next two sections. For now, I want to underscore two points. First, just because people's religious beliefs *can* be easily accommodated, it does not follow that they *should*. Sometimes accommodations reinforce sentiments that ought to be repudiated. Second, given that one of the best reasons for religious accommodations is the history of antireligious discrimination, religious accommodations ought not be used as a license to discriminate. It is to the topic of discrimination that we now turn.

2.4 DISCRIMINATION AND THE LAW

Bob Jones University is a private nondenominational Christian school in Greenville, South Carolina. Founded in 1927, it has a history of influence in American conservative politics, having hosted major Republican presidential candidates as speakers— including Ronald Reagan, George W. Bush, and, more recently, Ted Cruz.

Bob Jones University did not admit African or African-American students until 1971, and then only if they were married. When in 1975 it began admitting unmarried blacks, it also expanded disciplinary rules forbidding interracial dating and marriage, as follows:

There is to be no interracial dating.

1. Students who are partners in an interracial marriage will be expelled.
2. Students who are members of or affiliated with any group or organization which holds as one of its goals or advocates interracial marriage will be expelled.

3. Students who date outside of their own race will be expelled.
4. Students who espouse, promote, or encourage others to violate the University's dating rules and regulations will be expelled.[129]

These rules remained in place until the year 2000, when they attracted renewed attention after a visit to the university by then presidential candidate (later president) George W. Bush. Only then did the university rescind them.

Let me begin with what I take to be two uncontroversial observations. First, Bob Jones University's policy on interracial dating was *discriminatory*. Although it was worded neutrally, without reference to any particular race, it stemmed from, and contributed to, an unjust social regime.[130] The leaders of Bob Jones University have since admitted as much.[131]

Second, this racist, discriminatory policy was based on the sincere religious beliefs of the university's leaders. Here's Bob Jones Senior, the school's founder:

> Now, we folks at Bob Jones University believe that whatever the Bible says is so; and we believe it says certain fundamental things that all Bible-believing Christians accept; but when the Bible speaks clearly about any subject, that settles it. Men do not always agree, because some are dumb—some people are spiritually dumb; but when the Bible is clear, there is not any reason why everybody should not accept it. . . .
>
> Now, notice—this is an important verse—the twenty-sixth verse of the seventeenth chapter of the Acts of the Apostles, "And hath made of one blood all nations of men for to dwell on all the face of the earth . . ." But do not stop there, ". . . and hath determined the times before appointed, and the bounds of their habitation." Now, what does that say? That God Almighty fixed

the bounds of their habitations. That is as clear as anything that
was ever said. . . .

White folks and colored folks, you listen to me. You cannot
run over God's plan and God's established order without having trouble. God never meant to have one race. It was not His
purpose at all.[132]

The university reiterated this stance as recently as 1998, when a
spokesperson explained: "God has separated people for his own
purposes. He has erected barriers between the nations, not only
land and sea barriers, but also ethnic, cultural, and language
barriers. God has made people different from one another and
intends those differences to remain. Bob Jones University is
opposed to intermarriage of the races because it breaks down
the barriers God has established."[133]

Here, then, is a stark example of religion-based discrimination—
troubling, but hardly historically unique. Indeed, the university's
explanation echoed wording used by the trial court judge in
Loving v. Virginia, the case that led to the U.S. Supreme Court's
striking down of antimiscegenation laws: "Almighty God created the races white, black, yellow, malay and red, and he placed
them on separate continents. And but for the interference with
his arrangement there would be no cause for such marriages.
The fact that he separated the races shows that he did not intend
for the races to mix."[134]

Of course, other cases are more controversial today.
Consider:

- Posing in front of a Confederate flag, a Florida gun
  retailer posts a video declaring his gun shop a "Muslim-
  Free Zone."[135]
- An Indiana woman is fired from her job as a Catholic
  school English teacher after she and her husband used

in vitro fertilization (IVF) in an effort to have a second child.[136] Catholic moral teaching prohibits IVF.

- After "much prayer," a Michigan pediatrician declines to provide care for a lesbian couple's newborn baby; she sends a colleague as a substitute.[137]
- A New Jersey bridal shop refuses to sell a dress to a lesbian woman, telling her that her union would be "illegal" and "wrong." The woman had previously spent a day trying on dresses in the shop.[138]
- An Ohio baker cancels a birthday cake order after visiting a customer's Facebook page and realizing the cake was for the customer's same-sex partner.[139] "I'm sorry," the baker wrote in a text to the customer, "I just realized your [sic] in a same-sex relationship and we do not do cakes for same sex weddings or parties."[140]

At the most general level, to discriminate is simply to distinguish. In that broad sense discrimination is not necessarily a bad thing—thus we speak of "discriminating shoppers" or "discriminating tastes."[141] It is more common, however, to use the word in a narrower, negative sense: not merely differential treatment, but *unjust* differential treatment.[142] In what follows, unless otherwise indicated, I will use "discrimination" and its cognates in this more common, negative sense.

The controversies arise when people differ about what justice requires. Is it discrimination to refuse to hire someone simply because of their physical unattractiveness? But what if you're hiring a model? A receptionist? Is it discrimination to refuse to place someone in a leadership position simply because she's a woman? But what if the leadership position is that of Catholic bishop? Is it discrimination to decline to provide same-sex wedding services because homosexual conduct conflicts with your religious beliefs? What about interracial weddings? Interfaith weddings?

2.4.1 Material Harm and Dignitary Harm

It is worth distinguishing two ways in which discrimination harms people. One is *material harm*: Discrimination limits people's access to goods and services. For instance, employment discrimination limits opportunities for making a living. Housing discrimination limits opportunities for a safe and comfortable home. Healthcare discrimination limits access to medical treatment. Public accommodations discrimination limits the ability to participate fully in the public sphere, and so on.

Some deny that these limitations constitute harms, strictly speaking: If a gun shop owner refuses to sell a gun to a Muslim, or a bridal shop owner refuses to sell a dress to a lesbian, they make these people no worse off than they were before; thus, they do not harm them.[143] For the moment, it matters less whether we categorize these examples as harms than that we recognize the different ways that discrimination affects people, one of which is by frustrating their material interests. (If you don't like "material harms," substitute the phrase "material effects.") So for example, while there are various possible objections to Bob Jones University's interracial dating ban, one is that it *limited the educational options* of mixed-race couples.

But that's not the most important objection to the ban. After all, there were plenty of other schools willing to admit interracial couples, including other evangelical schools. Which brings us to a second and rather different type of harm: *dignitary harm*.

Although frequently mentioned in the literature, dignitary harm is seldom carefully defined.[144] The concept sounds prima facie odd, combining a typically deontological notion (dignity) with a typically consequentialist one (harm). Dignitary harm does not merely mean offense or hurt feelings, although it often correlates with those. It is rather the harm involved in treating people as having less than equal moral standing. The "separate but equal" regime of the Jim Crow South, along with its echoes in policies like Bob Jones University's ban, provides a paradigmatic example: By treating blacks as inferior, such policies were an affront to their dignity. This would be true even if these policies had not been accompanied by widespread material harm—even if, for example, the separate facilities had been truly equal (which they were not).

Some further clarifications are in order. First, borrowing from Pablo Gilabert, we should distinguish between two different senses of dignity: dignity as a *normative status* that people possess in virtue of their humanity or rationality or autonomy or some other (possibly innate) feature, and dignity as the *social condition* of having that status acknowledged or respected.[145] Dignitary harm is concerned with the latter of these: the social condition.

Failure to distinguish the two senses can lead to odd results. Consider Justice Clarence Thomas's dissent in the same-sex marriage case *Obergefell v. Hodges*. After noting that our country has long treated human dignity as God-given and inalienable, he adds: "The corollary of that principle is that human dignity cannot be taken away by the government. Slaves did not lose their dignity (any more than they lost their humanity) because the government allowed them to be enslaved. Those held in internment camps did not lose their dignity because the government confined them. And those denied governmental benefits certainly do not lose their dignity because the government denies them those benefits. The government cannot bestow dignity, and it cannot take it away."[146]

One might just as easily (and strangely) argue that because *rights* are God-given and inalienable, we do not deprive people of their rights by enslaving them! Of course governments cannot alter their citizens' normative status as persons. But when governments fail to recognize that status, they surely under-mine dignity as a social condition.

Second, dignitary harm receives much of its force from social context. A quirky, isolated insult is less likely to threaten a person's social equality than one made in the con-text of systematic exclusion. My grandparents, who arrived in the United States at a time when the country was rife with anti-Catholic sentiment, experienced a greater sting from anti-Catholic slurs than I do.[147] Calling my British colleague a "limey" would not have the same effect as calling my Asian colleague a "chink" or calling me a "faggot," given the differ-ent social contexts.[148]

Third, we should distinguish three related but distinct aspects of dignitary harm: (1) treating people as inferior, regard-less of whether anyone recognizes the mistreatment; (2) causing people to *feel* inferior, intentionally or not; and (3) contribut-ing to systemic moral inequality, intentionally or not. Although these aspects are related, they are not *necessarily* connected. A speaker might insult someone in a language the latter fails to understand, with no one else in earshot. A person may perceive an insult where none was intended. People may contribute to systematic moral inequality through ignorance or inattention.

Finally, note how material and dignitary harm are related: The sting of dignitary harm often functions to system-atically intimidate and exclude people in ways that have cumu-lative material effects.

2.4.2 Antidiscrimination Law and LGBT Equality

Antidiscrimination law addresses both material and dignitary harm. It prohibits unequal treatment on the basis of tradition-ally targeted characteristics: generally race, sex, and religion, and in some jurisdictions others, including marital status, sexual orientation, and gender identity. Such law aims to ensure equal access in the public sphere.

It may seem paradoxical that the law seeks to promote equality by giving special attention to certain characteristics: If the goal is equality, why not treat everyone the same?[149] But the paradox is specious. Sometimes the goal of equal treatment is best achieved by a process that gives certain factors extra scrutiny. And antidiscrimination law *does* treat all people equally with respect to those factors—after all, everyone has a race, a sex, a sexual orientation, and so on. (Not everyone has a religion, but antidiscrimination laws that enumerate "religion" generally protect agnostics and atheists too.)

Antidiscrimination law thus protects the conservative Christian heterosexual from unjust treatment by the gay atheist as much as it does the reverse. More so, in fact: Religion is a protected category at the federal level, whereas sexual orientation is not—indeed, fewer than half the states include it at the state level.[150]

In the current "culture wars," discussions of antidiscrimination law and LGBT equality tend to focus on wedding services. Unfortunately, this focus misleadingly suggests that the biggest problem facing LGBT people is the inability to buy cakes and flowers. On the contrary: Antidiscrimination laws are mainly about access to employment, housing, and basic goods and services. LGBT people have been and continue to be the victims of unjust discrimination in these areas. Recent analyses by the Williams Institute at the University of California, Los Angeles, find that LGBT people file complaints related to employment, housing, and public-accommodations discrimination at the same rate (adjusted for population) that racial minorities and women do for race and sex discrimination.[151] The powerful phenomenon of the closet makes it likely that such discrimination goes underreported.

Consider employment discrimination. The U.S. Senate Report on the Employment Non-discrimination Act provides some sobering statistics:[152]

- According to a 2008 report, 42% of lesbian, gay, and bisexual people have experienced at least one form of employment discrimination because of their sexual orientation.
- Twelve studies conducted in the last decade show that gay male workers are paid less on average than their heterosexual male coworkers. The wage gap identified in these studies varies between 10% and 32% of the heterosexual men's earnings.[153]
- Lesbian couples have a poverty rate of 6.9% compared to 5.4% for different-sex married couples. Poverty rates for children of same-sex couples are twice as high as poverty rates for children of married heterosexual couples.[154]
- A 2011 report found that 90% of transgender Americans experienced harassment, mistreatment, or discrimination at work because of their gender identity or took actions like hiding who they are to avoid it. Forty-seven percent of transgender Americans said they experienced an adverse job outcome, such as being fired, not hired, or denied a promotion because they were transgender or gender nonconforming. Twenty-six percent of transgender Americans reported losing their jobs due to being transgender. Fifty percent of transgender Americans reported being harassed.[155]
- Transgender respondents to a 2011 national survey were unemployed at twice the rate of the general population, and

15% reported a household income of under $10,000 a year, nearly four times the rate for the general population.[156]

For much of this nation's history, discrimination against LGBT people was not merely tolerated but in fact legally sanctioned. The exclusion from marriage made even long-term same-sex couples legal strangers to each other, sometimes with devastating financial, legal, and personal effects.[157] There has also been explicit governmental discrimination in employment.[158] And do not forget antisodomy laws, which turned most gay people into unapprehended felons, and had the further pernicious effect of limiting employment opportunities (because it's harder for felons, even presumed ones, to get jobs). Many of the loudest proponents of "liberty" today openly defended such laws, which were not struck down by the U.S. Supreme Court until *Lawrence v. Texas* in 2003.[159] Not coincidentally, these proponents defended them by appealing to religion. Here's Chief Justice Burger in *Bowers v. Hardwick* (1986), the decision that *Lawrence* overturned: "Condemnation of [homosexual conduct] is firmly rooted in Judeo-Christian moral and ethical standards. Homosexual sodomy was a capital crime under Roman law. During the English Reformation, when powers of the ecclesiastical courts were transferred to the King's Courts, the first English statute criminalizing sodomy was passed. Blackstone described 'the infamous crime against nature' as an offense of 'deeper malignity' than rape, a heinous act 'the very mention of which is a disgrace to human nature,' and 'a crime not fit to be named.' "[160]

Against this backdrop, antidiscrimination laws that enumerate sexual orientation and gender identity function to ensure that openly LGBT people, long marginalized, have a place at the table in public life. Although these laws are not mainly about wedding services, they include wedding services—which brings us to the current conflicts.

2.4.3 Cake Wars

Rachel and Laurel Bowman-Cryer are a lesbian couple in Portland, Oregon, having relocated from Texas.[161] They had been together for eight years when in 2012 they decided to marry. Laurel had previously proposed numerous times, but Rachel had hesitated. She finally acquiesced in order to provide "permanency and commitment" to their two foster children, whom they hoped to adopt. The children were disabled, with "very high special needs."[162] Rachel and Laurel had taken the children into foster care after the death of their mother, who had been Laurel's best friend. The adoption was finally approved in 2013, following a bitter and emotional custody battle with the children's great-grandparents.

Once Rachel agreed to the wedding, she became excited about its planning. She and her mother attended a wedding expo where they encountered Melissa Klein of Sweet Cakes by Melissa, the bakery that had provided a cake for Rachel's mother's wedding two years prior. Eager to order from Sweet Cakes again, they made a tasting appointment for January 17, 2013.

When Rachel and her mother finally arrived for their appointment, Melissa's husband, Aaron Klein, asked for the name of the bride and groom. (Melissa was out that day.) After Rachel explained that there would be two brides, Aaron stated that Sweet Cakes did not make cakes for same-sex weddings because of his and Melissa's religious convictions. This upset Rachel, who began crying and was escorted out by her mother, who attempted to console her. Rachel felt ashamed, and was particularly concerned that she had embarrassed her mother, who not long before had disapproved of her daughter's homosexuality. When Rachel's mother returned to the shop to explain to Aaron how "she used to think like him, but her 'truth had changed,'" he quoted Leviticus 18:22: "You shall not lie with a male as one lies with a female; it is an abomination."

(Leviticus makes no reference to lesbianism, but let's leave that aside.)[163]

Wedding planning can be emotional, alternately joyous and stressful. In Rachel's case, the refusal of service hit particularly hard. Given her sensitive nature, her prior relationship experience, and her religious background—she had been raised Southern Baptist—the incident stirred up painful emotions. She cried for days, fought with Laurel, and even doubted that she was "supposed to love or be loved, have a family or go to heaven."[164]

You might think Rachel Bowman-Cryer overreacted. Indeed, a different individual, with a different emotional makeup, might have told Aaron Klein where he could stuff his cake. But not Rachel: She was hurt. Her mother was present; her children might have been as well. As Andrew Koppelman explains, by advertising their services as open to the public, the Kleins induced Rachel "to participate in the activity of her own rejection."[165] It felt like a humiliating bait-and-switch. This wasn't what she bargained for when she made the appointment with Sweet Cakes.

As a result of their refusal of service, the Kleins were eventually found to have violated Oregon's Equality Act, which prohibits discrimination in public accommodations on the basis of "race, color, religion, sex, sexual orientation, national origin, marital status or age." Sexual-orientation discrimination is the most relevant category here, although one might also make a case for sex, or even marital status.[166]

The Kleins were fined $135,000 in damages for emotional distress. Some reports incorrectly claimed that this fine punished the Kleins for publicizing the Bowman-Cryers' address, but the labor commissioner's ruling explicitly said otherwise.[167] One could argue that the penalty was excessive, an example of the extremes of our litigious society. (I'm inclined to agree.) It's hard to deny, however, that the Kleins' refusal of service violated Oregon law.

Some (including my counterpoint authors) deny that refusing to sell a cake for a same-sex wedding constitutes sexual orientation discrimination: After all, the baker would equally refuse to provide a wedding cake for two heterosexual women or two heterosexual men. This objection overlooks the way in which some actions are constitutive of identity. It's like saying "I'm not discriminating against *Catholics*, I'm just discriminating against people who attend Catholic mass." Sexual orientation is a function of one's sex or gender and the sex or gender of those to whom one is romantically attracted; homosexual orientation is thus paradigmatically (though not solely) expressed in same-sex relationships. One reason these cases tend to arise in wedding contexts is that bakery customers' sexual orientation is generally not visible otherwise.

The Kleins are unwilling to sell cakes in precisely those instances where the cakes manifest their customers' sexual orientation. That's sexual orientation discrimination. By analogy, it would be religious discrimination if the Kleins said that they would sell cakes to Jews, but not for bar mitzvahs, or that they would sell cakes to Catholics, but not for First Holy Communion.

Thus far I've been examining this case largely from the perspective of the Bowman-Cryers; but what about the Kleins? Their interests matter, too. While most discussions focus on their *religious* liberty, it may be instructive to frame the discussion in terms of liberty more generally. Consider an analogous case in which a Colorado customer asked an LGBT-friendly baker for a Bible-shaped cake with the words "Homosexuality is a detestable sin—Leviticus 18:22" written on it.[168] The baker was willing to make the cake and even provide the customer with an icing bag, but not to write the words. Like that baker, the Kleins were asked to create a cake conveying a message that they morally disapprove. Should they be permitted to refuse to sell the cake?

2.4.4 Three Paths for Promoting Both Liberty and Equality

I believe in laws prohibiting discrimination on the basis of sexual orientation and gender identity.[169] And yet I'm also sympathetic to the argument that bakers and other business owners should be free to express their values in the conduct of their business. Is it possible to respect both equality and liberty in cases like these?

I think so, and in what follows, I want to explore three paths for doing so. In particular, I want to show that it's possible to respect the Kleins' interests without jettisoning the relevant antidiscrimination laws. In brief, the paths are as follows:

1. Fashion antidiscrimination law in such a way as to exclude certain businesses or services.
2. Legally prohibit discrimination and grant religious (and perhaps other conscience) exemptions, but require business owners who take advantage of such exemptions to post their position publicly, in order to give prior warning to same-sex couples.
3. Legally prohibit discrimination and *do not* grant religious (and other conscience) exemptions, but *permit* business owners who object to same-sex marriage to post their position publicly.

Although I favor some version of the first path, all three deserve thoughtful consideration. I shall examine each.

1. Fashion antidiscrimination law in such a way as to exclude certain businesses or services.

Path 1 suggests that we construct antidiscrimination law in such a way that it excludes certain types of business (e.g., "expressive," "wedding related," "small-owner-operated") or certain services. The law would still prohibit most businesses from discriminating, and would still send a signal to all businesses that antigay views conflict with the community's values.

The devil is in the details, though, and this approach has presented thorny line-drawing problems. Suppose that one wants to exempt "expressive" businesses. Wedding photographers would count, but would bakers? What about florists? Caterers? Limousine drivers? After all, the way drivers open car doors for newlyweds might express respect. Many businesses—and not just those offering wedding services—include some expressive aspect.

A more straightforward version of this approach restricts the built-in exemptions to businesses of a certain size. Such a proposal has been offered by a group of law professors consisting of Edward McGlynn Gaffney, Jr., Thomas C. Berg, Carl H. Esbeck, Richard W. Garnett, and Robin Fretwell Wilson.[170] They define "small business" as those made up of five or fewer employees. They then propose that no small business be required to "provide goods or services that assist or promote the solemnization or celebration of any marriage, or provide counseling or other services that directly facilitate the perpetuation of any marriage ... if providing such goods, services, benefits, or housing would cause such individuals or sole proprietors, or owners of such small businesses, to violate their sincerely held religious beliefs." They additionally propose that this rule will not apply if "a party to the marriage is unable to obtain any similar good or services, employment benefits, or housing elsewhere without substantial hardship."

The proposal attempts to balance some of the competing concerns in this case. Had such legislation been in place in Oregon, it would have allowed Sweet Cakes (a small business) to decline to bake a cake for a same-sex wedding, but only because numerous other local bakers were available for such purposes.

On the other hand, as Mary Anne Case has argued, the proposal's wording suffers from many of the problems that other exemption programs have.[171] It singles out marriage, which is but one of countless areas of law where people have sincere objections. It also singles out *religious* objections, which are but a subset of conscience claims.

What's more, it exempts small-business owners from assisting the celebration of "any" marriage to which they object. What about interfaith marriages, remarriages after divorce, marriages not solemnized by a church, or marriages not solemnized by the "right" church? Could a Baptist baker refuse to sell anniversary cakes to Catholics, or a Muslim to Jews? Would the exemptions extend to interracial marriage—and if not, why not? (Federal law already covers some of these categories in certain contexts, but should it?)

It's true that the proposal includes the provision that exemptions won't be granted unless the couple can find similar goods or services "without substantial hardship." But that provision only considers hardship to the couple, not the aggregate problem created when business owners can pick and choose which marriages to recognize when deciding whether to comply with relevant regulations. And how does one define substantial hardship? Would there need to be no other, willing baker within twenty miles? Fifty miles? What if the only willing baker has lousy Yelp reviews?

Another version of this path—one that I personally endorse—would draw the line not according to business size or type but according to business *service*: If the service is truly custom, the owners may at their discretion decline to provide it, but they must sell off-the-shelf or even catalog designs to any customer willing to pay the fee. Take bakeries. By "custom service," I don't mean cakes chosen from a catalog or requests such as "I want the same cake you made for my mother, but with green icing instead of pink." (The Kleins' blanket refusal to sell same-sex wedding cakes would thus not have been covered.) I mean unique artistic creations, of the sort one sees on shows such as *Cake Wars*.

Drawing the line at custom services helps to underscore an important principle: If a business is willing and able to sell an item to some customers, it is wrong for them to refuse to sell the *very same item* to other customers on the basis of the customers' race, religion, sexual orientation, and so on.[172] That principle helps us to distinguish the case at hand from that of the baker who refuses to sell a swastika-shaped cake to anyone, a kosher baker who refuses to sell a bacon-topped cake to anyone, or a vegan baker who refuses to sell a real buttercream cake to anyone, and so on—those are simply not items that these bakers provide *at all*.

For the same reason, I would protect the bakers' refusal to include writing that they don't want to provide, whether it's "Homosexuality is a detestable sin" or "Yay gay marriage!" Indeed, I think the LGBT-friendly Colorado baker handled the "Homosexuality is a detestable sin" Bible-shaped cake request perfectly, even generously: She agreed to make the cake, and even provide the piping bag, but not to write the words.[173] (My counterpoint authors discuss, and mischaracterize, this case in their Reply.)[174]

There are additional reasons for drawing the line at custom work. Custom services usually involve considerable artistry, and artists should have wide freedom from government intervention. Moreover, whereas people have a reasonable expectation that off-the-shelf goods and services will be sold to them at an advertised fee, custom work is more of an invitation to negotiation. And custom work generally (though not always) involves services that people want, but do not need.[175] No one starves for lack of a custom wedding cake.

Such a solution isn't perfect, of course. Imagine a baker who believes that physical deformities reflect "spiritual" deformities and therefore objects to working with the physically disabled.[176] According to my proposal, this baker would be required to sell any off-the-shelf or standard catalog designs to disabled people but would not be legally required to provide custom designs. This result is morally unpalatable.

There are line-drawing problems here too. How does one distinguish "custom" services from others? A portrait painter's services would seem to be entirely custom, and I would apply the same point to artistic photographers. But what about the operator of the mall portrait studio who essentially lines people up and announces "Say cheese!" And what about florists, who may copy catalog designs but often deviate from them depending on which flowers are available and fresh? Although I endorse this approach, I worry about whether "custom services" is a practically administrable legal category. We should consider alternatives.

2. Legally prohibit discrimination, grant religious (and perhaps other) exemptions, but require business owners who take advantage of such exemptions to post their position publicly, in order to give prior warning to same-sex couples.

For reasons discussed in previous sections, I'm not a fan of widespread exemptions. And I'm particularly opposed to granting them to antidiscrimination law, which protects vulnerable minorities' access to employment, housing, and goods and services.

One very important exception is the ministerial exception, which gives wide latitude to religions in hiring ministers—thus, for example, allowing Catholics to discriminate against women in choosing priests.[177] There are number of good reasons for the ministerial exception, but the main one is that it involves jobs whose required qualifications are beyond the purview of those outside the faith.[178] (Does a person need to be male in order to turn bread into flesh and wine into blood? I don't even know how to begin answering such a question.) The main worry about the ministerial exception is that religious officials abuse it by stretching the term "minister" to apply to a wide variety of employees, including those whose main duties have nothing to do with religion.[179]

But suppose exemptions to antidiscrimination law were allowed more widely. One way to reduce their negative effects on people like the Bowman-Cryers would be to adopt a policy suggested by Andrew Koppelman, Douglas Laycock, and others: Businesses that take advantage of exemptions should be required to post this fact prominently, on their websites (if applicable) and at the entrances to their premises, in order to give prior warning to those affected.[180] For the Kleins, such a posting might look something like this: "We welcome a diverse group of customers for a wide variety of baked goods. However, we also believe in a traditional definition of marriage as the union of one man and one woman. *Accordingly, notwithstanding the Oregon Equality Act, we do not provide cakes for same-sex weddings.*" This posting requirement would achieve two aims. First, it would ensure that those seeking exemptions are serious about whatever commitments render them unable or unwilling to adhere to applicable law—serious enough that they're willing to state their opposition publicly, even though doing so might cost them some business. Second, and more important, it would help to prevent the awkward, uncomfortable, and painful personal encounters in which owners *directly* reject the couples. It would thus prevent the sort of humiliating bait-and-switch at the heart of this case. This avoidance is something that both sides should welcome.

Of course, if the exemptions became too widespread, as they might in certain conservative towns, then the same-sex couples would lack access to services. Perhaps path 2 could be modified with a "without substantial hardship" clause, as discussed in path 1. Even so, I favor the third path over the second.

3. Legally prohibit discrimination, do not grant religious (and other conscience) exemptions, but permit business owners who object to same-sex marriage to post their position publicly.

The third path resembles the second, except without exemptions to the relevant law. Nevertheless, it allows business owners like the Kleins to make their opposition to same-sex marriage clear. Such business owners might post announcements of the following sort: "We comply with all applicable laws, including laws that prohibit discrimination on the basis of sexual orientation; we thus provide cakes for same-sex weddings when requested to do so. However, we also believe in a traditional definition of marriage as the union of one man and one woman and personally oppose same-sex marriage." Path 3 is in fact an existing legal option: Although the Kleins may not refuse service on the basis of sexual orientation, they are, and always have been, free to express their views about marriage. There was some confusion about this point in media reports about a "gag order," a confusion that was encouraged by ambiguity in the labor commissioner's statements and the Kleins' own public remarks.[181] And the fact that it's an existing option doesn't mean that it's uncontroversial: Some would argue that such signs create a hostile workplace environment. But free speech must include freedom for those who hold minority viewpoints, even offensive ones.

Andrew Koppelman favors this path.[182] It builds on a suggestion by the New Mexico Supreme Court in its ruling on a wedding photography case, *Elane Photography v. Willock*: "Businesses that choose to be public accommodations must comply with the NMHRA [New Mexico Human Rights Act], although such businesses retain their First Amendment rights to express their religious or political beliefs. They may, for example, post a disclaimer on their website or in their studio advertising that they oppose same-sex marriage but that they comply with applicable antidiscrimination laws."[183]

This path has much to recommend it. It gives conservative religious business owners the freedom to express their views. Yet it also guarantees access for same-sex couples in towns where few businesses might otherwise serve them. Meanwhile, in towns with many gay-affirming options, it alerts same-sex couples that other businesses may better share their values. Thus, even without granting exemptions, this option makes it unlikely that people like the Kleins will ever have to make cakes for same-sex weddings: Why would gay couples want to spend their money there, given knowledge of the bakers' position and good available alternatives?

There are potential disadvantages. Some may worry that encouraging businesses to post signs opposing same-sex marriage would simply perpetuate the negative environment that antidiscrimination laws aim to ameliorate. Perhaps so. But remember, these are not "No Gays Allowed" signs: Unlike path 2, which allows exemptions, this path requires all businesses to follow the relevant antidiscrimination laws.

A second and more serious worry is that this path doesn't quite address the central concerns of conservative religious business owners like the Kleins. Yes, part of their worry is expressive—they do not want to condone same sex marriage—and this path helps remove any doubt about where they stand. But they also worry about complicity: They don't want to participate in something of which they disapprove. Doesn't this path simply respond to the complicity concern by saying "Tough luck"?

I don't think so. To see why, we must consider what exactly the Kleins would be complicit in. Assume for the sake of argument that same-sex marriage is wrong. Normally, one is complicit in something by causally contributing to it or failing to prevent it when one ought to have done so. If Moe announces that he intends to murder Larry, and Curly offers him a gun, Curly is complicit in Moe's shooting Larry. If Curly knows that Moe intends to murder Larry and fails to call the police when he could and should, Curly is complicit in Moe's shooting Larry. If Curly knows that Moe murdered Larry and fails to tell the police what he knows, he's complicit in the cover-up and in Moe's escaping justice.

With respect to the Bowman-Cryers' marriage, the Kleins' situation is quite different. Marriage happens with or without cake: Unlike, say, the minister or the judge, the baker is in no way causally responsible for the marriage. And it's not as if the Kleins could have prevented it by, say, calling the police. So the Kleins cannot plausibly claim that baking the cake would make them complicit in the Bowman-Cryers' *marriage*. The most they can claim is that baking the cake would make them complicit in the *celebration of* the marriage. And indeed, perhaps celebrating a wrongful act is another way of being complicit in it.[184] That's what the Kleins want to avoid.

But the Kleins are not being asked to join the celebration; they are being asked to provide a cake. Wedding cakes convey a celebratory message, yes, but that message is the couple's and their guests', not the baker's. The same can be said of many other wedding services: As the New Mexico Supreme Court put it in *Elane Photography*, "it is well known to the public that wedding photographers are hired by paying customers and that a photographer may not share the happy couple's views on issues ranging from the minor (the color scheme, the hors d'oeuvres) to the decidedly major (the religious service, the choice of bride or groom)."[185] The posting option of path 3 simply removes any doubt—and thus further undermines the plausibility of any complicity claim. My point is that the complicity claim in this case is inextricably tied to a speech claim: To celebrate is to express enjoyment; this path, however, allows the bakers to express disapproval.

Of course, the Kleins might still *feel* complicit in the celebration, reassurances about causal distance and contrary messages notwithstanding. But offering legal exemptions in the face of such weak complicity claims would wreak havoc on antidiscrimination law. What about the Ohio baker who didn't want to sell a *birthday* cake to a lesbian (who was purchasing it for her partner), presumably because she felt complicit in the act of affectionate gift-giving between them? What about bakers who disapprove of interracial marriage, interfaith marriage, or remarriage after divorce? And what about off-the-shelf items, which are similarly used for celebration? This is a serious problem with the argument for exemptions for wedding services: It proves too much.

Such sweeping deference would undermine support for complicity claims in cases where virtually everyone supports them: cases where the claimant is directly causally connected to the disapproved behavior, and where that behavior has life-or-death consequences. Think of nurses who don't want to assist in abortions, or prison doctors who don't want to perform executions.

A third and final worry is that such laws should not exist in the first place, because it is not the government's job to curtail discrimination by private business owners. This is the libertarian position: Government's proper function is to protect people's rights against force or fraud, and no more. Market forces should take care of the rest.

This is a large objection, and it is beyond this book's scope to provide a full answer. Instead, let me make a few observations that should go some way toward blunting its force. First, notice how the libertarian position elevates liberty over all other values, including equality. Its appeal stems partly from the assumption of equal starting points. But people often come to market negotiations from dramatically unequal starting points, economically and socially, and the libertarian position offers little to address this inequality.

Second, and related, note that the libertarian position rules out virtually all antidiscrimination law, not just where it's related to sexual orientation and gender identity: If the Kleins want to refuse to sell cakes—even off-the-shelf cakes—to Jews, or Catholics, or Asians, or single mothers, and so forth, there is no libertarian argument for the government's stopping them. The only exceptions are for government actors, public utilities, common carriers, or monopolies. Some libertarians would also make exceptions for laws combatting racial discrimination in the Jim Crow South, the idea being that "Jim Crow segregation involved the equivalent of a white supremacist cartel"[186] and was thus inconsistent with a truly free market. But even if that argument could be made consistent with libertarian principles—and it's quite unclear that it can[187]—it does not explain why such laws should be retained now, or why they should include other, less controversial categories such as religion or national origin.

Third, the libertarian position would eliminate far more than simply antidiscrimination law. Consider the various uncontroversial ways in which laws restrict bakers' liberty, including their "religious liberty," broadly understood. For example, it is against the law for bakers to operate in the nude, even if they're nudists for religious reasons. That's not because their doing so would violate anyone's rights but because people have a reasonable expectation that shopkeepers in commercial spaces will be clothed. The bakers cannot smoke, even if both they and the customer mutually agree to assume any risks inherent in their doing so, and even if—like Alfred Smith of the famed peyote case—they have religious reasons for smoking. They must carry liability insurance, even if they believe that "God will provide" and that insurance is a form of gambling or usury. If an employee gets pregnant and the business is of a certain size, the owners must offer her maternity leave and allow her to return to work, even if they have religious objections to mothers' working outside the home.

There are also safety regulations, tax regulations, insurance laws, minimum wage laws, and a host of other relatively uncontroversial features of modern business that are inconsistent with the libertarian position. Anyone wishing to invoke libertarianism must bite the bullet on these other examples; very few do.

Fourth, it matters whether a business operates as a sole proprietorship or as an incorporated entity. Businesses incorporate in order to formally distance the relationship between the owner and the business entity, thus limiting the owner's liability in various ways. As philosophy professor Dale Miller asks, "if the business owner is willing to accept less responsibility for her decisions, then why should she expect as much freedom in making them?"[188] Justice Ginsburg makes the same point in her *Hobby Lobby* dissent: "In a sole proprietorship, the business and its owner are one and the same. By incorporating a business, however, an individual separates herself from the entity and escapes personal responsibility for the entity's obligations. One might ask why the separation should hold only when it serves the interest of those who control the corporation."[189]

Of course, one need not be a libertarian to think that certain laws go too far, and that laws covering wedding cakes are among them. Because of legal line-drawing challenges, however, it is difficult for the law to distinguish between "essential" foodstuffs and nonessential ones, let alone between wedding cakes and birthday cakes. So the law requires that businesses open to the public must be open to the entire public, without getting into the details of whether particular services are necessities or luxuries.

The law is an imperfect instrument. Oregon's antidiscrimination law strikes me as one reasonable way to promote both liberty and equality in the commercial sphere, especially when coupled with a posting option. I myself would go even further and would offer exemptions for truly custom services.

I also want to emphasize that zealous legal enforcement is not called for in every case. The fact that a law is good to have does not mean that it is good to enforce whenever possible. It's against the law for people who are not postal workers to go into other people's mailboxes; that's a good law to have. But if a friend drops a birthday card in your mailbox, you'd have to be a jerk to report them to the police. It's against the law to possess nude photographs of minors; that's a very good law to have. But when two North Carolina sixteen-year-olds consensually "sexted" each other nude photos of themselves, there was something absurd about prosecutors' charging them (as adults!) for possession of child pornography and threatening them with thirty years on the sex-offender registry.[190] Notwithstanding the wisdom of the relevant law, its application was disproportionate to the offense.

By refusing service, the Kleins spoiled what should have been a happy process for Rachel Bowman-Cryer and caused her considerable psychological distress. Not every case is like this. Take Baronelle Stutzman, owner of Arlene's Flowers in Washington state. For years Stutzman provided flowers to her customer Rob Ingersoll and his partner, Curt Freed. She did so gladly; she considered him a friend. But when he asked her to provide flowers for their wedding, that was a bridge too far. As Stutzman explains, "if all he'd asked for were prearranged flowers, I'd gladly have provided them. If the celebration were for his partner's birthday, I'd have been delighted to pour my best into the challenge. But as a Christian, weddings have a particular significance."[191] She politely explained her reservations, and then suggested three other nearby florists that she "knew would do an excellent job for this celebration that meant so much to him." They parted on apparently good terms. Then Ingersoll sued Stutzman for discrimination.

Washington state's antidiscrimination laws, like Oregon's, strike me as good laws. But from where I stand, it seems there were better ways to handle this situation.

2.5 BIGOTRY AND SOCIAL PRESSURE

Cases like Stutzman's and the Kleins' have led to a common complaint on the right: that those who maintain a traditional male/female understanding of marriage are being unfairly branded as bigots. The word "bigot" and its cognates tend to get tossed around without much precision. In this section I want to clarify the concept and also say more about the role of social pressure in combatting discrimination.

Dictionary definitions of "bigotry" are notoriously unhelpful: They sometimes suggest that anyone who feels strongly about something is a bigot.[192] I take bigotry to consist in stubborn and unjustified animus toward people, typically (though not always) in the context of a larger system of subordination. This definition is somewhat controversial, especially in its inclusion of "animus": Many would argue that those who hold certain views are bigots even if they hold them without ill-feeling: Recall Keith Bardwell, the Louisiana justice of the peace with "piles and piles of black friends" who opposed interracial marriage. And some have questioned whether bigotry is necessarily stubborn: the philosophy professor William Ramsey offers the counterexample of the "wishy-washy racist" who is nevertheless a bigot.[193] What is clear is that bigotry admits of degrees; that it often infects those, like Bardwell, who seem like otherwise nice people; and that it sometimes stems from, and is reinforced by, religion.

Rather than focus on the word "bigotry"'s *meaning*, it may be more illuminating to focus on its *use*. To call people bigots, or their viewpoint bigotry, is not merely to say something about them; it is also to say something about oneself. It is to express, in very strong terms, one's deep moral disagreement. It is to mark their views as beyond the pale: more worthy of silencing and shunning than thoughtful engagement.

Sometimes this stance is entirely merited. Take racism. Decent people treat racist views as not merely wrong, but toxic—both infected and infectious. That's one reason why many people were surprised during the 2016 U.S. presidential campaign when House Speaker Paul Ryan referred to some of Republican nominee Donald Trump's comments as a "textbook definition of racism" yet continued to endorse him: Racism generally disqualifies people from polite company, let alone the presidency.[194]

At other times, such ostracism is misdirected. Not long ago, many people shunned interracial couples with the same antipathy that most of us now feel toward racism, with even judges describing interracial marriage as "revolting, disgraceful, and almost bestial."[195] Similar disgust was long directed toward LGBT people—and still is.[196] Consider these words from Pastor Kevin Swanson at his National Religious Liberties Conference in 2015:

> There are families, we're talking Christian families, pastors' families, elders' families from good, godly churches, whose sons are rebelling, hanging out with homosexuals and getting married and the parents are invited. What would you do if that was

the case? Here is what I would do: sackcloth and ashes at the entrance to the church and I'd sit in cow manure and I'd spread it all over my body. That is what I would do and I'm not kidding, I'm not laughing. . . .

These are the people with the sores, the gaping sores! The sores that are open, pussy [i.e., puss-filled] and gross, and people are coming in and carving happy faces on the sores! That's not a nice thing to do! Don't you dare carve happy faces on open, pussy sores![197]

Notice how Swanson explicitly uses the language of outrage and disgust to refer to same-sex relationships—"Don't you *dare* carve happy faces on open, pussy sores!" It's the mirror image of the sentiment that one appropriately expresses toward bigotry: In both cases, the object is treated as loathsome. Swanson also reiterated his view that homosexuality should be punished by death, although he conceded that the time was "not yet" at hand for carrying out this biblical injunction.[198] His conference was attended by major Republican presidential candidates, including Senator Ted Cruz.

Calling someone a bigot thus functions as a conversation stopper: It marks them as unworthy of dialogue. While that stance is entirely appropriate in certain cases—I'd apply it to Swanson—it should be used judiciously. Dialing every single conflict up to the "outrage" level is not only disproportionate; it's also counterproductive, precluding opportunities for dialogue with the "movable middle."

The question of when to shun and when to engage involves a judgment call, and in a diverse society, that call is often difficult. We've moved rapidly from a time when many people thought homosexuality so obviously wrong as to not merit further inquiry—that's Swanson's position—to a time when many people think *opposition* to homosexuality so obviously wrong as to not merit further inquiry.[199] Dialogue between such groups is virtually impossible; hence the polarization in the "culture wars."

Consider the case of Brendan Eich, cofounder of the tech company Mozilla. After Eich was named Mozilla's CEO in March 2014, it was revealed that back in 2008 he had contributed $1,000 to California's Proposition 8 campaign, which successfully revoked same-sex marriage in that state for a time. Eich was widely denounced, and he eventually resigned his post. At *Slate*, J. Bryan Lowder wrote that Eich's firing

> may be a sign that we are nearing a point at which it will no longer be acceptable to publically articulate opinions about what LGBTQ people do and do not "deserve," that we have matured such that we understand (once again) that groups of human beings with intrinsic characteristics may no longer be used as conversation pieces. Tim Teeman wrote on Friday that "the 'shame' axis around homosexuality has positively shifted from those who are gay to those who are anti-gay." He may be right about that, but speaking personally, I am not interested in shaming anyone; it would be enough for me if those people who are so ignorant or intransigent as to still be anti-gay in 2014 would simply shut up.
>
> Or at least, for the majority of Americans to agree that they should do so and to object with the appropriate vehemence when they try to run their mouths. Money being speech, this is actually what happened in Eich's case. A man offered an opinion on an issue about which opinions should not be entertained, did not indicate that he was interested in amending it, and was duly dismissed.[200]

Some of Lowder's claims strike me as contradictory: I'm not sure what "shaming" means if the treatment he proposes for Eich doesn't count. (If you're going to do it, at least own it.) In a follow-up piece, Lowder makes it clear that he thinks we should treat Eich no better than we treat racists.[201]

My own view on the Eich affair is more conflicted. By all accounts, Eich interacted well with LGBT employees—that's one reason people were surprised by his donation—and he made strong statements of his commitment to equitable treatment in the workplace.[202] That he should be dismissed for political views about marriage he expressed outside the workplace troubles me, especially as someone old enough to remember when it was very common for people to fear losing jobs on the grounds of being gay or progay. (It still happens, just not as often.)

Of course, even this last point has its limits. If it had been discovered that Eich had been giving money to neo-Nazi groups or the Ku Klux Klan, I would have joined calls for his ouster, no matter how well he behaved toward minorities at work. Again, that's how we treat bigots: as infected and infectious, in need of quarantine. But in his words and actions, Eich did not strike me—or for that matter, his LGBT fellow Mozilla employees—as a bigot.[203] He struck me as a decent man for whom same-sex marriage was still a bridge too far. At the time of his ouster, that's a view he shared with 42 percent of Americans.[204]

I prefer to engage rather than ostracize people like Eich, and in the wake of his ouster I even signed an open letter urging greater tolerance and engagement.[205] I take this stance not only because such engagement helps to win political battles or because it's more charitable than the alternative—although both are true. Most important, I take it for the sake of those who come after us. Remember that same-sex marriage opponents have children, and some of them may turn out to be lesbian, gay, bisexual, or transgender. J. Bryan Lowder would prefer that those who disapprove of homosexuality simply "shut up," but the more likely scenario is that upon being silenced in public they'll go home and vent their frustrations in private—in ways that may hurt LGBT youth even more. I thus reject Lowder's view that this is an issue "about which opinions should not be entertained."

On the other hand, I think that social conservatives have dramatically overplayed what happened to Eich. In his more nuanced moments, Lowder has a point: While Eich was free to express his views, so too are the rest of us free to express our strong disapproval of such views. More to the point, Mozilla stakeholders were free to do so, and they did. Eich contributed to an ugly, scaremongering campaign that portrayed gays as threats to children and took away legal rights. His support for that campaign is one reason why comparisons to President Obama, who also opposed same-sex marriage in 2008, fall flat: Even before he "evolved" on marriage equality, President Obama opposed Proposition 8. Mozilla is an "open source" company, part of a movement that shares its code freely and emphasizes community values; Eich's stance was incongruent with those values. Freedom to express one's views is not tantamount to freedom to be CEO of a company whose stakeholders find those views deeply troubling. So while I myself would have preferred a path of greater tolerance, I don't think what happened to Eich can fairly be characterized as "reverse bigotry."

The Eich affair underscores another important point: Sometimes otherwise good people promote bigotry. I wouldn't call Eich a bigot, because he showed no apparent animus. But the scaremongering campaign to which he contributed both drew from and fostered animus. An important step in fighting bigotry—whether racism, or sexism, or homophobia, or anti-religious bigotry, or any other—is recognizing that we all have moral blind spots. Bigotry is not just something that nasty, hateful people do. When we look carefully—as we should—we find it in people like Eich, and our families, and ourselves.

Before concluding this section, I want to say a bit about analogies to race. Because racism is a paradigmatic case of bigotry, people often use it to illuminate other forms.[206] The LGBT rights movement, for instance, often finds inspiration in the civil rights movement.

Opponents object that the analogy is inapt, claiming that race is not the same as sexual orientation or gender identity. Of course it isn't. An analogy doesn't mean that two things are *the same*; it means that they're similar in some relevant respects. They may be quite dissimilar in other respects, and both the similarities and the differences can be instructive. In any case, from the true premise that sexual orientation and gender identity are *importantly different from* race, we should not leap to the false conclusion that they are *nothing at all like* race.

According to opponents of LGBT rights, one key difference is that race is an immutable, nonbehavioral characteristic, whereas sexuality and gender expression involve chosen conduct; thus it's wrong (even insulting) to compare them. But even putting aside evidence for biological contributions to sexual orientation and gender identity, this objection is badly misguided. It misrepresents the nature of racism, the nature of anti-LGBT prejudice, and the point of various analogies between the two.

Although race may in some sense be an immutable, non-behavioral characteristic, racism is all about chosen behavior. Racists don't simply object to minorities' skin color: they object to minorities' moving into "our" neighborhoods, marrying "our" daughters, attacking "our" values, and so on. In other words, they object to conduct, both real and imagined. What's more, discriminating on the basis of race—dividing up the world according to skin color and treating people differently because of it—is most certainly a chosen behavior. Calling race "nonbehavioral" misses that important fact.

At the same time, calling sexual orientation and gender identity "behavioral" misses quite a bit as well. Yes, both sexual orientation and gender identity are typically expressed and realized via behaviors. But one need not engage in any of those behaviors to fall victim to anti-LGBT discrimination: Merely being perceived as "queer" is enough. Moreover, anti-LGBT discrimination involves restricting people according to their biological sex, which is at least as "innate" as race is.

My point is that the biological/behavioral distinction—or the status/conduct distinction, as Anderson and Girgis render it—won't do the work that social conservatives want it to do in undermining analogies between race and LGBT identity. Whether such analogies are apt ultimately depends on what they aim to accomplish. That's one reason why I avoid referring to "*the* race analogy": It suggests a single point of comparison, whereas in fact there are many. Both race and LGBT identity involve powerful systems of social pressure. Both tend to elicit other people's moral judgment. In both cases people invoke "God's plan" and notions of what's "natural" to back up those moral judgments. Both can deeply affect one's sense of self vis-à-vis others.

There are differences between race and LGBT identity, too, just as there are differences between the various overlapping communities included under the umbrella term "LGBT." As a group, LGBT people don't experience the cumulative generational effects of discrimination that racial and ethnic minorities do; their parents and grandparents and great-grandparents seldom share their LGBT identities. (Of course, individual LGBT people may intersectionally possess other generationally transmitted minority statuses.) The flip side is that, unlike most racial and ethnic minorities, LGBT people cannot always count on their families for sympathy in the face of discrimination; their loved ones are sometimes their worst enemies. Historically, LGBT people have also experienced severe rejection from their own religious communities. And while antimiscegenation laws were struck down in 1967, "homosexual sodomy" remained illegal in parts of the United States until 2003.[207] There are also differences in opportunities for "passing," which affects when and how discrimination occurs.

What does all of this have to do with religious liberty and discrimination? I'd like to emphasize two points. The first is a reminder that people have used, and continue to use, religion to justify race-based bigotry in ways disturbingly similar to how they use it to justify anti-LGBT bigotry: They hide their fallible prejudices behind "God's infallible word."

The second is that because analogies are instructive yet imperfect, one should consider several when trying to understand other people's experiences. In order to understand discrimination against LGBT people, for instance, one might look not only to race-based discrimination but also religion-based discrimination. Doing so might help mitigate some common blind spots.

Consider, for example, the following passages by scholars Paul McHugh and Gerard V. Bradley in an essay arguing against the Employment Non-Discrimination Act, which would prohibit discrimination on the basis of sexual orientation and gender identity by most larger employers:

> But social science research continues to show that sexual orientation, unlike race, color, and ethnicity, is neither a clearly defined concept nor an immutable characteristic of human beings. Basing federal employment law on a vaguely defined concept such as sexual orientation, especially when our courts have a wise precedent of limiting suspect classes to groups that have a clearly-defined shared characteristic, would undoubtedly cause problems for many well-meaning employers. . . .

> Nor is there any convincing evidence that sexual orientation is biologically determined; rather, research tends to show that for some persons and perhaps for a great many, "sexual orientation" is plastic and fluid; that is, it changes over time. What we do know with certainty about sexual orientation is that it is affective and behavioral—a matter of desire and/or behavior. And "gender identity" is even more fluid and erratic, so much so

that in limited cases an individual could claim to "identify" with
a different gender on successive days at work. Employers should
not be obliged by dint of civil and possibly criminal penalties to
adjust their workplaces to suit felt needs such as these.[208]

Both of these passages have been cited approvingly by my
counterpoint author Ryan Anderson.[209] Put aside the fact that
their claims about sexual orientation and gender identity—as
well as race, color, and ethnicity—are at best controversial and
at worst demonstrably false: "Color," for instance, is about the
furthest thing from a "clearly defined concept."[210] The thing
I want to highlight is how the logic of their argument also commits them to denying *religious* protections in the workplace.
That's because every single one of their claims about sexual
orientation and gender identity here applies with equal or
greater force to religion: Religion is "neither a clearly defined
concept nor an immutable characteristic." It is not "biologi-
cally determined"; rather, "for some persons and perhaps for a
great many, [religion] is plastic and fluid; that is, it changes over
time." Religion is "behavioral." It is "fluid and erratic, so much
so that in limited cases an individual could claim to 'identify'
with a different [religion] on successive days at work."

And yet, social conservatives generally endorse workplace
protections against religion-based discrimination. Such inconsistency reveals a dramatic failure of intellectual imagina-
tion and moral sympathy. Worse, it betrays a stubborn moral
blind spot.

2.6 CONCLUSION

Religious liberty is a core value of our nation and of any just
society. No one in this debate disputes this point. But religious

liberty should not morph into religious privilege, licensing discrimination and fostering exclusion and inequality. Such distortion betrays religious liberty's greatest legacy.

In this essay I have tried to provide clarity about both conceptual and practical puzzles in current debates over religious liberty. If I have done that much, and given the reader some food for thought, I'll consider the essay a success.

Among my more specific recommendations, I argued that RFRA ought to be modified. The "compelling interest" and "least restrictive means" requirements should be loosened: I would allow exemptions from generally applicable rules that burden religious beliefs unless denying the exemption is "substantially related" to an "important government interest." In other words, I endorse an intermediate scrutiny standard for indirect burdens on religion. I would propose the same boundaries for state RFRAs, if they are deemed necessary. I would strike down all remaining blue laws. And I would extend any RFRA-granted exemptions to comparable secular conscience claims.

I also argued that religious exemptions should seldom be given to antidiscrimination law, except when business owners are being asked to provide genuinely custom work. I suggested that if exemptions are to be granted more widely, a posting requirement should be considered, and that even when exemptions are denied, posted signs might address some of the interests of both owners and potential customers. Throughout the discussion, I emphasized that the most important functions of antidiscrimination law have little to do with cakes, flowers, and other wedding flourishes.

The law is not the only way to address religious liberty and discrimination. Education, including interfaith dialogue, can go a long way toward increasing sensitivity to diverse groups of citizens. The business community can and often does use its power to exert positive pressure, because it recognizes that diversity and inclusion are good for business. Customers can make choices about where to shop, as well as how to raise objections when businesses act unjustly.

One troubling aspect of this debate is that the loudest voices in favor of religious liberty often seem all too happy to deny liberty to others when they themselves hold the power. Of course, neither side is immune from this all-too-human tendency. In that sense, when it comes to the Puritan mistake, we are all potentially Puritans. But the rhetoric of "religious liberty" today is more often invoked by those who seek to exclude than by those who favor a big tent. Kim Davis's ardent defenders would be all too happy to deny gays not only the freedom to marry but also the freedom to engage in consensual sex: As noted, it was not long ago that most social conservatives openly defended laws prohibiting "homosexual sodomy."[211] Many would deny to Muslims and other religious minorities in America the very liberties that they insistently demand for themselves: the freedom to offer public prayers, for example, or to build houses of worship where they see fit.[212] The Puritan mistake lives on: Religious liberty means the liberty to do things *our way.*

The most rhetorically effective arguments from the other side are those that accuse the proequality side of a similar Puritan mistake, insofar as we exert social and legal pressure on those who discriminate. "Bake me a cake, bigot!" is a chapter title in my counterpoint author Ryan Anderson's last book; it employs this rhetorical strategy.

Such accusations simply ignore the fact that antidiscrimination laws cut both ways: They prohibit the LGBT business owner from firing, evicting, or refusing service to the conservative Christian on the grounds of identity just as much as they prohibit the conservative Christian from firing, evicting, or refusing service to the LGBT person on the grounds of identity. In my preferred world, the gay florist must give equal service to Christian conservatives; the reverse is not true in Anderson and Girgis's preferred world. And Anderson and Girgis never adequately explain why we should outlaw discrimination on the basis of religion, as most everyone agrees, while permitting it on the basis of sexual orientation or gender identity. I return to this "double standards" theme in my Reply.

A final note about consistency: Doubtless some readers will have noticed that when discussing Kim Davis, I never mentioned that she herself has been divorced three times. Many observers have argued that her personal history proves her hypocrisy and renders her position untenable.

I mostly disagree. As a philosophy professor, I strongly believe that the soundness of an argument depends on its content and logical structure rather than on who offers it. If a moral principle is true, it should be true in anyone's mouth: saint or sinner, friend or foe. Besides, most of us have fallen short of our ideals. Davis says she's a changed woman; I have no reason to doubt her.

But I do think it's relevant that when reporters reminded Davis that the Bible condemns most divorces and asked her whether she would deny licenses to divorced people, she demurred: "That's between them and God," she insisted.[213]

It's easy for Christians to protest that the two issues are different: Divorce is in the past, they say, but homosexuality is ongoing. Easy, but unbiblical. In the Gospel of Mark, Jesus states: "Whoever divorces his wife and marries another commits adultery against her; and if she divorces her husband and marries another, she commits adultery" (Mark 10:11–12). Notice that Jesus does not say that people who divorce and remarry *did sin* (past tense) and then had their slates wiped clean. He says that they *are sinning*, as unrepentant adulterers.

Now this standard is very demanding, and I don't in fact agree with it. On the other hand, I don't go around substituting my reading of "God's law" for the laws of the state.

My point is not to argue theology with Kim Davis but to highlight how self-serving theological scruples can be. The plain fact is that Kim Davis wanted to hold gay people to a different standard than her fellow divorcees: For gays, she would enforce "God's law" here on earth. For divorcees, "That's between them and God." Like so many of her fellow social conservatives, she selectively cited the Bible to justify discrimination against a marginalized group while giving a free pass to those in the majority like herself.

Such inconsistency suggests that this case was less about the Bible than about simple antigay prejudice. It betrays a moral blind spot, much like that which South Carolina exhibited when it denied unemployment benefits to Saturday sabbatarians while requiring them for Sunday sabbatarians. It insists on freedom—"That's between them and God"—but only for those who do things *our way.*

The law should not give force to such discrimination. It should especially not do so under the venerable mantle of religious liberty.

3

Against the New Puritanism

Empowering All, Encumbering None

RYAN T. ANDERSON AND SHERIF GIRGIS

■■■

IN THE WEST, RELIGIOUS LIBERTY today leads a double life. You'll find it toasted and praised in every realm—until you hit territory occupied by the culture wars over abortion and contraception, gender and sex, marriage and childrearing. No national organizations campaign against allowing the Amish to opt their children out of high school, or Muslim inmates to grow short beards, or Native Americans to ingest peyote, each in the name of conscience. There is no media outrage over these outcomes. They find favor with the Left and Right alike.

But things are different when it comes to sex. As progressives gain ground, some of them have challenged the freedom of conservatives to live by their beliefs that sex is for marriage, that marriage unites a husband and wife, that children deserve a father and mother, that abortion is wrong, or that biological sex is to be accepted, not altered. Against the best of the liberal tradition itself, and with portentous wider implications, a progressive Puritanism has arisen on these issues—an effort to coerce conscientious dissenters to live by the majority's views; to punish the moral heretic.

We start by exploring four stress points in these debates: the freedom of private adoption agencies and hospitals, schools and universities, wedding and relationship professionals, and civil servants who embrace a traditional ethic. Leaving them free under law to live by their convictions has become ferociously controversial, but we think both sides of these particular disputes can afford to live and let live. In these cases, society can honor moral and religious liberty, and promote pluralism and social peace, without undoing anyone's legitimate policy goals. Pressing others into the service of progressive social outcomes is therefore gratuitous.

Nevertheless, some will disagree on these cases, and many will differ with us on harder ones. We owe readers an account of the principles behind our conclusions. So in the next section, we lay out our premises in open view. We develop an ethical framework for thinking about civil rights and liberties and about associations: political and voluntary; civic, religious, and otherwise. Within that framework, to which we return throughout this book, we first consider the proper place, and the hazards, of religious liberty. Picking up where our introductory essay left off, we mount a fresh philosophical defense of the decision to single out for protection religious liberty and conscience rights in scores of national and international charters and major statutes.[1] We use that defense to explain exactly when, why, and in what sense these interests might require sturdier protection than others. Insofar as liberty claims in today's debates spring from moral and religious convictions, then, the case for respecting them is especially strong.

But more is at stake. Freedoms of religion and conscience are part of a delicate ecosystem of liberties that includes freedom of speech and association. As we show, these rights together protect the soil of civil society, in which associations can sprout and thrive as expressions of private initiative and self-determination. Together, these rights serve what we call a principled pluralism: the natural social variety rooted in the range of good and honorable ways to live—variety that some of the coercive policies we discuss would try to eradicate.

The same civil liberties also serve what we call pragmatic pluralism: variety stemming from errors or harms that the law cannot uproot without doing more harm. We show why a society open to reform must put up with certain sorts of wrongs—and how it can, without abetting injustice. In that connection, we address the objection that respect for religion and conscience inflicts material and dignitary harms that no decent society would allow. Third-party harms can justify some limits on liberties. But there are some harms that it would be perilous for the state to try to suppress. Here we will distinguish two senses of dignitary harm, arguing that a just and open society will use legal coercion to target the one but never the other. Our arguments on conscience and pluralism, civil society and social dynamism, furnish still another case for robust liberty protections, even in these culture wars.

Next we turn to American history, sifting it for lessons for today's policy debates on religious liberty and antidiscrimination. Drawing on that history, and building on the ethical framework developed earlier, we defend new policy proposals for protecting religious liberty. We offer an account of discrimination in general and of when it is invidious in particular. And we propose a test for telling when it makes sense to use antidiscrimination laws to fight material and dignitary harms to certain groups. But no law is without its costs, and antidiscrimination laws are no exception, so we also discuss when they cost too much, how they should be drawn and defined to minimize these costs, and when it makes sense to grant exemptions from them.

Finally, we use this analysis to decide if, when, and how the law should give sexual orientation and gender identity protected status. So far, such "SOGI laws" have done harm to free expression and conscience, as some progressives concede. To be sure, coercive policies would be needed anyway if discrimination were rife, so that LGBT people were locked out of the market or out of the public square or into second-class status. But we argue that this isn't the case, not in the United States today. New evidence might prove otherwise, in which case we'd support laws to fight those harms as explained below. In that scenario, we show, the best grounds for enacting them would leave plenty of room for exemptions in cases like those with which we begin. In fact, good laws soundly applied wouldn't classify the actions in those cases as unlawful discrimination in the first place.

Again and again, we show that this debate happily offers a surfeit of win-win solutions, ways of protecting conscience without unraveling progressive policy goals. Again and again, we address our opponents' compelling concerns and challenge them in turn to produce reasons for rejecting solutions in which society can empower the oppressed without encumbering the legitimate freedoms of others.

3.1 PUBLIC POLICY AFTER SAME-SEX MARRIAGE

In the United States, adults are free to enter or refuse almost any relationship—personal, civic, commercial, romantic—without legal interference. Freedoms of association and contract are presumed. As we argue below, these civil liberties are intimately related to freedoms of religion and conscience, and even the freedom of speech. For analysis, it's useful to pull apart these strands of the First Amendment and other protections, but their contributions to justice are hard to distinguish. Their cumulative effect is this: if the state is going to curb your freedom to associate with others on your own terms, by your own moral and religious lights, it carries the burden of proof. Government action that strains these mutually supporting freedoms must not be gratuitous. It must support a meaningful public interest, with minimal fraying of freedom.

So businesses and charities and other civic associations have ample freedom to run by their own values: to choose employees or customers or members, and standards of conduct. They're free to express and act on their own beliefs in ways that others might find compelling or trivial or deplorable. Freedoms of association and contract *just are* freedoms to "discriminate" in these ways. We tolerate such differences for the sake of creativity, initiative, vitality, and reform.

What does this presumption of liberty urge after the Supreme Court's *Obergefell* decision? This presumption of liberty favors implementing that decision with as modest a burden as necessary on freedoms of association, religion, conscience, and speech.[2] *Obergefell* was about state recognition and its effects: legal rules for hospital visitation and medical decisions, inheritance and taxes, and eligibility for a number of public programs and benefits. It was also meant to curb what many saw as the social harms of being denied public recognition of an enduring romantic relationship.

These material and social effects of legal recognition can be achieved without curbing private parties' freedoms of religion, conscience, or association. Indeed, respect for these freedoms flows naturally from ideals so often cited by same-sex marriage advocates: toleration for people's differences and support for their freedom to live with integrity. These ideals are not to be discarded just when they would protect what the *Obergefell* majority itself called the "decent and honorable religious or philosophical premises" behind traditional views on marriage.

For these reasons, the law after *Obergefell* should treat those who believe that marriage unites man and woman (or that sex is for marriage, or that children are owed a mother and father, or that biological sex is to be accepted) as it has treated prolife hospitals, doctors, and others in the wake of *Roe v. Wade*. These institutions and professionals are held to the same standards as others of their kind, but not to a litmus test on abortion. The state refrains from using its power to subsidize, license, and contract to coerce their consciences for being heretics on abortion. The same should go for dissenters from the state's new vision of marriage. The political settlement that has worked for four decades on abortion can work on marriage. In this first section we canvass the case for extending it to four types of claimants: private hospitals and other charities, private educational institutions, wedding and relationship professionals, and public employees.

3.1.1 Private Adoption Agencies, Hospitals, and Charities

Adoption agencies have been casualties in battles over religious liberty for charities and are perhaps the rawest reminders of the gratuitousness of coercion in these culture wars.

In Massachusetts, Illinois, and the District of Columbia, religious adoption agencies and foster care providers have been forced to shut down rather than comply with government orders to place children with same- as well as opposite-sex couples or else lose their licenses and grants.[3] Their closure did nothing to help a single child in need of a home, or a single couple in search of a child. (In no state do private agencies enjoy a monopoly on adoption and foster care.) Pressuring them to close only scored a political point, making vulnerable children victims of an adult culture war.

A former president of the National Council for Adoption warned that "if all faith-based agencies closed due to such laws, the adoption and child welfare field would be decimated, depriving thousands of children growing up in families."[4] Some one thousand private providers handle more than a quarter of the unrelated domestic adoptions in the United States each year.[5] Many are faith-based agencies that provide spiritual and emotional support that state bureaucracies are ill-equipped to offer. In the words of John Shultz, who with his wife, Tammy, adopted four foster-care children through an evangelical agency later forced to shut down: "One of our main things we were looking for in an agency was one that shared our religious and faith beliefs." Without one, he doubted they could have "weathered the storm of the foster care system."[6]

People of every persuasion can agree that having many adoption agencies is better than having fewer; and that offering some adoptive parents tailored support is better than offering none. Respecting private agencies' conscience claims serves the believers who run them and the children who might otherwise wait longer for a home. And it imposes no material harm on anyone, by anyone's score—liberal or conservative. (We'll consider dignitary harm below.) This is one of those rare policy issues on which all the arguments seem to point in one direction.

The same goes for medical care. We should allow reproductive technology providers to choose to lend their services only to homes headed by a mother and father if they feel bound to do so. When the California Supreme Court in 2008 forced one private clinic among many to provide artificial insemination for a lesbian couple—over the doctors' moral objections to creating children fatherless by design—it clipped conscience rights without making a material difference to a single couple.[7]

Likewise, some religious hospitals and staff object to providing sterilizations, sex-reassignment surgeries, and direct abortions. Sensibly enough, they would sooner shut down than use their healing arts for what they regard as mutilation or murder. Yet none could thwart patients seeking these services elsewhere. Hospitals should certainly have to provide emergency services. But religious liberty took a gratuitous hit when HHS reinterpreted laws banning discrimination based on "sex" to require healthcare plans to cover sex-reassignment therapies, and physicians to perform them. Offering no religious exemptions, this regulation would force many hospitals and providers to offer such treatments against their consciences or medical judgments. With a single decree never approved by lawmakers—indeed, in a gross distortion of duly enacted laws—it would do away with conscience rights for providers long championed by both sides.

In these cases, and in those we discuss below, the sheer fact that the entities seeking protection open their doors and services to the public should not count against them. The only question should be whether exemptions for them would impose too high a cost on others. Yes, those costs are *likelier* to occur, the more these institutions interact with the public. But once we tally such concrete third-party harms, it isn't an *extra* point against these claimants that they've stepped into the public square. To treat it that way is gratuitous—and counterproductive. The public square exists to bring a variety of voices together. It can't serve its function unless dissenters feel free to step into it. Nothing could be more at odds with that goal than counting it against dissenters' conscience claims that they choose to serve the public.

3.1.2 Educational Institutions: Creeds and Codes of Conduct

What we have said about adoption agencies and hospitals applies to educational institutions. We think even progressives can grant that it promises little public benefit—and does palpable harm—to deprive competent institutions of accreditation, nonprofit tax status, public contracts, subsidized student loans, and other forms of support unless they violate the religious convictions of the communities they represent, in hiring, housing, or otherwise.

Here we see the intersection of multiple civil liberties, as we did in our joint essay's discussion of *Pierce v. Society of Sisters. Pierce* affirmed parents' authority to guide their children's education. But neither parents nor students are free to choose a religious education unless institutions are free to embrace their convictions—unless we let Notre Dame be Catholic, and Wheaton be evangelical, and Zaytuna be Muslim, and Yeshiva be Jewish. To cripple these schools for building a community around a creed—by pulling their nonprofit tax status or accreditation or denying them subsidized student loans or research grants—is to rob families of the choice for a certain moral and intellectual formation, in a supportive environment.

But allowing them to keep to their mission serves us all, religious or not. It gives strength and clarity to more voices in our public discussions, with intellectual benefits all around. To allow Liberty University to be fundamentalist in the broad sense of enforcing agreement about evangelical fundamentals—by hiring only faculty who share its creed—enables it to create a scholarly community more apt to deepen Christian thought, including the social teachings of the gospels of Matthew, Mark, Luke, and John. The same goes for allowing private schools to embrace a secular-liberal fundamentalism, the better to refine the social gospel of Sanger, Hume, Mill, and Rawls. Allowing each to incubate its own intellectual tradition populates the wider public debate in which they all take part. Local agreement enhances global debate.

Meanwhile, in a nation with thousands of institutions of every persuasion, at every level of quality, allowing some to operate by religious creeds needn't deny anyone a suitable education. So we bring no one to ruin by allowing religious schools to foster a milieu supportive of their values: to require teachers to share their marital or prolife ethic or to make rules against nonmarital sexual activity (straight and gay) or to refuse to recognize groups that reject their ethical commitments. These measures are not gratuitous or controlling. They empower incoming students and scholars by giving them the freedom—the live option—to join a community that offers support for living by a demanding moral vision of their own choice.

And they welcome anyone who shares that vision. We haven't found a single school unwilling to employ gay or lesbian teachers who support and try to live by its message and mission. Some have dismissed teachers publicly opposed to their teachings and unwilling to try to live by them. We must acknowledge how painful and disruptive that can be for the people dismissed, and for their families, colleagues, and friends. We must do what we can to minimize those harms. But eliminating those harms would curb the freedom of all—secular and religious, *including* those who leave after a change of heart—to choose institutions with a particular vision.

This isn't a conservative point. Progressives who defended Mozilla Firefox's right to oust CEO Brendan Eich over his traditional views on marriage understood the toll this would take on him. But they thought his values out of step with those that had drawn many of Mozilla's stakeholders. Concern for those parties also urges concern for students who want a school supportive of their efforts—and their struggles—to live by their creeds. Leaving schools free to provide that support will serve those students while depriving no one of an institutional home. The burden of proof is on those who would brandish the law against these schools and students and families, despite the costs to everyone of a world less rich with rival intellectual traditions and supportive communities.

3.1.3 Wedding and Relationship Professionals

Wedding vendors and relationship counselors have also been targets in the religious liberty wars. Elane Photography's owners were fined more than $6,000 for declining on religious grounds to photograph a same-sex commitment ceremony. A small family bakery was fined $135,000 for refusing to bake the wedding cake for a same-sex wedding. And seventy-year-old Barronelle Stutzman was sued for declining to make floral arrangements for a same-sex wedding.[8] Stutzman, who has employed gays and lesbians since opening her store, had for ten years designed arrangements for the couple that sued her. Her only objection was to lending her artistic talents to their wedding celebration.

Here again the pattern holds: legally coercing professionals serves no serious need but works serious harms. Conservative wedding providers are few and dwindling, due to market pressures; and most important, they don't refuse to serve LGBT patrons. In case after case—with only one exception we know of, in a news climate that would thrust any exception right up to national headlines—bakers have had no problem designing cakes for gay customers for every other occasion. It's just that an exceedingly small number can't in good conscience use their talents to help celebrate same-sex weddings, by baking a cake topped with two grooms or two brides. And while coercing these cultural dissidents has vanishingly small effects on the supply of products for any given couple, it impinges seriously on particular vendors' freedoms of conscience or religion. If any harm remains in leaving these wedding professionals free, it is only the tension we all face in living with people who disagree with us on the most personal matters.

The same goes for counselors morally opposed to sexual relationships between boyfriend and girlfriend, or two men or two women. Consider Julea Ward, a graduate student dismissed from Eastern Michigan University's counseling program for asking her supervisor to assign another counselor to a gay client seeking relationship help.[9] Ward, whose religious convictions kept her from affirming same-sex sexual relationships, tried to place the client with a counselor who could. She did so ahead of time, based simply on his file. Meeting her request would have been a win-win, protecting her liberty without embarrassing him. Society should aim for these outcomes. Here again, it isn't simply that the benefits of liberty barely outweigh the costs. It's that the benefits to people's integrity or livelihood are great; and the costs vanishingly small.

3.1.4 Government Employees

Institutions of civil society—charities, schools, and businesses—are the easiest cases. If same-sex marriage policy is about the benefits of *legal* recognition, we can afford to let others hold back their private recognition. But that same fact makes it harder to accommodate dissenting employees of a *government* convinced that justice requires its own recognition of same-sex couples.

Clearly, the government must give all citizens easy access to their legal entitlements. That is the only tenable position, and the only fair one. If this requires every employee in an office to offer same-sex marriage licenses, so be it. On the other hand, personal integrity matters for public officials as much as anyone else. So where the government can accommodate dissenting officials *at low cost* to those served by its policies, it should.

In short, there is no *independent* significance to the fact that the claimants are officials, seeking exemptions from official duties. The law should ask the same question as it does when judging private actors' claims: will granting exemptions impose too high a cost on others? Some progressives believe that beyond such concrete harms, *the sheer fact* that the claim arises in an official context is an extra point against granting it. For reasons elaborated on in our rebuttal, we disagree.

So does federal law. The absolutist standard pushed by some progressives today—perform every last part of your job description, whatever your beliefs, or resign—has long been rejected in the United States. Under Title VII of the Civil Rights Act, for example, the government, like other employers, must take reasonable steps to accommodate its employees' religion. Applying this legal rule, courts have required accommodations for pacifist postal workers opposed to delivering draft cards,[10] for example, and for IRS officials opposed to processing non-profit applications for abortion clinics.[11]

Are the latest culture wars the *one* context where otherwise competent and willing employees should quit or go to jail when there are easy alternatives? Some same-sex marriage advocates, like Illinois Law School professor Robin F. Wilson, say no. Entitlement to a certain public service, she writes, creates no right to receive it "from each and every employee in the office who is available to do it."[12] At the same time, Title VII doesn't entitle employees to win every time. They can—and should—lose if a court finds that there was no burden on the employee or no reasonable accommodation available. Religious objections aren't trump cards. The law only demands a careful and subtle balance.

A police officer is asked to ride his motorcycle at the front of a gay pride parade—not to provide security but to participate on the department's behalf. Should he be forced to violate his beliefs?[13] Of course, everyone deserves the protection of the police department, and every officer must be willing to take any *call* for such protection. But what about assignments requiring something besides protection and enforcement? Here, too, we should accommodate conscience as we can.

That brings us to Kim Davis, a county clerk who had been issuing marriage licenses for decades when the U.S. Supreme Court redefined civil marriage in 2015. Should she have been forced to violate her objection to signing off on same-sex marriage licenses? Kentucky had accommodated conscience in other licensing schemes; thus, it exempted objecting clerks from issuing hunting licenses. And after *Obergefell*, it changed marriage licenses to read "Party 1" and "Party 2" rather than "Bride" and "Groom." That suggested that it could fulfill its duty to give every eligible couple easy access to a marriage license without burdening the head clerk's conscience, simply by removing her name from the form. Yet Governor Steven L. Beshear issued a mandate taking that option off the table. That's why Kim Davis ended up in court.

It needn't have come to that. Kentucky lawmakers could have followed North Carolina's example. A law passed there in June 2015 provided that no eligible couple could be denied a marriage license but that officials could recuse themselves should they have sincere objections. By notifying a superior of their objections ahead of time, they could keep their integrity without inconvenience to anyone. We favor such compromises. Citizens seeking their legal entitlements shouldn't have to clear any more hurdles than the entitlement itself requires. And consistent with that aim, government employees should be accommodated—as federal law demands.

3.1.5 First Amendment Defense Acts

Our law protects moral and religious liberty in two ways: by exemptions from a wide range of laws across a number of areas, and by accommodations for narrower contexts. Some statutes—like RFRAs—authorize judges to grant exemptions from any law that burdens a person's conscience, but only after balancing her liberties against the public interests at stake.

Other statutes provide narrower but categorical protection for one set of convictions. And they can afford to do so because the legislature can be sure in advance that in a certain realm, coercing an objector won't be needed, or therefore justified.

In the modern era, the United States has offered such categorical protections on abortion. In 1973, just months after *Roe v. Wade* was handed down, Congress passed the Church Amendment, named for Senator Frank Church, a Democrat from Idaho. While *Roe* shielded the choice to have an abortion, the Church Amendment protected doctors' and nurses' choices not to perform one. It provided that healthcare organizations receiving federal funds could not force their doctors or nurses to perform or assist at abortions.

Some twenty years later, Congress passed and President Bill Clinton signed the Coats–Snowe Amendment. It prohibits the government from discriminating against medical students who refuse to perform abortions and medical residency programs that leave out abortion training. And in 2004, Congress passed the Hyde–Weldon Amendment, which keeps the government from discriminating against healthcare institutions that don't offer abortions. Since 1973, then, U.S. policy has protected a right to choose an abortion right alongside an individual and institutional right to choose against facilitating one.

Our law should now do the same on marriage. It needn't and shouldn't penalize private associations for their beliefs on this issue. Doing so would make no appreciable difference to the ability of same-sex couples to receive the goods and services they seek; but it *would* undermine conscience rights for some. So lawmakers can and should grant a categorical accommodation. A bill now pending in Congress would do that. Much like the Church, Coats–Snowe, and Hyde–Weldon Amendments, the First Amendment Defense Act (FADA) would protect the freedoms of citizens and organizations who hold a belief at odds with one enshrined by courts.

Protecting prolife conscience did not violate the Constitution, by establishing a religion or engaging in viewpoint discrimination or otherwise. Nor do laws protecting pacifists or animal welfare advocates. Their only aim is peaceful coexistence in the face of disagreement. The same goes for FADA. It would enact a bright-line rule to keep government from penalizing someone just for acting on her belief that marriage is the union of husband and wife. It protects people who hold that belief for religious *or* secular reasons. And it shields organizations from losing nonprofit tax status or licensing or accreditation for operating by these beliefs.

But even FADA's categorical protections reflect a careful balance. They protect individuals, nonprofit charities, and privately held businesses but not publicly traded corporations, or federal employees or contractors in the course of their work. The First Amendment Defense Act makes clear that it does not relieve the federal government of its duty to provide services, medical care, or benefits to all who qualify; it must simply respect conscience in the course of doing so.[14]

Mississippi passed a state version of FADA that also struck a delicate balance in its choice of whom to protect and when. In Roger Severino's words, it protected only the following persons and institutions, in the following contexts:

- Religious organizations, like churches, cannot be forced to use their facilities to celebrate or solemnize weddings that violate their beliefs.
- Religious convents, universities, and social service organizations can continue to maintain personnel and housing policies that reflect their beliefs.
- Religious adoption agencies can continue to operate by their conviction that every child they serve deserves to be placed with a married mom and dad.

- Bakers, photographers, florists, and similar wedding-specific vendors cannot be forced to use their talents to celebrate same-sex weddings if they cannot do so in good conscience.
- State employees cannot be fired for expressing their beliefs about marriage outside the office, and individual state clerks can opt out of issuing marriage licenses so long as no valid marriage license is delayed or impeded.
- Counselors and surgeons cannot be required to participate in gender identity transitioning or sex-reassignment surgeries against their faith and convictions while guaranteeing that no one is denied emergency care or visitation rights.
- Private businesses and schools, not bureaucrats, get to set their own bathroom, shower, and locker room policies.[15]

This was a reasonable bill. It protected the consciences of people on the losing end of the marriage debate while avoiding the awful outcomes that critics fear. Yet the Mississippi FADA was struck down by a district court judge in June 2016. We say more about that, and our counterpoint's criticisms of it, in our rebuttal. For now, we note the unwillingness of some progressives—progressive Puritans—to take carefully laid paths to peaceful coexistence.

3.2 ETHICS AND POLITICS

How did we reach these conclusions? How would we extend them to harder cases? Here we offer a framework for our reflections on moral rights and wrongs in private and public life. We can think of both realms as filled and shaped by the human good. There is, of course, no *single* good life, but a range of good lives: countless ways of blending the basic ingredients of human thriving. And we can discern and identify the ingredients themselves—the most basic ways in which people can be well, or flourish. We call these "basic human goods." They are ways of being and acting that it makes sense for us to want for their own sake. Health, knowledge, play, aesthetic delight, and skillful performances of various sorts are a few examples. Knowing the history of the Russians or the Houston Rockets, appreciating Vivaldi or Dylan, perfecting your craft as a writer or woodworker makes you better off in one dimension of life even when it gives you nothing else.

A few basic goods are especially relevant to this book. We can think of them as forms of integration or integrity, or harmony between different elements: within the self, between the self and others, and between the self and the transcendent. For any of *these* goods to be authentic, they must be freely chosen. So a just society will enforce rights to protect the freedom for each. Harmony or integrity between one's convictions and actions grounds our concerns with the rights of conscience. Harmony between the self and others is about friendship and solidarity and social respect, rights of association and assembly, and antidiscrimination interests. And harmony between the self and the transcendent grounds our concern with religious freedom.

Most people understand the second form of harmony: friendship and solidarity. But what do we mean by the first, harmony within the self; and by the third, between the self and the transcendent? How do these give rise to rights of conscience and religious liberty?

The first is about personal integrity. It comes from trying to harmonize your choices, actions, and expressions with your moral convictions: your best judgments about what morality requires. It's the unity of life that we often praise in others even when we disagree with them (within limits) about what morality really requires. ("Agree with her or not, you've got to admit that she lives by her principles.") Of course, it's best to have and live by the *right* moral principles. But it is also good for rational agents to act in keeping with their best rational judgments. Living by your best judgments about the right and the good—even when those judgments are mistaken—inherently makes you better off, *in one respect*, than ignoring or flouting them. The self, like the body, is wounded by division. For both, harmony is health.

The third form of harmony is between the self and whatever transcendent source of meaning and value there might be. What is our origin, and what is our end? Do we have an ultimate creator or ultimate judge? Has it communicated with us or made demands on us? These are the questions that begin the religious search, the effort at harmony with transcendent sources of meaning, being, and value. We say more about this form of integrity below.

Note that these two forms of harmony overlap. Conscience calls for fidelity to your religious as well as moral obligations, including those moral obligations you come to accept on religious grounds. Even if your only "religious" conviction is that religion is bunk, moral integrity requires you to stand firm against pressures to profess creeds you find hollow. And again, both religion and integrity hinge on freedom. Both demand the freedom to judge the truth about moral and spiritual obligations, and the freedom to live by your conclusions. Both kinds of freedom are needed to protect what we might group under the summary label *moral and religious integrity*.

Finally, your integrity—as a real dimension of your well-being, even when your underlying convictions are off—gives the rest of us *some* reason to respect and promote it. Forcing a death penalty opponent to assist at an execution would harm her—not only from her perspective, but objectively. Not only because the death penalty does harm, but because the fragmentation of the self—the splitting of actions from convictions—is itself a harm. Of course, the reasons for respecting anyone's conscience can be overridden by other demands of justice and the common good. Our point is only that even mistaken conscience counts for something.

And concern for it, as we will see, gives rise to rights of conscience and religious liberty. For political morality, like all of morality, requires concern and respect for these and all the basic goods of everyone we affect. It bids us to act on what the Aristotelian tradition has long called right reason: on reason unfettered by contrary feelings; on our rational appreciation of basic goods, undistorted by partiality or hostility that would blind us to some of the people or goods before us. Thus, morality rules out invidious discrimination, or callousness toward the goods of some. And it rules out trampling some basic goods on our way to others—or more precisely, *intending* harm to someone's most basic interests as a means to other benefits. This explains how there can be *absolute* rights, such as those against torture or intentional killing of the innocent.

As an affirmative matter, concern for the human good calls for political authority, since individuals and families and neighborhoods can't realize their own all-around good on their own. They need to cluster in groups large enough to enable a rich division of labor for meeting everyone's basic needs. Cooperation across large numbers, in turn, requires ways of resolving coordination problems for all; defense against aggressors; general rules for punishing private wrongs and enforcing binding agreements. The state exists to promote these and other conditions that are needed to enable people and the communities they freely form to pursue their all-around good.[16]

Of course, we can't expect it to set us up for becoming *complete* in any basic good, since the basic goods are inexhaustible. There's always more to know about the world, more art to appreciate, more muscle and skill to build up, more to love in family and friends, and so on for each of the basic goods. And yet there is a difference between a shallower experience of any such good and a deficient one. That fuzzy but real boundary separates, say, being less informed about the world from being deceived; or being a slow runner from being paralyzed. So while the state can't set us up for completeness in any basic good, it can and should allow us to pursue each of the basic goods *adequately*. And it must do so *fairly*, without imposing onerous and gratuitous burdens on some. As much as possible, it must empower without encumbering.

That job description limits as much as it authorizes. It entails that the state should *not* do for individuals and communities what they can do well enough on their own initiative. For self-determination is itself a good to be respected. So the very human good that calls for political order also limits the state to setting the stage for people to pursue the good *for themselves*.[17] Only then will people and the associations they form—companionate, familial, religious, recreational, artistic, and commercial—have room to shape their identities by acting on their own initiative.

Finally, civil rights and liberties keep the state to its basic task, by protecting basic goods that the state exists to serve. These rights reflect the broad limits that the state must observe to allow people the opportunity for all-around fulfillment without itself quashing some of their basic goods in the process.[18]

Some civil rights or liberties serve basic goods by picking out for special protection a mere means to one or another of them. Freedom of speech is an example. To speak isn't inherently valuable: there are worthless forms of expression. But the freedom to communicate is indispensable for pursuing all of the basic goods. Without it, friendship never gets off the ground. Without new ideas and free dissent, knowledge shrinks and groupthink grows. Political authorities are cut off from the needs of those they serve. So any state concerned with the common good will respect robust liberties of speech and expression.[19]

Other civil rights and liberties directly pick out a basic good for respect and promotion; it's in this way that the rights of conscience and religious liberty protect aspects of our integrity. We now consider why they should have the peculiar form and strength that they normally do.

3.3 RELIGION AND CONSCIENCE, CIVIL SOCIETY AND PLURALISM

Most democracies single out religious liberty for special protection. For this one might cite a variety of reasons. Though peripheral at best to some, religion is central to many people's deepest commitments and communities. It has a singular power to inflame conflict, but also to propel people over their hardships and faults and beyond themselves in service to those in need. Religious communities, as typical targets of discrimination, need special support.

Here we suggest that two other reasons are central. First, as the site of efforts to achieve harmony with the ultimate source(s) of meaning and value, religion has basic value. It's a basic element of our good. To fail to attend to this dimension of life—if only to conclude that there is no transcendent reality—is to let one branch of your flourishing wilt. But respect for *this* basic good requires respect for your freedom to pursue it by your best lights. It rules out direct attacks on your religious freedom. It even gives the state some reason to avoid indirect burdens on religious liberty in more stringent ways than the state protects other liberties, as we'll show.

And when cultures accept these limits on the state, they come to see its jurisdiction—the field of activities it can justly coerce—as limited in principle. This brings us to a second point in favor of protecting religious liberty: its singular *instrumental* benefits for our common life. History and sociology show that religious liberty fosters appreciation for the character-forming associations of civil society, as prior to the state; and for other civil rights and liberties, as limits on its power—which in turn advances the same associations that form us in virtue, including the virtues needed for a thriving civil society, and so on in an upward spiral.

Freedom of conscience, too, protects a basic facet of our well-being (integrity), and promotes principled and practical limits on the state that give civil society room to blossom.

We unpack these points in four sections below. In the first two, we say more about the nature of the basic goods of religion and integrity and why they require separate and in some ways more stringent legal protection than civil liberties that serve other basic goods. In the third, we show how religious liberty rights have given civil society room to breathe; and in the fourth, how their ongoing protection serves pluralism and tolerance in the best senses.

3.3.1 Religion Gives the State Reason to Protect Religious Liberty

A Mesopotamian city raises a temple to Ishtar and a Mayan one to the sun god. A pharaoh pays homage to Aten and a Hindu to Brahma. A carpenter in Palestine takes up itinerant preaching and crowds begin to follow. A Buddhist monk fingers his prayer beads and a Catholic nun her rosary beads. Supplications rise up from ancient Zoroastrians and modern Rastafarians; from medieval Muslims and Renaissance Mennonites. Augustine searches and Luther protests and Wesley preaches. For all their differences, this splendid range of people from every corner of every culture across thousands of years would agree that much hangs on exploring religious questions and living by the answers. Even those who end up atheist or agnostic are compelled to search by a sense of the value of achieving harmony with whatever ultimate source of meaning there might be.

As a basic human good, religion consists of efforts to align your life with the truth about whatever transcendent source (or sources) of being, meaning, and value there might be. It's about efforts to honor or find harmony with that source—call it the "divine." Relationship with the divine, like human friendship, must be freely chosen to be authentic. To coerce it is to produce a counterfeit. So respect for your basic interest in religion demands respect for your freedom in pursuing it. For this basic good, religious liberty is a precondition.

And hence the state, which exists to protect the ability of people to pursue all the basic goods, must never directly attack this freedom. It must never require or forbid an act on religious grounds—for example, on the ground that its religious rationale is true or false, or that the associated religious community should shrink or grow. But the same basic good also requires the state to avoid needless incidental limits on religious freedom. These arise where your faith calls for you to shape your whole life by the divinity's demands: in preaching and conversion, pilgrimage and prayer, building and worship, ritual and ascetical struggle, charitable work and sabbath rest. All of these might conflict with legitimate laws. The state can't avoid a conflict every time. It has to protect the wide range of basic goods for all of society, even at the expense of some instances of them, religion included. But because religion, like moral integrity, is itself one of the basic goods to be protected, the state should avoid impositions on it wherever reasonably possible.

This quick argument leaves questions hanging. Recent debate has centered on two that ask, in different ways, whether and how religion and conscience are special.

To see the force of the first question, note that most basic goods don't get protection under their own civil liberty. Most freedoms—like speech and association—indiscriminately serve all the basic goods. Religion and integrity are just two basic goods among others. So why shouldn't they have to settle for protection under the same generic, all-purpose civil liberties of speech, association, and the like? Why should the law set freedoms of religion and conscience apart? For that matter, why treat religion differently from other deep commitments? Most legal systems' separate provisions for freedoms of religion and conscience end up shielding moral and religious commitments more than commitments to becoming a master chef or a chess master, to making art or making the Olympics. Is that a fair result? In short, should we really enforce moral and religious liberty, over and above the other civil liberties we normally protect?

A second question: Should the law worry about incidental burdens on religion more than incidental burdens on other basic goods? Consider law professor Marci Hamilton's hypothetical, slightly tweaked: if you speed, is the reason to give you a ticket any weaker if you're late for a Bible study that you really care about than if you're late for a Pilates class that you really care about? Or take "time, place, manner" restrictions on speech. Do we have more reason to grant you an exemption from a law banning the use of bullhorns at midnight if it's the Koran that you want to proclaim, and not the benefits of a new diet? Health is as much a basic good as religion, after all.

For reasons related to these, many progressives now think religion shouldn't get special protection. But most of them would still object to *some* incidental burdens on religion, even some that don't actually *force* people to violate their religion. Laws requiring a prolife physician to perform abortions wouldn't force her to violate her conscience—she could always become an accountant—but they would trouble even many skeptics of expansive religious liberty.

In our view, each side in these "(how) is religion special?" debates gets something right and something wrong. Religion and conscience do require a separate civil liberty, enforced by its own set of rules, because moral and religious integrity demand more stringent protection than other deep commitments—but only in certain cases, to be specified below. Hamilton is right, for example, that we needn't avoid the burden of a ticket on someone speeding to meet his Sunday Mass obligation. On the other hand some regulations that burden conscience deserve extra scrutiny even when they are merely conditional—like a law requiring doctors to perform abortions or else find a new job. And to add one more wrinkle: even among religious liberty protections, some are more stringent than others. The need to avoid interfering with a religious community's choice of leaders (embodied in U.S. law's "ministerial exception" from legal interference) is and should be nearly absolute,[20] and certainly weightier than the need to avoid other incidental burdens on religion, or interference in secular associations.

A simple idea brings all these fragments together. Rather than starting with cases where religion seems to carry more weight and then trying to find a principle to tie them all together, begin at the foundations. Start with the idea that the state's most basic duty is to empower and not encumber people's pursuit of the basic goods. That means leaving us free to pursue each of the basic goods adequately—that is, better than deficiently.

The state does that partly by protecting civil rights and liberties. But these limits on the state's power will inevitably conflict with its *affirmative* policies in service of the same basic goods, and too often to allow scrutiny of every last conflict. So we need a procedure for deciding when to give laws that invade our liberties extra scrutiny. Since the reason for having any civil liberty is to serve the human good, we should scrutinize those incursions on liberty most likely to do serious harm to associated goods.

Applying this standard involves a great deal of guesswork, because most civil liberties serve a range of goods in hard-to-measure ways—and what counts as "serious" harm to those goods is also hard to quantify. How much of a burden on speech and expression will seriously harm the goods of knowledge and aesthetic experience? The most we can say for these two goods is that the law must leave you a rich range of options for pursuing them, even if its affirmative policies close off this or that avenue for doing so. That standard tells us something about how stringently courts should enforce the civil liberties that serve these goods.

And in fact, the tests that courts have devised to enforce most civil liberties hew to this standard pretty well. In the United States, for example, they ask whether a law "substantially" burdens a given liberty, or leaves "ample alternative channels" for exercising it—as do some "time, place, manner" restrictions on speech (like laws banning noise in neighborhoods at night). For most liberties, that's as good a proxy as one can find for when burdens on those liberties—and thus on the underlying basic goods—are too onerous to pass over nonchalantly.

But a more determinate (and in *some* cases more stringent) rule is available for freedoms of conscience and religion, and it flows from the distinctive nature of these goods. It is this: if a law would penalize you for meeting any of your (perceived) moral or religious obligations, its application to you merits extra scrutiny. The question is why. The short answer is that the underlying goods—religion and integrity—are more fragile than others. Since the state exists to protect and promote all your basic goods alike, it must guard fragile ones more closely.

Consider, for example, how moral integrity is more fragile than the basic good of self-determination. To respect the first, integrity, the state needs to let you obey the specific convictions you already have. To respect the second, self-determination, it simply needs to let you choose and pursue *some* projects—not necessarily the ones you already have or most prefer. After all, if you're barred from pursuing one project, you can adopt another, live out that new one, and your self-determination doesn't take much of a hit. You need only a respectable range of options. But if you're pressured into flouting even one of your perceived *obligations*, you're stuck; your integrity is cracked. So integrity is more fragile than self-determination. That's why we should scrutinize legal burdens on conscience more exactingly than legal burdens on other commitments or projects. The same goes for burdens on obligations you have on religious grounds.

Now we'll unpack this account of how religion and integrity are special, to make it more general and more precise. Again, we'll treat first principles first: the state must enable people to pursue basic goods adequately—better than *deficiently*. What do we mean by "deficiently"? Consider health. This basic good has a threshold. Dip beneath it, and you don't have simply less health but deficient health. There's a qualitative difference between running a sub-Olympic mile and being paralyzed. Integrity and religion, too, have thresholds. You have more or less integrity to the extent that your feelings line up with your moral convictions. But you're deficient in this basic good if you *act against* your convictions. The same goes for religion. You might pursue it more or less, but your pursuit is deficient if you flout what you judge to be your religious obligations.

Thus, when it comes to moral and religious integrity—obeying your conscience and adhering to God as you understand God—you need to avail yourself of *particular* options to avoid becoming deficient. Having a wide range isn't enough. The moral and religious conclusions you reach are what they are. Violating one of them makes you deficient in religion or integrity even if you work harder on living by the others. If the law pressures someone into flouting her Muslim obligations, she can't make up for that—and escape deficiency in religion—by fulfilling a Mennonite duty instead. There are no alternative channels for *her* to pursue religion in full. The same is true if the law pressures her into violating only *one* religious duty. She can't make up for violating the teaching against eating pork by redoubling her efforts to live out her separate duty to pray at certain times. Her religious life still suffers. Likewise with moral integrity. Imagine an Abortion Endorsement Law that said, "To promote women's freedom by fighting the stigma around abortion, every adult must sign a statement affirming abortion access as a basic right." As soon as we know that someone objects to complying with this law, we know that compliance would make her deficient in integrity.

This illustrates the sense in which moral and religious integrity is fragile. Taking away certain options for pursuing it doesn't simply diminish integrity but damages it. Because the law should keep the way clear for adequately pursuing the basic goods, it should leave you free to obey your conscience and religion unless doing so would chip at other facets of the common good. Another way of saying that is this: applying laws to you that would penalize you for living with integrity should trigger heightened scrutiny; our presumption should be to exempt you.

Thus, we've arrived at a bright-line rule for when to scrutinize burdens on religious liberty and conscience rights. It doesn't apply to other liberties, and it's more *stringent* than tests that simply ask whether a law burdens other liberties "substantially." And in both ways, treating moral and religious liberty differently from other freedoms makes sense. After all, of no other civil liberty can we say that (1) an easily identifiable burden on it would (2) pressure you into *deficiency* in a whole basic good (as opposed to denying you *some* ways of pursuing it).

And so at last we see why religious liberty and conscience rights need their own set of protective legal rules. There is an easier-to-spot—and more easily triggered—condition for heightened scrutiny of laws that weigh on them. If we simply merged them into other civil liberties, two of the basic goods served by freedom—religion and integrity—would lose the safeguards that all the goods deserve.

Another legal rule peculiar to religious liberty—lost if we merge it with other freedoms—flows from the same analysis. In Western legal thought it was born as *libertas ecclesiae* (freedom of the church). A modern variation in U.S. law is the "ministerial exception," which protects the freedom of religious groups to decide on their leadership, free of legal interference even by antidiscrimination law. Again, our analysis makes sense of this rule. You can pursue friendship or aesthetic fulfillment or knowledge adequately even if the state imposes *some* limits on related associations. It's rare to find yourself with an unchosen (perceived) *obligation* to join any given secular association. But the stakes are higher with religious association, where interference can easily make you slip into deficiency in a basic good. If your religion *requires* you to plug into a community governed by a certain creed, then you aren't free to live by your convictions unless that group is free to organize itself. A Catholic can't meet her obligation to receive the sacraments from priests chosen according to the Church's teachings if the state gets to meddle in their selection. If the mayor gets a veto on who will preach in local mosques, a Muslim can't find a cleric to preach to her about what *she* believes are the prophet's teachings. So your freedom to pursue religion adequately turns on a religious community's freedom to organize itself adequately.

By contrast, again, protection for civil liberties serving other goods can be more pliable. For most basic goods, most of the time, you can replace some options for promoting them with a range of alternatives, without falling into deficiency in those goods. If your Crossfit class can't get exercise by doing lunges on the White House lawn, if your orchestra can't promote aesthetic experience by calling itself to order on a residential street at midnight, you can always exercise and perform elsewhere. If a law burdening freedom of movement makes it costlier for you to stay in touch with one friend, you needn't become deficient in the good of friendship overall. You can pursue that friendship in other ways and friendship with other people. Even if more options would leave you better off with respect to such goods, these restrictions on your civil liberties don't shove you into deficiency. The state need only leave you enough options for exercising the liberty in question; being deprived of any particular option doesn't raise red flags.

Relatedly, as we began this section by noting, our framework clarifies how religion differs from other deep projects or commitments. You can pick your projects at will, but not your moral and religious convictions. That is, even if living by projects of your own choosing serves the basic good of self-determination, that good doesn't require pursuing *particular* projects. If one option is off the table but enough alternatives remain, you can pursue another without seeing your self-determination suffer. To protect the latter, the state need only leave you a rich range of options. Not so with religious and moral integrity.

3.3.2 Freedoms of Religion and Conscience: What's a Substantial Burden? What's Coercion?

Our analysis so far might seem silent on the cases most common in today's cultural clashes. Those are cases in which the law gives you an out for preserving your integrity: namely, bowing out of a certain corner of the public square. In *Hobby Lobby*, a case we discuss below, the law didn't require owners of the arts and crafts store chain to violate their conscience by supporting abortifacients through insurance coverage for their employees. It required them to do that *or* pay a fine *or* give up their business. The requirement that went against their conscience was *conditional*. Can we still say that it penalized them for living by their convictions?

We can. That conditional rule had the same problem as the *un*conditional requirement in our imaginary example of an Abortion Endorsement Law. In one sense, the latter would leave prolifers an out: they could refuse to sign and suffer a fine. It's clearly still a violation of their consciences, though, because it *raises the cost* of the only option their consciences allow. Not just by accident, in combination with outside factors, but by design. That is the sense in which it penalizes prolife citizens for living with integrity; that is why it merits scrutiny.

But the same harm inheres in some *conditional* requirements, including the HHS mandate. If the Abortion Endorsement Law would leave prolife citizens two options—surrender your money or your integrity—the HHS mandate left the Greens three equally unsavory ones: surrender your money *or your business* or your integrity. The problem with the Abortion Endorsement Law is that it would raise the price of preserving integrity as applied to prolifers. But so did the HHS mandate. It meant that the Greens' and other prolifers' only ways of living with integrity involved giving up something of great value. It didn't simply *happen* to do that, in some cases, in combination with a number of factors external to the law. It imposed those costs itself, for anyone refusing to comply. The penalties flowed right from the regulation.

Thus, if an Abortion Endorsement Law should raise red flags, so should the HHS mandate. To drive the point home, imagine if the Abortion Endorsement Law were framed this way: "Sign this statement supporting abortion access, or we will punish you by confiscating your business (or fining you) if you have one, or legally disabling you from ever forming one if you don't." That would hardly make it less objectionable, less of a "fine" on living with integrity. But it would have the same range of effects as the HHS mandate itself. It would leave pro-life citizens with the grim choice between paying a high cost or wounding their own integrity.

The same problem can arise when the government imposes harsh conditions on receipt of its own benefits. Tax-exempt status, for example, is essential for U.S. universities. If donors and universities both had to pay taxes on gifts to the latter, endowments would plummet. Most schools would have to close. So tax-exempt status is of enormous value to universities and the communities they serve. Yanking it from some schools but not others amounts to, well, a tax. And yanking it from religiously conservative schools unless they violate their religion—but not from others—entails a tax on their religion. To require an otherwise qualified Muslim college seeking tax-exempt status to violate Islamic norms by offering married housing for cohabiting couples is to force its community to choose between deficiency in religion and a loss of millions.

Yet not *all* conditional requirements force such a choice. As we've suggested, a law that fines you for speeding to church, when you feel obligated to get there on time, doesn't force a choice between paying a fine or becoming deficient in the basic good of religion. That's because it leaves you an *affordable* alternative for avoiding a violation of your religious duty: leaving the house on time. So it does *not* meaningfully raise the cost of keeping your religion—of pursuing this good adequately.

Taking this last wrinkle into account, then, we can make our proposed legal rule more precise: The decision to apply a regulation to someone should trigger heightened scrutiny whenever that application by itself would raise the cost to her of keeping her moral or religious obligations. For then the regulation would penalize her for pursuing some basic goods adequately (nondeficiently)—which the state must avoid doing if it can without eroding the common good.

Against this, a critic might note that all kinds of factors can stick a high price tag on integrity. Sometimes the costs come from the demandingness of your convictions; sometimes from the ferocity of your contrary desires; sometimes from outside forces; and sometimes from the law. Why is the last case worse than the others? But we could say the same of the Abortion Endorsement Law—that it would simply impose costs that might have arisen for any number of reasons. It can be wrong for the law to foist costs on you that misfortune could also impose. Chance costs for living with integrity are unlucky; fines for doing so can be unjust.

You might fear that by our logic, *any* legal restriction might become a fine on religion or conscience. Even the speeding law would, if leaving minutes earlier to keep your duty to get to church on time would cost you your job. But there's a difference. In that scenario, the speeding law by itself *does* leave you a way out. Alone it wouldn't raise the cost of living by your religious duty. It does so only in combination with outside factors—including your work schedule and your fussy boss. But the HHS mandate, like the Abortion Endorsement Law, *all by itself* raises the cost of living by prolife convictions. In both cases, that cost isn't the unhappy result of a pileup of factors, the law being only one of them; rather, the penalty *flows entirely from the law itself.* That's what makes these laws fines on prolife conscience—rather than one factor among many forcing prolifers into a corner.

Critics might finally answer that if we were right, we'd have to say that all regulations "fine" any number of worthy pursuits. Well, they do. But unless those regulations are very onerous, they won't pressure you into deficiency in a whole basic good. Sometimes they do put up significant obstacles to your pursuit of other goods, which is why serious burdens on other liberties also merit scrutiny. The difference here is that burdens on freedoms of religion and conscience become "serious" more immediately—and in a more immediately ascertainable way—because the goods they serve are fragile. Your pursuit of religion and integrity more easily dips into deficiency.

The framework built in this section, then, offers a unified account of (1) why unconditional burdens on religious liberty and conscience rights deserve heightened scrutiny, (2) why some conditional burdens do (as in *Hobby Lobby*) while others do not (as with speeding laws), (3) how to tell the difference (i.e., which burdens are substantial), (4) why freedom of religious *association* has singular importance (as with the ministerial exception), (5) why conditions on legal benefits as much as restrictions can merit heightened scrutiny, and (6) how the dictates of conscience differ in these respects from the demands of other deep commitments. Below we also use this framework to address another debate, showing that (7) the law cannot respect the conscience of flesh-and-blood human beings unless it also recognizes conscience claims brought by the corporations they form. None of this analysis is based on an empirical guess about religion's social utility. It's based on a vision of the human good and of the unique demands of moral and religious integrity within it.

Here we should pause to note a few things about the case we've made for moral and religious liberty. First, it is neither statist nor libertarian.[21] It sees moral and religious liberties as rights grounded in preexisting moral principles—not free bequests of the state, but natural rights. Yet it also doesn't treat freedom as an axiom. It grounds liberties in human goods and our duty to attend to them. As applied to the good of religion, this duty isn't specific to any theology; it isn't the duty to any particular creed. You fulfill it by paying careful attention to ultimate questions, answering them sincerely, and living authentically, whatever your answers.

Second, and relatedly, our argument is neither relativistic nor sectarian. It doesn't assume that all religions are equally true or all simply false, nor does it make truth a condition for protection. On anyone's view, of course, most religions are wrong about a great deal. But even religious acts based on intellectual mistakes can have the value of religion as a natural human good and virtue. A person is better off for having performed sincere religious acts even when they rest on false premises. Far from relativistic, this view is found in some traditions that claim for themselves the fullness of divine revelation.[22] But neither is it sectarian; reasoned reflection supports it.[23] And so, again, the value specific to religion shows up *whenever* people act with a view to coming to know and align themselves with the highest source of meaning.

Third, though we think you'll see more of religious liberty's value if you see religion as a basic good, you could accept our political-theoretical and policy conclusions even if you deny that. Those conclusions rest just as easily on the value of obeying conscience, secular or religious. Perceived religious obligations are, after all, perceived obligations. And we offer many instrumental reasons for specially supporting religious associations—ways in which religious vibrancy benefits believer and unbeliever alike. We turn to those now.

3.3.3 Civil Liberties, Civil Society, and Limits on the State's Jurisdiction

Appreciating these demands of the good of religion will drive home an insight that (it is no exaggeration to say) transformed human history, giving rise to the civil rights and freedoms now cherished throughout the West and beyond. It gave rise to the idea of civil society as something separate from the state that matters in itself and limits the law's claims to power. And it solidified a conviction that serves everything from congregations and clubs to whole economies: the state shouldn't quash intellectual difference. It must free us of physical deprivation and violence precisely to clear the arena for differences over mission and creed; for rival experiments in living, even beyond religion; for vitality and innovation in every part of life.

The American founders saw the first point clearly. They celebrated religious integrity as a source of moral limits on government, grounded in each person's duty to seek the truth about ultimate matters and to live by it. As James Madison wrote in his *Memorial and Remonstrance*, "the Religion then of every man must be left to the conviction and conscience of every man,"[24] because of a prior *duty* to seek out the truth about God and the created order: "What is here a right towards men, is a duty towards the Creator. It is the duty of every man to render to the Creator such homage and such only as he believes to be acceptable to him. This duty is precedent, both in order of time and in degree of obligation, to the claims of Civil Society."[25] If religious integrity makes it inherently unjust for the state to coerce religion directly, to enforce theological orthodoxy in worship, to select ministers, and the like, it follows that morality imposes universal limits on the state's authority to coerce, on its proper ambitions and goals. Respect for this right sears into political culture an image of the state as limited by higher laws: transcendent moral norms, and timeless truths about humanity's prepolitical needs and duties. The state has no natural general mandate to coerce us, with our rights coming merely from its gracious self-restraint. It's the other way around: civil society has moral claims on the state.

And this points to the second instrumental benefit of religious liberty mentioned above. It plays a crucial role in preserving civil society as something separate from the state. It makes conceptual room for—and promotes in practice—private associations and self-determination, the rights and liberties on which both depend, and the social and economic vitality that flows from all of these. Where religion has flourished under a regime of ordered liberty, other civil liberties have been more apt to get the protection they deserve. Religious freedom is the root, and civil society the outgrowth. The former really is our "first freedom," historically as well as conceptually. Thus, Professor Michael McConnell of Stanford Law School: "Long before liberalism ... the division between temporal and spiritual authority gave rise to the most fundamental features of liberal democratic order: the idea of limited government, the idea of individual conscience and hence of individual rights, and the idea of a civil society, as apart from government, bearing primary responsibility for the formation and transmission of opinions and ideas."[26] In short, freedoms of religion and conscience together—and the division of spiritual and temporal spheres that they created—made room for other civil liberties that we now cherish under the banner of the First Amendment. Once people saw clearly the distinction between the state and society, and saw that the first exists to serve the needs and rights of the second, there emerged other civil liberties, each serving human goods in its own way.

These rights are crucial for civil society's own diffuse form of governance: the private order created by the free choices of people and communities; by commerce, custom, and culture. Associations that populate the space between individuals and the state—religious congregations and institutions, but also civic institutions like the Boy Scouts and the Salvation Army, Oxfam and Greenpeace, charities and hospitals, clubs and businesses and schools—can have their own value, as expressions of private initiative and self-determination. And as cultural authorities separate from the state—relying on their own network of norms, serving their own purposes—they too check the state's ambitions. They create the private sphere. They shield it from tyranny. And they emerged from and still find reinforcement in our resolve to recognize the autonomy of religious and other expressive associations that the U.S. Supreme Court rightly calls "crucial in preventing the majority from imposing its views" on dissenting minorities.[27]

Freedoms of conscience and religion, fortified by association and speech, have thus fenced in the state's claims and let civil society bloom. Governments get this. Take this statement: "A church should not become a power which can promote radical change. . . . Otherwise, the church is not engaged in religion but in politics, which is not allowed for a church."[28] That statement came from a state-owned newspaper in China, in response to the Shouwang Church's campaign for liberty for itself. The Chinese government feared that the church could be a potent rival culture authority—a hunch that sociology confirms. Thus, sociologist Brian Grim:

> Religious freedom is embedded within a much larger bundle of civil liberties. At the core of religious expression is the freedom of speech and at the core of freedom to worship is the freedom to assemble. To claim freedom of speech without allowing for a freedom to express religious beliefs quickly erodes freedom of speech in other areas. Likewise, allowing for restrictions on the assembly of religious groups opens the door for curtailing activities of other groups as well. The denial of religious freedom is inevitably intertwined with the denial of other freedoms.[29]

Grim goes on to document statistically significant—and in some cases really striking—correlations between religious liberty protections and social goods as varied as political freedom, freedom of the press, women's equality, levels of income and GDP, and economic freedoms. Social science thus confirms what reflection suggests: that the freedom to embark on your own search for the deepest truths for which the human spirit yearns, to join your neighbor in the effort, and to live by your honest conclusions is the ribcage of a healthy civic culture. Our most

important liberties—the most important limits on the state—
rise or fall with that one.

3.3.4 Pluralism and Tolerance

A tolerant society protects civil liberties; doing that serves pluralism. So another social benefit of religious liberty protection
is a tolerant and pluralistic society—a point best grasped by
thinking about what we might call *principled* and *pragmatic*
senses of pluralism.

Pluralism means variety; and tolerance (in some sense) is
required where it would be a mistake to stamp out that variety. But this might be for either of two reasons. Some variety
is a valuable expression of differences worth celebrating. Call
respect for it "principled pluralism." But some social variety
is tragic, resulting from immorality or error or privations of
other sorts, and we must tolerate it only because the risks of
enforcing uniformity make attempts to cure it even worse. Call
respect for this sort "pragmatic pluralism." Its value is instrumental: we can't enjoy principled pluralism in full without
the buffer provided by pragmatic pluralism. Respecting the
first demands respect for the second. And our civil liberties
serve both.

Within a family, for example, a variety of talents and interests would be good. There's nothing inherently regrettable
about one child becoming a doctor, and another a carpenter.
For parents to impose one career on all their children would
violate their rights and drain the family's life of a splendor
good in itself. But the same family might also have "variety" of
a regrettable sort: in degrees of personal freedom (because one
kid is stuck in jail), say, or in levels of maturity (because one
is stuck in adolescence). Still, these forms of variety would be
worth *tolerating*, given the alternatives. Breaking your son out
of jail would be wrong; browbeating your immature adult-child

would be pointless and harmful; and achieving harmony at the cost of kicking either kid out of the family would be wrong and beside the point.

Likewise, there are two kinds of cases in which the state ought not to quash social variety. On the one hand, the human good is textured and open-ended. There are many honorable ways to blend the elements of human flourishing. Even in a civilization of saints, there would be a range of valuable ways of life, with people and associations giving priority to different goods, pursued in different ways. Civil liberties exist partly to protect that valuable variety by slowing the state's ambitions to achieve important social goals at its expense. This highlights the need to empower, not encumber, the civic associations that arise in free societies: principled pluralism.

On the other hand, the state should also tolerate some things that really are erroneous or harmful or immoral, where the alternative would risk doing still more harm and little good. This pragmatic pluralism is born of a healthy humility and a healthy fear. Our powers of reason are limited; our evidence is limited; and so is our experience—and in different ways for different people. So where people are free to come to their own conclusions about matters of right and wrong, religion, and the like, they come to *different* conclusions, even when they all act in good faith. Add to this the universal temptation to hoard and abuse power, and we all have good reasons to want our governments limited even in their efforts to promote true moral standards. That's why we should keep many avenues open for the expression of dissent.

So we have both principled and pragmatic reasons to avoid the Puritan mistake. Policies that violate pluralism, and forfeit its evident benefits for no good reason, are *illiberal* as we'll use the term here. And we'll have all too many occasions to use it.

Of course, there must also be limits to the state's self-limitations, for the sake of justice. We have to trim our liberties for the sake of the common good. And we will often disagree on where those cuts should be made; there's no getting around it. So we have to address skirmishes in the culture wars one by one. But we all have some reason—based on the truth about the common good—to structure our law to give individuals and private associations some breathing room to get things wrong. Not because variety on matters of right and wrong is valuable in itself but because accepting some degree of it is the lesser evil.

Thus, if the law is entitled to ban vices, it should do so only where they're pervasive enough, and hard enough for private entities to clean up on their own, that the common good will otherwise suffer greatly. And contrary to what some liberal commentators may claim, this isn't the Johnny-come-lately position of conservative culture warriors in the face of political defeat, but the considered judgment of the central tradition of Western political thought, most fully articulated by no less a religious and political-perfectionist thinker than Thomas Aquinas.[30]

The value of self-determination thus tells against efforts to hurry the task of moral and political reform—and smooth over its messiness, and dull its raw emotions—by the cold and heavy hand of the state. In a word, it urges us, wherever possible, to cure social ills not by official fiat but by free choices and communities, by custom and culture.

3.4 OUR FIRST FREEDOM AT WORK

But is it feasible to leave so much space for people to get things wrong? Can we give believers latitude without making the sky fall? The best evidence we have comes from American practice from the founding onward. And it lends support to the idea that one source of the dynamism of American society is its long, vigorous respect for moral and religious liberty.

We noted in our introductory essay that above all, the founders intended to protect religious liberty in the same way as other liberties: by limited and localized government. The First Amendment and the tests applied under it by courts have been secondary. So too are legislative religious liberty protections, including accommodations and exemptions. But these secondary protections become all the more important as government grows beyond the size and scope envisioned by the founders. A larger, centralized, and more active government has more occasions to violate religious liberty—even unintentionally—and thus a greater need for conscience protections.

These come in two varieties, as we explained above. Where it's clear in advance that leaving dissenters free to act on this or that view won't wound the common good, the law gives them categorical protections, as it does for prolife individuals and institutions on abortion. But it also provides for judges to grant exemptions on a case-by-case basis where exempting believers wouldn't gut the law's purposes. As we noted in the introductory essay, there is a long American history of giving dissenters both kinds of shields. Whether or not the U.S. Constitution requires them, it certainly does not forbid them. It does forbid special burdens on religion, require *certain* exemptions (e.g., the ministerial exception), and allow those created by legislatures and agencies.

3.4.1 Religious Freedom Restoration Acts

As we've noted, broad liberty protections can prevent any number of burdens that might be unintended and unimagined at the time of legislation. This purpose animates the federal RFRA, the various state RFRAs, and RLUIPA. These laws require judges to grant citizens exemptions from regulations that curb their exercise of religion, except where denying exemptions is the least restrictive means of serving a compelling government interest.

We discussed the concrete effects of RFRAs over the last quarter century in our introductory essay—effects that we think confirm their wisdom and fairness. Some opposition to religious liberty seems based on the idea that laws ought to and can be one-size-fits-all. But most regulations allow any number of exemptions for reasons unrelated to conscience or religion. There is no general reason to avoid exemptions for the sake of the latter, which virtually no one rejects across the board. (Consider, e.g., the draft.) The real questions are: When should we grant them? And who should decide?

We could entrust the decision to lawmakers alone—leave it entirely up to them to carve out religious accommodations from any particular law, as they have where vulnerable groups were visible enough when the law was being written. That may have been enough before the administrative state swelled to its present size. Indeed, the Supreme Court didn't require judicially granted religious or conscience exemptions until the 1960s, and statutes requiring them in many contexts didn't come until the Court changed course in the 1990s.

But the need for those exemptions remains. Statutory accommodations aren't enough in a society as religiously diverse as ours, with state and federal policies as far-reaching as ours. *State* lawmakers can't foresee all the reasonable accommodation claims that might arise. It would be all the more difficult for the U.S. Congress to imagine the claims that might arise from Anchorage to Atlanta and from Austin to Augusta. Besides, without a provision for case-by-case exemptions, any group seeking protection would have to wait until the legislature had heard its case; minority groups might never attain the political muscle to grab the legislature's attention at all. Such a regime would be inefficient and unfair—especially given the importance of following the dictates of conscience, and of protecting conscience for minorities.

So it's better if those burdened by government actions can bring their claims to local courts and seek relief from judges. But there are problems with this approach, too. If there's no way for a legislature to foresee all the reasonable objections to a particular policy, there's equally no way to capture all reasonable claims in a single rule that would give judges clear direction in almost every case. Their guiding norm would need to be a broad standard, like "grant religious exemptions when doing so would be *reasonable*." Yet if this standard gave judges the last word, it would wrench too much power from lawmakers. Every law passed by any legislature would be subject to free-ranging manipulation by courts, which could choose to gut laws they didn't like.

This problem suggests its own solution.[31] In passing statutes, lawmakers could carve out accommodations that they foresaw and thought important and affordable. They could frame those forward-looking protections as narrowly or widely as they saw fit, within constitutional limits. And these protections would be part of the law that judges applied but had no power to repeal. Beyond that, lawmakers could give judges a general power—by statute, not constitutionally—to grant reasonable exemptions from laws that burdened religious activity.

And finally, to keep the judiciary from grabbing this power and running with it—essentially undoing the legislature's work and undermining all its aims—lawmakers would remain free to rein in the courts. Because the power given to judges would be statutory, the legislature could always enact new statutes to hem that power in for certain purposes. It could pass a law to bar exemptions from particular statutes, or allow them only where the claims cleared a still higher hurdle. So the political branches would have the final say. But once they had enacted a law, the political burden would be on them to foreclose exemptions from it.

This is a balanced approach. It protects religion and conscience against incidental burdens, as any sensible regime sometimes must—but it does so more efficiently and fairly than a system requiring lawmakers to foresee and care enough about every possible reasonable claim. It also avoids wresting all power from lawmakers. If lawmakers deem a policy goal important enough, and vulnerable enough to gutting by exemptions, they can do something about it. But the burden is on them to defend their view to voters and pass laws accordingly—rather than shifting to minority believers the burden to prove that their religious claims really count.

In fact, this is the U.S. approach, in the federal government and nearly half the states. It has a name: RFRA. The statutes we call RFRAs give general instructions to judges to provide religious exemptions. But precisely as statutes, they can be overridden when lawmakers worry enough about the effects of exemptions to take the trouble to disallow them. Thus, as Eugene Volokh has argued, RFRAs provide for religious liberty the sensible, balanced regime of protections—the steady rhythm of sallies and volleys between judges and lawmakers—that has worked well to shape Anglo-American torts, property, and contract law for centuries by common law. Such a regime should quell Justice Scalia's fears in *Smith*. Indeed, you can think he was right there about the Constitution's requirements *and* think Congress was right to pass RFRA.

Note that most RFRAs, as written, require exemptions except where denying one is the "least restrictive means" to serving a "compelling state interest." These are terms of art from other areas of law. Elsewhere they enshrine the "strict scrutiny" test for legislation—the most demanding constitutional test. But some legal observers argue that in practice, courts have applied a weaker test under RFRA.[32] What we endorse are RFRAs as applied. There are different ways to embody the principle that we think political morality requires (see our rebuttal for more detail); and if RFRA ever leads judges astray, lawmakers can always correct them.

As written, RFRAs may seem to give conscience claims too much latitude, by setting too high a bar for legal coercion of conscience to clear. If we accommodate the baker who refuses to participate in celebrating same-sex weddings, and employers who refuse to pay for insurance to cover abortifacient drugs, where will it stop? Religious objections proliferate. There are countless possible claims to bring. Some involve minor burdens on conscience. So even if the public benefit to burdening conscience is slight in any given case, isn't it more efficient overall to allow no exceptions to most laws? Isn't the resulting burden on any given citizen quite slight?

This is the wrong way to look at these cases, as we suggested above, in our discussion of the differences between what it takes to protect integrity as opposed to other basic goods. Conscience claims don't present a choice between a trivial interest for the state and a trivial interest for the claimant. They are not simply about weighing interests on both sides—the public's interest in efficiency, against the claimant's interest in a clear conscience. They're about finding a way to respect each—to serve each adequately. The burden of proof should favor moral and religious integrity not because it matters more but because of what we've called its fragility. Yet that presumption must be applied on a case-by-case basis, since integrity's demands—and the social harms of honoring those demands—will depend on the content of each claim. RFRAs enshrine just such a system of case-by-case application of a presumption for integrity.

That sensible balance once drew remarkably wide support. Nadine Strossen, president of the National Board of Directors of the American Civil Liberties Union, testified before Congress in support of RFRA:

> To paraphrase the great bard, I think it is all in the name: the Religious Freedom Restoration Act. That is an accurate description of what this legislation would do, no more and no less. It is hardly a radical proposal to restore religious freedom. Indeed, I think the only radical thing at issue here is the Supreme Court's

decision in the *Smith* case which took religious freedom effectively out of the Constitution.

Now all we are asking this legislature to do is to restore to Americans the religious liberties that we took for granted under our Constitution until that Supreme Court decision in *Smith*, and let me describe. Basically, what this would do would be to restore to religious liberty the same kind of protection that the Court has given and still does give to other fundamental freedoms under our constitutional system. They are not absolutely protected, but in order for government to infringe on a liberty, including religious liberty, it has to show some compelling interest, and it has to show that the measure is narrowly tailored so as to do as little damage as possible to religious liberty.

Under that kind of strict scrutiny approach in the past, some religious freedom claims were sustained and some were not; this is hardly a radical approach.[33]

Let that sink in: The president of the American Civil Liberties Union championed RFRA for restoring to religious liberty the shield we use for other freedoms. Indeed, she celebrated the very applications of RFRA that progressives now say are abuses never imagined by its advocates. As Strossen wrote in her testimony for RFRA, under the heading "Without H.R. 2797 [RFRA], Religious Liberty is Gravely Threatened":

In the aftermath of the *Smith* decision, it was easy to imagine how religious practices and institutions would have to abandon their beliefs in order to comply with generally applicable, neutral laws. At risk were such familiar practices as the sacramental use of wine, kosher slaughter, the sanctity of the confessional, religious preferences in church hiring, establishing places of worship in areas zoned for other use, permitting religiously sponsored hospitals to decline to provide abortion or contraception services, sex segregation during worship services, exemptions from mandatory retirements laws, a church's refusal to ordain women or homosexuals, exemption from landmark regulations, and the inapplicability of highly intrusive educational rules to parochial schools. These were decisions in areas that society had previously assumed that religious groups had the right to make for themselves and could not be compelled to change just because society thought otherwise.[34]

So Strossen explicitly cited religious hospitals refusing to provide contraception among "familiar practices" that "society had previously assumed that religious groups had the right to make for themselves and could not be compelled to change just because society thought otherwise." Only yesterday did this go from being a cool observation to a white-hot provocation.

Of course, as we noted in our introduction, RFRA-style laws have been used to protect a wide variety of minority claimants: Apache Indians told they can't wear headdresses with eagle feathers, Sikhs told they can't carry a kirpan if they work for the government, Santería priests prevented from performing their sacrifices, inner-city black churches zoned out of existence, Muslim prisoners forbidden to grow short beards, and Jewish inmates denied kosher meals. They only became controversial when the federal RFRA protected a business against the federal government's mandate to provide coverage to which its owners objected, and when it seemed that state RFRAs might protect bakers, florists, and photographers who objected to same-sex marriage. We've said something about the latter. Now we'll address the former.

3.4.2 Hobby Lobby and the Little Sisters

Both Hobby Lobby, a corporation, and the Little Sisters of the Poor—a nonprofit religious order of nuns—invoked RFRA against a federal agency's mandate that employers offer insurance covering abortion-inducing pills. In *Hobby Lobby*, the Court ruled that Hobby Lobby was a "person" under RFRA, that requiring it to offer insurance coverage of abortifacients against its owners' objections substantially burdened religious exercise, and that another of the government's own policies revealed a narrower path to its goals: the accommodation it offered religious nonprofits.

Then in the case brought by the Little Sisters of the Poor, the Court considered what RFRA entailed for those nonprofits burdened by the mandate whose objections were not addressed by the accommodation offered them. The Court asked for additional briefing to see if a more adequate accommodation could be granted without putting cracks in the widespread coverage of contraceptives sought by the government. When both sides filed response briefs essentially saying yes, the Court decided unanimously to have the parties agree on such an accommodation for lower courts to consider—an outcome that all sides can celebrate.

Let's unpack all of this.

The first legal issue in *Hobby Lobby* was whether family-owned, closely held business could exercise religion under RFRA. The Supreme Court held that they could, as a matter of statutory text and history. Setting aside the interpretive question, we focus on the philosophical question whether the law *should* extend civil liberty protections to corporations.

The purpose of the legal fiction of treating corporations as persons is, as the Court noted, "to provide protection for human beings" by allowing them to do more than they can by solitary pursuits, or social pursuits without legal status. That is why nonprofits have legal rights. So do individuals in their profit-seeking activities. So what is it about the combination of the corporate form and profit-seeking that should disqualify an entity from protection? After all, for-profit corporations needn't pursue profit alone. As the Court pointed out, some

"take costly pollution-control and energy-conservation measures that go beyond what the law requires"; why can't they take
steps to operate by religious values?

Yes, Hobby Lobby's owners opened their stores—and their
job offers—to people of other creeds or none. But why should
that disqualify them from bringing a claim in the first place? If
it means that granting their claim would unduly harm others,
then the claim will be denied under RFRA's test. But apart from
those harms, there's nothing mystical about stepping into the
public square that should further count against these owners.
Yes, there are benefits to legal incorporation, including limited
personal liability for the corporation's debts. But that doesn't
stop corporations from exercising other civil liberties. Thus,
for-profits like the *New York Times* enjoy freedoms of speech
and press.

These are all arguments from analogy for why for-profit
corporations should enjoy the rights that nonprofits and individuals exercise. Here's another, more direct way to see the
point, building within the framework we developed above.
Corporate rights matter because—and only because—we must
recognize them to respect the civil rights of the human beings
who form them. Being able to organize under the corporate
form provides many important legal and financial protections.
To condition those protections on people's willingness to violate their moral or religious convictions is—for the reasons we
gave above—to penalize them for the opportunity to pursue
all of the basic goods (including moral and religious integrity)
adequately. It would be as if a law punished people unwilling
to facilitate abortifacients by banning them from owning businesses. Such regulations needlessly pressure people into deficiency with respect to a basic good, in violation of the state's
most basic duty.

And there would be no legal obstacle to the most flagrant
violations of that duty, if corporations couldn't bring religious

or conscience claims at all. As the Supreme Court noted, the state could then "require all employers to provide coverage for any medical procedure allowed by law in the jurisdiction in question—for instance, third-trimester abortions or assisted suicide." With one decree, an agency could shutter the doors of thousands of small businesses. As Justice Kennedy wrote in concurrence: "In our constitutional tradition, freedom means that all persons have the right to believe or strive to believe in a divine creator and a divine law. For those who choose this course, free exercise is essential in preserving their own dignity and in striving for a self-definition shaped by their religious precepts. Free exercise in this sense implicates more than just freedom of belief. It means, too, the right to express those beliefs and to establish one's religious (or nonreligious) self-definition in the political, civic, and economic life of our larger community." As evangelical and Mennonite Christians, the Greens (who own Hobby Lobby) and Hahns (who own Conestoga Wood, another party to the litigation) believe it gravely wrong to participate in killing human beings even at the earliest stage. So the HHS mandate burdened their religious exercise by forcing them to offer insurance coverage of four (out of twenty) specified contraceptives that, as the FDA itself notes, could work by causing the death of embryonic human beings.[35]

The next issue the Court tackled was whether that requirement substantially burdened religious exercise. To operate their businesses in keeping with their religious beliefs, the Greens and Hahns had two options under the mandate. They could offer health insurance that did not cover four of the twenty contraceptives specified and pay $100 per day per employee in fines: $475 million a year for Hobby Lobby and $33 million a year for Conestoga. Or they could drop health insurance altogether, with Hobby Lobby paying $25 million and Conestoga paying $1.8 million a year for that. Either way, the Court judged that they faced substantial burdens under RFRA.

Anyone applying the framework we sketched above would agree. Supporting abortifacients would violate the Greens' and Hahns' religious conscience. But paying fines or going out of business would cost the Greens and Hahns millions of dollars in value. (Either way, they faced a penalty—it was just payable in two ways: their cash or their business.) And being forced to violate your religious conscience, on pain of paying stratospheric penalties, is surely a "substantial burden" on religious exercise, on any sensible reading of that term.

And it was needless. As the Court found, applying the mandate to the Greens and Hahns was not the least restrictive means of giving employees free access to contraceptives. There were numerous less onerous alternatives, including one that the government itself had provided for religious nonprofits. Under RFRA, then, HHS was required to offer the same accommodation to the Greens, the Hahns, and their businesses. Our framework would urge the same result, since the mandate needlessly penalized these families for pursuing basic goods adequately.

In the Little Sisters of the Poor case, the question was whether the accommodation that the government created for religious nonprofits was *itself* the least restrictive means of achieving its goals. Everything else was the same: The Little Sisters were judged "persons" under RFRA, and they faced the same fines for noncompliance. They objected to the requirement to fill out a form notifying the government of their objections—a form that would then legally authorize (and require) the insurance provider to offer the coverage. They believed that taking a step that legally triggered the objectionable coverage would make them complicit.

The Court took the Little Sisters at their word about what their religious conscience required, once again focusing on the least restrictive means test. The Court asked both parties—the government and the religious nonprofits—if there was a way to meet the government's goals without forcing religious nonprofits to act against conscience. To revert to our own terms and framework, it asked whether the interests of both sides to the dispute could be realized *adequately*. When both parties filed responses essentially saying yes, the Court vacated the lower court rulings and instructed the courts to reconsider the case in light of a new accommodation that the government was to provide. In other words, the Court instructed the administration to try to find a win-win solution. This reflects the value of the common-law, iterative process that we defended above as a merit of RFRA.

Some thought the Court should've ruled that the Little Sisters' religious exercise wasn't "substantially" burdened, because signing a form that required the insurer they hired to offer the coverage wouldn't *really* have made them complicit in contraception. But that wasn't the question. The Religious Freedom Restoration Act doesn't tell courts to decide what moral complicity really involves, or what your religion really deems sinful. It says nothing about complicity or sin at all. Neither word shows up in the statute.

The Religious Freedom Restoration Act only requires courts—it only allows them—to say what counts as a "substantial burden" on religion. And substantial burdens on your religion surely include *forced violations* of your religion. In other words, it's a substantial burden if the law threatens you with serious penalties unless you do what *you* believe your religion *forbids*. Why you believe that is none of the courts' business, as U.S. jurisprudence has always held. So leave "complicity" out of it: the Little Sisters believed it would be sinful for them to sign a form triggering others' provision of contraception coverage. *That* is why fining them for refusing substantially burdens their religion. It isn't for the Court to tell them what their conscience *should* have told them.

In general, believers decide what status a certain action or refusal has in their religion: whether it's required or optional.

Courts get to decide whether penalizing actions *with that status* imposes a "substantial burden." Thus, if stopping by church for the occasional prayer after work is optional for Catholics—according to Catholics—then a legal curfew that incidentally requires them to stop by a few hours earlier (or less often overall) is no substantial burden. But a law that exacted a high cost for their refusal to violate their religion surely would be.

The outcomes for both Hobby Lobby and the Little Sisters should appeal to progressives, too. They are victories for each of the parties at the cost of none. They tell government wherever possible to protect everyone's interests adequately. If you think contraception crucial for women's equality, that's no reason to object: private employers had never been required to cover contraceptives; they're available in countless other ways; and there was no serious evidence that anyone would lose access altogether. If you think religious liberty also matters, as both sides do, you should celebrate its protection. Benefits redound to all, and burdens are reduced to the point of vanishing. This is legislatively mandated and judicially managed compromise at its best.

3.5 FALLACIES REGARDING DISCRIMINATION, COERCION, AND DIGNITY

But some people find such compromises pernicious. They see burdening certain conservative convictions not as a tragic side effect but as a victory for social justice. What we would count as a gain for everyone's interests, they would see as a loss for some people's dignity. In their view, traditional ideals on sex and marriage should be pressured out of existence, socially and legally, because they're invidious. Respecting claims that spring from them would mean enforcing a "right to discriminate." That's a serious charge, and a serious mistake.

We'll say why in the next section, by developing and deploying a general framework for thinking about what discrimination consists of, when it is invidious, what sorts of material and dignitary harms justify antidiscrimination law, and how those laws should be framed. But first, in the remainder of this section, we clear some brush. We dispel three fallacies or hasty assumptions common in these debates: that in certain contexts, all differential treatment is wrongful discrimination; that all wrongful discrimination must be banned; and that emotional pain or moralized offense alone can justify banning it. Addressing each of these in turn over the next three subsections will set the stage for our positive account of what discrimination does involve, when it is worth banning, and what kinds of dignitary harms do justify coercion.

3.5.1 Wrongful Discrimination

It's common to think that discrimination is always wrong. It isn't. Discrimination in the broad sense is simply the making of distinctions, which we do all the time. It's a necessity of life. The question is whether the discrimination is on the right basis. Discrimination based on relevant factors is good—as when we require recipients of driver's licenses to be able to see. It's wrong when it's based on *irrelevant* factors—as when the United States once required voters to be white.

But when people talk about discrimination in this moralized sense, they don't usually mean just *any* arbitrary and immoral distinction in treatment. A teacher giving grades based on the color of his students' T-shirts is treating them differently based on irrelevant factors, but there would be something odd about calling his treatment of them "discrimination." The further element of "discrimination" in the familiar moralized sense is that it involves mistreatment based on a stable, socially salient trait around which many forms of arbitrary treatment have clustered.

Mistreatment clusters around stable traits because their stability enables human beings to do what they have always been disposed to do: create stable in-groups and out-groups; define a clan and prefer it to others in systematically unjust ways. That involves disadvantaging others in several realms, based on traits that are stable and easily detected—and morally irrelevant in most contexts.[36] When a particular trait is the site of many unfair burdens, people coin an "-ism" (sexism, racism) to label related wrongs. They speak of the creation of social castes and second-class citizens. In this subsection, we'll generally use "discrimination" in this pejorative sense.

The fact that abuses bunch up in this way gives rise to a persistent temptation for those trying to fight discrimination. If a group has long been oppressed, it becomes natural to think that every decision based on related traits is just another thread in the web of wrongs. But that's a bad inference. There might be some legitimate forms of "discrimination" (differentiation) based on the same trait. Disentangling the two can take work. Sexism is wrongful discrimination based on sex, but that doesn't tell us whether it's sexist to give men and women separate bathrooms. Policies rejecting school vouchers in favor of government-run schools might measurably harm the economic prospects of poor minority students, but that doesn't make these policies racist. And the sordid history of abuses against the LGBT community doesn't prove that traditional marriage was part of the oppression. Indeed, as we'll show, history proves just the opposite.

In general, how we define concrete instances of discrimination depends on our underlying moral judgments about particular cases. A charge of discrimination is not just a perfectly neutral observation about how someone has reasoned her way to a particular decision. Nor is it based only on claims about past patterns of mistreatment. It always hangs on substantive moral claims about the rightness (or not) of reasoning in a certain way *here and now.*

3.5.2 How to Respond to Discrimination

In fact, where conscience and charges of discrimination intersect, there are *two* moral judgments at issue. Consider the charge that the Greens and the Hahns discriminated by refusing to offer their employees insurance coverage for abortifacient drugs. This verdict can't rest only on the fact that sexism has been historically pervasive. It also makes assumptions about the moral status of abortion—and about the moral duties of those who facilitate healthcare.

To start with the latter: even if you thought abortifacients morally good, you could well support allowing employers like the Greens and Hahns to refuse to cover them. Maybe abortifacients are like dental care: coverage is good but not required. Or maybe they're like emergency care, which it's unjust to deny. Or maybe there's no duty to cover *any* birth control for women, unless you already cover vasectomies for men. But all of these possibilities assume that abortifacients *are* morally good. If you disagreed, you wouldn't have to weigh the pros and cons of making others pay for them. Refusing to participate in something immoral can never be wrong *in itself.*

Our point is simply this. Where Jones refuses to deal with Smith on the ground that Smith's actions are immoral, the charge that this makes Jones guilty of wrongful discrimination rests on not one but two moral judgments: (1) of Smith's underlying action, and (2) of Jones's refusal to be linked to it. And the policy view that we should therefore coerce Jones against his conscience depends on the separate political and empirical judgments that (3) the law must penalize his discrimination to preserve others' ability to pursue their basic interests adequately, and that (4) granting conscience-based exemptions from such a ban would unravel that goal. The last two points follow from our discussion of the state's central duty to ensure adequate access to the basic goods in general.

So what can we *immediately* infer about the right policy response to wrongful discrimination? Nothing. Politics is about keeping up the social conditions that allow people to pursue goods for themselves, not about making us pure of heart. Law should not ban every vice or enforce every virtue. So there are scenarios in which all things considered, *it should remain legal* to fire you for how you look or walk or talk or on any number of bases it's clearly wrong to consider. That sounds paradoxical but follows, on reflection, from almost any serious theory of the proper limits of law. We have to get used to the sound of it if we're to think carefully and accurately about when antidiscrimination laws are justified. On our own view, only when discrimination impedes a group's ability to meet basic needs or join public life does it call for policy solutions. In a word, antidiscrimination laws always hang on moral *and* empirical *and* policy judgments that are all far more controversial than the idea that we should treat each other as subjects of dignity and worth—a principle on which we and Corvino agree without hedge or hesitation. So in Corvino's essay and rebuttal, we'll look for arguments on four issues that any good defense of SOGI laws must address:

1. The moral status of the acts from which objectors seek to disengage (e.g., gay marriage)
2. The moral status of their refusal (e.g., to offer wedding cakes)
3. The public need for a law coercing private parties in the first place (e.g., SOGI laws)
4. The public harm of granting exemptions from that law (e.g., for evangelical florists)

But for now, we turn to consider when the last two criteria, which are empirical, are met. And since we discuss below the case of SOGI laws in particular, here we go back to the question whether the law should coerce Hobby Lobby. To justify that conclusion, again, you need to judge (1) that using abortifacients is morally acceptable, and (2) that there are strong reasons to have health insurance providers cover them, so that business owners wrong their employees by refusing them coverage. You then need to show (3) that the failure to cover abortifacients is so widespread and harmful that it justifies a coercive policy. And *then* you must go on to show that (4) the public need is so sensitive that exemptions would enfeeble any policy meant to meet it.

There are plenty of possible reasons to get off the train at step (3). Maybe contraceptives are critical, but *abortifacient* contraceptives are not. Or abortifacients are critical, but they're already reasonably accessible. Or they're inaccessible, but we can change that without coercing others. Or legal coercion here wouldn't be effective or prudent or worth the costs. We won't dwell long on the different ways that the third criterion might fail, because our opening discussions of four flashpoints in these debates show that step (3) is satisfied in none of them.

Step (3) *is* satisfied if the world is rife with wrongful discrimination against a group. It might be tempting to say that in those cases, step (4) is *automatically* satisfied as well: If fighting discrimination is the goal, exemptions will always undermine it; every exemption will be a partial unraveling of the law's legitimate purposes. Right?

Not necessarily. Often the best reason to fight discrimination is to keep it from passing a tipping point, beyond which people aren't simply inconvenienced here or there but are locked out of markets for meeting basic needs. In *these* cases, allowing exemptions for a small subset of providers who refuse to offer a service for reasons of conscience wouldn't upset the law's goals *even a bit*—since those goals all depend exclusively on keeping refusals below the tipping point.

Thus, suppose that abortion access is a basic right but that the vast majority of surgeons refuse to perform one—most to free up their schedules for more lucrative procedures. Only 1 percent refuse because they are prolife; and they are spread out geographically. In this scenario, the best reason for the state to force surgeons' hands would *not* be to pressure out of existence the prolife minority's moral dissent. Reeducation efforts like that are illiberal. The best reason would rather be to guarantee each woman access to a willing surgeon somewhere nearby. That would only require keeping the rate of refusals below a certain number. In that case, exempting the 1 percent who refuse in conscience wouldn't put even the tiniest dent in the law's goals. It would promote integrity without doing any material harm by anyone's tally.

So even when antidiscrimination policies are needed, we can often afford to grant conscience-based exemptions. And we *must* do so where the material harms are nil since we'll then have no reason to deny them, and some reason to grant them (which even erring conscience always provides). But what about discrimination's nonmaterial harms? We turn now to a common mistake about those.

3.5.3 Discrimination and Dignitary Harm

Many argue that discriminatory actions, even when they have no tangible, material effects on others, do public harm that the state is right to try to eradicate. Douglas NeJaime and Reva Siegel have offered one influential argument for this view. They propose that judges and lawmakers weigh religious liberty and conscience claims now arising (in which claimants seek to disengage from what they see as others' sins) against the *dignitary harm* these liberties might inflict. Conscientious refusals, they say, are salvos in a culture war. A certain message resounds from them, whatever the refusing party might mean or say. Refusals to provide morning-after pills, for example, tell women that their choice is sinful or wrong—even that they are sinners.[37] This is stigmatizing. And many such refusals, mobilized by zealous generals in our culture wars, only intensify what one might call *moral stigma*—the harm of being told (even by polite refusals) that decisions central to your identity are immoral.

In the section below, on antidiscrimination law, we'll discuss a cousin of moral stigma that we do think it appropriate for law to fight. Here we concentrate on the problems with taking into account moral stigma itself. First, counting it can be self-defeating because fear of it can be self-fulfilling. The more that we—or officials, in weighing complicity claims—say that a policy or belief expresses disdain for a group, the more it will take on that social meaning. Lawmakers or judges trying to fight the harm might thus extend it. This is not to blame the victims as hypersensitive. Quite the opposite. It's to acknowledge that social meaning depends not on any one person's state of mind but on diffuse social facts. Feminists for Life certainly don't think their convictions are sexist, and some prochoice people might agree for now. But the more that professors and officials declare—and act on the assumption—that opposing abortifacients is sexist or stigmatizing, the more it will take on that social meaning.

Second, in many disputes, both sides could claim with equal force that a decision against them would morally stigmatize them. Grant that exemptions from baking same-sex wedding cakes tell gay couples that intimacies central to their identity are immoral. What about denying the bakers' claims? Won't that tell them—and *all* traditional Muslims, Orthodox Jews, and Christians—that acting on beliefs central to their identities is immoral? Wasn't Brendan Eich told that convictions central to his religious identity were oppressive? If exemptions from performing abortions tar women who've had abortions, coercing prolife doctors must brand them enemies of women's equality. On most serious issues, any side might feel deeply stigmatized by rival actions or policies, which is one reason to simply favor freedom over coercion on such matters.

One might reply that sometimes the stigma is justified, because the targeted view is deplorable. Maybe it is deplorable. But to stymie rights to expressive conduct on that basis alone is illiberal. It forfeits the fruits of what we have called pragmatic pluralism—and of what most call classical liberalism.

Note first that clipping our liberties for imposing dignitary harm would actually require trimming the whole field of religious liberty (and *other* civil liberties), and not just that small corner of conscience claims centered on complicity in the shadow of a culture war. In a diverse society, after all, religious liberty *always* creates moral stigma. Religious freedom includes nothing if not the rights to worship, proselytize, and convert—forms of conduct (and speech) that can express the conviction that outsiders are wrong.[38] Perhaps not just wrong, but deluded about matters of cosmic importance around which they have ordered their lives—even *damnably* wrong.

This can hold within religions, too, and even among those Christians allied in the culture wars. On the Catholic view, for instance, worship of the Eucharist ought to be the organizing principle of one's life.[39] For evangelicals, making it so might entail idolatry, a violation of literally the first commandment.[40] In a world full of conflicting faiths and denominations, then, religious freedom is the ultimate source of moral stigma.[41] Freedom of conscience is another. Actions based on *secular* moral views held as universal truths might also stigmatize. At a dinner out with friends, a vegan's order of tofu might suggest judgment of her friends' choice of beef. That hardly favors her ordering tenderloin—as her carnivorous friends should agree.[42]

To be sure, in the religious context, most progressives would deny that we should whittle away at rights to worship or convert wherever their exercise implies that others are sinning. They might set different standards for *these* facets of religious liberty. But on what ground? Yes, these are central to religious freedom, but so is conscience—which many progressive policies would effectively fine, as we've seen. If the power to stigmatize should count even a little against the latter, why not against the former? But since we certainly *won't* suppress the former and far more pervasive exercises of religious liberty, how much good would it do to stamp out only the moral stigma created by complicity claims caught up in culture wars? The reduction in public rancor would be slight, while the cost for each person coerced against her conscience would be quite grave.

So far, we see little public good, and some inconsistency or harm, in legally counting moral stigma—painful though it can be, culture war or not. But moral stigma also has benefits. It can lead to moral reform. Personally, it does us the painful but needed service of disturbing our dogmatism about ultimate questions. Politically, it prevents victories or defeats from ossifying into orthodoxies. If civil society's ideological currents are allowed to run freely, we all enjoy a steadier flow of fresh ideas about morality, religion, and politics. Mainstream assumptions are challenged by countercurrents; no cultural tide becomes too strong to turn. That is why some of our greatest reforms first sprouted in the soil of civil society, long irrigated by religion. The greatest examples in the United States are the movements for abolition and civil rights.[43]

Thus, it is the pride of U.S. public culture that the law shields even quite offensive speech, because protections are most needed for expressions that most offend the majority. Some offensive speech is socially worthless, but the socially valuable kind—the kind that spurs moral reform—will always debut in social life as an offense to a majority. We protect it because a policy of silencing today's dissent will always mute the voice for tomorrow's reform. As the Supreme Court explained in a unanimous opinion, the "point of all speech protection" is to "shield just those choices of content that in someone's eyes are misguided, or even hurtful."[44]

Agreement on this point creates a dilemma for progressives who would curb religious liberty to fight dignitary harm. Most progressives lend their voices to the American chorus in praise of shielding even offensive speech. Yet offensive speech can inflict far more of the dignitary harm that progressives would cut down *religious* freedoms to suppress. Think of the slurs of a white supremacist pamphlet, or the slander of the Westboro Baptists' antigay picketing. Why accept immense dignitary harms to make room for free speech, but not for freedoms of conscience and religion, where the dignitary harms are often lighter anyway? Why the double standard of counting dignitary harm (*in addition* to material harms) against conscience claims, but *not at all* against speech? This is a challenge to which progressives have no response.

That challenge is all the more pressing because freedoms of conscience and speech build off each other. John Stuart Mill famously argued that a marketplace of ideas allows us to test our views against rivals and appropriate the truth more deeply.[45] But freedoms of conscience and religion also serve that market. As we've seen, they furnish ideas traded on the intellectual market, and empower those hawking them. But to do so, these rights must be protected with an ideologically even hand. The state cannot play the crony capitalist with ideas, giving stronger protections to those it finds congenial. Or as Justice Robert Jackson wrote, in a case that (fittingly) combined religion and free speech: it is a "fixed star in our constitutional constellation ... that no official, high or petty, can prescribe what shall be orthodox in politics, nationalism, religion, or other matters of opinion."[46] We imperil political reform by weighing dignitary harm against religious liberty—assuming that "dignitary harm" refers to the pain of being told that you're acting immorally.

Targeting it also threatens *personal* reform. People are roused from dogmatism not simply by the detached observation that someone somewhere might disagree with them. More important is what Andrew Koppelman, a veteran advocate of socially progressive causes, calls "the open collision of moral views," which liberalism has long seen as a benefit:

> When John Stuart Mill's classic defense of free speech balances liberty against harm, Jeremy Waldron has observed, that balancing cannot count as harm the moral distress of having your most cherished views denounced. . . . A core value of free speech is that it will and must induce such distress. Mill, and liberalism more generally, places great value on "ethical confrontation— the open clash between earnestly held ideals and opinions about the nature and basis of the good life." Moral distress, "far from being a legitimate ground for interference . . . is a positive and healthy sign that the processes of ethical confrontation that Mill called for are actually taking place."[47]

The distress of having your ideals challenged is a boon, even when it's also a bane. Counting moral stigma against a claim doesn't simply choke political reform. It also shelters us from the moral confrontation that might force us to rethink and reform our lives.

In short, what many progressives see as legally cognizable harms of complicity claims—the spread of moralized offense and the empowerment of contrarian social movements—have promoted reform for individuals and societies. They don't advance it every time. But in any given case, almost by definition, the majority is in no position to tell. So we must give them a wide berth.

Just how wide? Isn't it *sometimes* necessary to turn down liberty claims on account of the boost they give evil movements, or to use the law to fight moral stigma? Aren't some moral principles certain enough that we can entrench them— by protecting them against political turbulence—without risking a missed opportunity for social reform?

For a real-life test case, take the IRS's decision in 1970 to revoke Bob Jones University's tax-exempt status because of its campus ban on interracial dating. Today we are rightly certain that Bob Jones's principles were wrong. Punishing the university for holding them didn't silence a voice for genuine reform. But wouldn't our argument condemn the IRS's decision as illiberal? (Set aside its legality.) Tax exemption, after all, fosters charities that span the ideological spectrum. It subsidizes civic associations that—on our argument—can serve social reform only if we don't punish them for the mere offense of morally offending us. Yet you might see the IRS's revocation as an attempt to do just that: to punish action for the degrading ideas behind it.

Indeed, the *Bob Jones* decision was controversial when it was decided—on the bench and beyond—and remains so today. But set aside the legal-interpretive question it raised, and consider the policy issue. Even the justices who voted for the result were eager to quarantine it,[48] and for reasons like ours. As Justice Powell wrote, "the provision of tax exemptions to nonprofit groups is one indispensable means of limiting the influence of governmental orthodoxy on important areas of community life."[49] So while the Court upheld (as legally authorized) the IRS's finding that the dating ban was against public policy, it implicitly set a very high bar for such findings in the future. It made much of the fact that every branch of the federal government had opposed racial segregation firmly and for decades. It thus sought to ensure that tax exemption wouldn't later be revoked whenever the IRS commissioner found a group's values demeaning.

That caution—whatever the unpopular moral view in the majority's crosshairs—is what our argument calls for. It would be a mistake to allow ourselves easier ways to punish offensive views as beyond the political pale. After all, we often disagree as vehemently about what should lie beyond ordinary politics as we do about the right answers on issues within it. Nor is the perceived importance of a principle a barometer of its correctness: Avid prolife and prochoice citizens agree that abortion is a question of the highest moral importance, but they would entrench exactly opposite regimes and would find exactly opposite views to be demeaning of some group or other. Indeed, history shows that humanity's most certain, centuries-long consensus can be wrong, and disastrously so: Witness the world-historical record on the "necessity" of slavery, or on the social status of women. One benefit of our constitutional democracy is that it makes political entrenchment hard. We see no footing, above the fray, from which to decide which matters should be exceptions to that norm. Certainly, the monumentally controversial questions of our culture wars are not candidates.

Nonetheless, there is a grain of truth in the call to use the law to fight dignitary harm. We discuss it below, in the course of explaining what sorts of social harms are worth fighting by law.

3.6 ANTIDISCRIMINATION LAWS

Our opening saved for later discussion a prominent exception to the rule that the law leaves people free to deal with others on their own terms, by their own lights. That is the case in which refusals to deal with certain parties involve discrimination based on one of a small number of protected traits. Many progressives think that wrongful discrimination is just what happens when wedding vendors, schools, hospitals, and charities act on traditional convictions about sex and marriage. Indeed, some think that a proper aim of *state* recognition of same-sex marriage is to contain and ultimately eliminate the idea among *private* parties that marriage is opposite-sex.

From this perspective, cutting into private actors' freedoms of conscience really is narrowly tailored to serving a compelling public interest. That interest is social equality for gays and lesbians; it requires punishing those who would act on traditional morals that are (progressives would say) inconsistent with that social equality. On this view, completing the work begun in *Obergefell* requires adding SOGI to the list of legally protected traits. We address this proposal (to enact "SOGI laws") in the next section. Here we discuss antidiscrimination laws in general.

Antidiscrimination laws forbid private actors—individuals, businesses, and certain other associations—from treating people differently based on traits deemed irrelevant to most choices. They put the power and prestige of the law, and the threat of civil penalties, behind the ideal of social equality. That is an important goal—in general, of course, but also in the debates prompting this book. No one should be put to shame or marginalized for the shape of their sexual desires or their gender identity, any more than for their race or sex—or, for that matter, their height or hair color or a thousand other traits. But that isn't enough to justify a ban on anything just yet. The law isn't about siphoning evil out of every heart. It's about setting up and keeping up the conditions under which everyone can adequately pursue the basic goods of human life.

Based on that standard, we begin with a general test for telling when to pass antidiscrimination laws and how to shape them. Anybody devising one has to contend first with freedoms of contract and association—freedoms that throw up important hurdles for antidiscrimination laws to clear. Indeed, these civil liberties just *are* freedoms to "discriminate"—to make your own decisions about your own dealings with others. Does that make them inherently dangerous? Legal scholar Maureen Markey recites a litany of horrors that she fears would follow from giving people too much latitude in contract and association: "Could a landlord ask about, assume conduct, or refuse to rent to (or a business owner refuse to do business with) someone who did or might ... practice birth control, have an abortion or advocate the right to an abortion, ... commit adultery, ... drink alcohol, use drugs, gamble, smoke, eat meat, ... dance, play cards, swear or curse, celebrate birthdays and holidays, dress or speak or conduct themselves in a suggestive manner ... ?"[50] And we could pile on. What about landlords turning people away because of their political party? Or out of annoyance at how they talk or walk? Or because the applicants are think tank fellows, whom the landlords consider hacks; or lawyers, whom they consider social menaces? But the truth is that discrimination on virtually any of these grounds is legal in any context on almost every square inch of U.S. soil: housing, employment, public accommodations, education, licensing, credit, and more.[51]

Thus Koppelman, a longtime progressive advocate: "The general rule that governs business transactions, both public accommodation and employment, is contract at will. In most states, most businesses have the privilege of refusing service to anyone for any reason or no reason. They need not justify these actions to any official. Antidiscrimination laws, such as the Civil Rights Act, are exceptions. So long as economic actors do not engage in the enumerated types of discrimination, they have the privilege of being as arbitrary as they like."[52] Here Koppelman points to what we've called the presumption of liberty that the state has to justify overriding. As we've noted, laws generally ban private discrimination on just a few grounds (e.g., race or color, ethnicity or national origin, sex, religion, age, disability, pregnancy, marital status), and only in some contexts. In every jurisdiction in the United States, the vast majority of bases for discrimination that all would consider manifestly unjust are perfectly legal.

This tells us two things. First, since there is no epidemic of, say, partisan-political discrimination by landlords, employers, and vendors, something besides law must be containing most forms of wrongful discrimination. In the case of partisan discrimination, it certainly isn't lack of motivation. It's probably the market. Employers competing for the best employees have incentives to consider only those factors that matter for their mission. And companies competing for customers have every reason to take any form of business that they can in good faith.

Second, given that most governments haven't banned most forms of discrimination anyway, just in case, there must be real costs to banning even egregious forms. And there are. Coercion is always inefficient. Even where legal limits would seem most urgent, they *can* be counterproductive. Take employment. A thicket of regulations against layoffs can make businesses slow to hire for fear of being stuck with unproductive workers. That isn't bad for some abstract thing called the free market. It's a tangible harm to people out of a job—to the very people the law was meant to help. One recent study found that in France, where more severe legal limits on layoffs apply to businesses with fifty or more employees, more than twice as many French manufacturers have forty-nine employees as have fifty.[53] In general, antidiscrimination laws in the labor context put dents in the rule of at-will employment that has made the U.S. labor market stronger than those in Europe. Our law's enduring presumption of liberty serves important goals.

So it's too quick to glide right from the injustice of some form of discrimination to the conclusion that we should ban it. Nonetheless, presumptions can be rebutted. Liberty isn't a basic good. It's only a means. Two facts are needed to rebut this presumption: the need for the ban must be high, and the cost of enforcement low. Specifically, the presumption of liberty is overcome—and a given antidiscrimination bill should be passed—only when:

1. Private treatment of a particular group imposes
    a. material and/or
    b. social harms
    c. which the law can best cure; and
2. The particular proposed antidiscrimination provision is drawn narrowly enough to
    a. suppress interactions that inflict those material and social harms,
    b. avoid banning too many legitimate or harmless interactions, and
    c. avoid treading too far onto other interests like conscience, religion, and speech

We can say a bit more about each prong.

As for (1): a group faces (a) *material* harms of the sort that justifies antidiscrimination law when private discrimination against it is so pervasive that (i) it can't meet *basic needs* for housing, lodging, loans, jobs, education, healthcare, and the like; (ii) it's excluded from the *markets* for other goods and services; or (iii) its *social or professional mobility* or *political influence* is seriously curtailed. These material harms overlap and interact with each other—and with social harms that also justify antidiscrimination laws.

These (b) social harms consist of cultural ideas and attitudes unfairly impugning a group's abilities, actions, character, proper social status, or moral worth. Call these ideas and attitudes—even when the person acting on them isn't hateful himself—"social contempt." As social contempt for a group metastasizes, others find it harmful, dangerous, socially improper, or wrong to deal with the group on equal terms.[54] That's why the state has reason to fight social contempt, by curbing conduct whose social meaning fosters it.

To flesh this out, we need to do what few on either side of this debate have bothered to do: Say what "social meaning" *means*, and in what sense and why it's something the law should care about. Recall that the state's job is to protect the social conditions in which everyone can thrive. Social contempt as we've defined it upsets those conditions. If people think ill of your abilities, character, or worth—if they think you're incompetent, vicious, criminal, or beneath them morally or socially—they'll be less likely to hire you, trust you, or include you. They'll think it unwise, dangerous, or wrong to mingle with you on equal terms at all. You'll have a hard time exchanging freely, rising professionally, participating politically, or doing anything else that hangs on the cooperation of others. That's why the state should take note when people are unfairly robbed of social respect in what we'll call these socially debilitating ways. (We say "unfairly" because it's sometimes appropriate to deprive a group of social respect. Banning larceny tarnishes the name of convicted thieves, but that's no argument against it.) That's why actions that breed a culture of contempt have social meaning of the sort that the law can fairly oppose.

It's one thing to detect a climate of contempt, and another to figure out which actions contribute to it—which of them carries a harmful "social meaning." Since law is about preserving the social conditions for flourishing, the question *for law* isn't what this baker secretly thinks, or how that patron happens to react. The question is: What lesson will others draw from this sort of interaction? Specifically, the refusal must be one that *observers would think was motivated* by a group's perceived inferiority or incompetence. That's what bestows on it a certain *social* meaning.

That social meaning can have material effects insofar as motivations are contagious. If you think your neighbor has a certain motive, you might pick it up—consciously or not. So actions can contribute to a culture of contempt by sending a message that leads others to adopt demeaning attitudes or ideas. To recap, then, an action's social meaning is harmful when (whatever the person's *actual* motives might be) others would infer that it is motivated by unfair and socially debilitating ideas or attitudes about your actions, abilities, social status, or moral worth.

Of course, they might draw that inference *unreasonably*. Even then, if the action they misread is one you can easily afford to give up, you ought to do so anyway. Even if there's nothing inherently wrong with a choice, the fact that others see it as disrespectful is a good reason to desist. If belching after a meal gives you moderate relief but gives offense to your host, you should bear the slight gastrointestinal discomfort for the sake of decency. It is, so to speak, cheaper for you to restrain yourself than for others to get used to the idea that belching shows no disrespect.

But here we aren't debating trivial choices that social conventions happen to render disrespectful. We're dealing with choices people make to preserve their integrity. It's unfair enough to assume that their refusals spring from contemptuous ideas or attitudes if benign readings are available. But then it's unjust for the state to add injury to that insult—to impose on people's integrity based simply on society's *unfair* reading of their motivations. (Material harms are a separate matter.) Of course, even if people are wrong to draw harmful lessons from certain refusals, the lessons will harm. But then it would be fairer to contain that harm by promoting more charitable interpretations of the refusals at issue. It's fairer to expect the rest of us to adjust, to exercise intellectual sympathy, to embrace more charitable—and quite natural—interpretations of the ideas or attitudes driving them. That's the easier path to an equilibrium allowing everyone to pursue the goods adequately. And it calls on a skill that pluralistic communities have to hone anyway. Charity in interpretation may be the social skill par excellence on which pluralistic societies will flourish or fail.

So we've worked up from political-theory foundations to the following rules: In deciding whether the social meaning of someone's action justifies brandishing the law against her, *at the price of her moral or religious integrity*, we should limit ourselves to asking how *reasonable* observers would interpret a refusal to offer the relevant good or service. In these scenarios, we shouldn't ban the refusal unless it could only be seen as rooted in attitudes or ideas that unfairly impugn a group's abilities, character, social status, or moral worth. If its roots are simply moral convictions we find false or offensive, its social meaning alone won't justify legal coercion.

How do we figure out if the interactions discussed in this book inflict social harm of the sort we can ban? We don't have good surveys about how observers interpret them. But even if we did, that wouldn't suffice. The question isn't simply how actions *are* interpreted but how it's *reasonable* to read them. Answering that requires reflection and inference. It requires looking at where the ideas behind these conscience claims come from and where they lead. That is, reasonable interpretations of particular actions will be sensitive to their intellectual history and the patterns they form.

As for part (1)(c) of our test for telling when antidiscrimination laws are justified, the law is the best cure for social *or* material harm when media, market forces, and social pressure of other kinds aren't treating the harm themselves. That happens when so many people discriminate across so many sectors of society that potent opposition never gets going, and competition never pushes out offending providers. Thus, refusals create the sort of material and social harm that justifies antidiscrimination law only when *they reach a tipping point.*[55] Short of that, isolated instances of wrongful discrimination never coalesce to create the kind of harm the law ought to fight—unless we slip back into the illiberal notion that purging the expression of offensive messages is a legitimate public goal of its own.

Finally, on condition (2) above: Once antidiscrimination laws become imperative, they should be drawn to avoid sweeping away too many legitimate practices (like the separation of male and female locker rooms for the sake of privacy), or imposing too much on other public goods (like the integrity at stake in conscientious dissent). Of course, to be worth any costs at all, the law must do some good. It must (2)(a) succeed at banning some wrongful discrimination. But lawmakers should limit its collateral damage in two ways. They should authorize exemptions based on (2)(c) civil liberty claims to freedom of conscience, religion, and speech. They should also (2)(b) keep the legal ban narrow in the first place by defining discrimination more precisely. It's one thing to let a small, Muslim-owned bed and breakfast bring a RFRA claim against having to put up a boyfriend and girlfriend. It's another thing—and more efficient—to leave small bed and breakfasts beyond the reach of bans on marital-status discrimination from the start. And it's still another to see that distinctions based on moral convictions about premarital sex aren't invidious or socially debilitating discrimination requiring legal coercion.

By all these standards, the case for banning discrimination against African Americans could not have been stronger. Individuals, businesses, and associations across the country excluded them in ways that caused material and social harms, without justification or reprisal by the market. They were denied housing and loans and kept out of fancy homes and office suites of every sort—except as servants, janitors, and bellboys. These material harms both built on and fortified the social harms of a culture that considered them less intelligent, less skilled, and less important. They didn't just make it harder for blacks and whites to mingle on equal terms. That was their whole point. And discrimination was rampant enough that no one lost his money or sullied his reputation by engaging in it. Social and market forces didn't punish discrimination but rewarded it. Given the irrelevance of race to almost any transaction, there were hardly benign alternative motives. So the law had to step in. And yet the result—the Civil Rights Act of 1964—was quite narrowly drawn, leaving out a surprising number of providers based on type and size. It steered clear of imposing costs it didn't absolutely have to impose. It was content to keep even the most wicked form of discrimination beneath a tipping point, rather than chasing after every last perpetrator. Once the law gave a good shove, markets and culture could continue their work.

In short, because of the nature of racism and the design of the Civil Rights Act, the latter fought a social evil without banning legitimate choices or exacting serious social costs.

3.7 SEXUAL ORIENTATION AND GENDER IDENTITY ANTIDISCRIMINATION LAWS

The same isn't true for SOGI laws. And now we can explain why by applying our general framework on antidiscrimination laws to the question of whether and when SOGI laws are justified and how they should be crafted.

These analyses often begin with analogies to race. Race and SOGI are indeed alike in some ways. As with one's race, the sheer experience of gender dysphoria or of desire for members of the same sex is irrelevant to a host of transactions: buying, selling, hiring, firing, and so on. So it is unjust for people to take them into account in public life, or to shun others for them in private life. Abuses of both sorts—by relatives and friends, colleagues and neighbors and governments—have left deep scars, and made scapegoats and outcasts of many.

But in other respects, the case of SOGI is quite different. Discrimination faced by gays and lesbians was never as acute or common or stubborn as that faced by blacks. According to George Chauncey and other historians of the LGBT experience, who submitted their research to advance gay rights litigation, "widespread discrimination" based on "homosexual status developed only in the twentieth century . . . and peaked from the 1930s to the 1960s."[56] Today, market and social forces are fast at work to curb the mistreatment. And proposed SOGI laws are far broader than the Civil Rights Act. And their unintended costs are higher.

Indeed, the most important difference between laws on SOGI and race—or religion or disability or sex or virtually any other protected status—is this: over and over, SOGI laws impose gratuitously on important personal and social goods. They're not simply about preventing "no LGBT people allowed" policies. They're designed and applied to needlessly penalize conscientious refusals to participate in morally controversial actions to which many people reasonably object, wounding moral and religious integrity and depressing pluralism. And that's a sharp contrast indeed. How often has the Americans with Disabilities Act forced anyone to violate her conscience? When has it burdened any basic good, or dimmed any element of our society's vibrant pluralism, or harmed anything but the profit margins of a business forced to install a wheelchair ramp? When have evangelicals wielded legal bans on religious discrimination to force a secular-minded Wellesley College to bend its mission or code of conduct or housing policy toward their own values? Yet as we've seen throughout these pages, SOGI laws are continually used in ways that press down on the conscience and mute the minority witness of moral and religious dissidents daring to open a shop or a charity or a school.

These costs are our main reason for opposing the SOGI laws proposed so far. Regardless of costs, of course, we'd support any well-drawn policy that proved essential for meeting LGBT people's needs (e.g., if providers actually did have "no LGBT people allowed" policies). So we'll start by asking if the need is there. Following the framework sketched in the previous section, we'll consider whether there are (1)(a) material or (1)(b) social needs that are (1)(c) best addressed by SOGI laws. First we'll argue that there is no good evidence that LGBT people are locked out of markets for jobs or material goods, and some contrary evidence. Next we'll show that of the legitimate (i.e., not illiberal) policy goals that might fall under the heading of "fighting social harms," none would justify banning refusals based on traditional marital and sexual ideals. And even if you disagreed on both points, you could agree with our third: that the gales of market and culture are blowing discrimination out of the public square. Remaining harms aren't so firmly planted as to require legal coercion.

Based on these points alone, one might see no great need for SOGI laws, but also no great harm. We would agree, were it not for the toll these laws take on civil liberties and basic goods. So having shown below that the case for SOGI laws is anemic, we'll look more closely at the costs of a sample of SOGI bills proposed so far. Then we'll show that even if we are wrong about all of this—even if the empirical case for SOGI laws is strong overall—the case for leaving out the refusals with which we began this essay remains stronger still. Punishing the conscientious choices at stake there would penalize some people for keeping their moral and religious integrity intact, while letting them be wouldn't impede others' ability to meet their own needs.

If anything were needed, then, it would be something narrower than existing SOGI laws. We'll end by testing the current need for *that* with a challenge to SOGI law supporters. We think that challenge suggests that even by their count, there may be little that society needs *the law* to eliminate, once the refusals we would exempt are off the table. Or more precisely, that the main thing left for *legal coercion* to accomplish would be the symbolic value of making outlaws of their ideological opponents. It would be the illiberal goal of stifling moral dissent.

3.7.1 Material Costs and Market Forces

The strongest case for SOGI laws is this: Unless we coerce private parties, LGBT people will be kept out of markets for key goods and services, and off the highest rungs of political and professional ladders. That argument would move us to support *whatever* coercion was needed, if its empirical claims checked out. But the evidence doesn't support that conclusion. And we aren't alone in noticing this. So have some gay rights advocates, like Andrew Koppelman. On denial of services to LGBT people, he wrote: "Hardly any of these cases have occurred: a handful in a country of 300 million people. In all of them, the people who objected to the law were asked directly to facilitate same-sex relationships, by providing wedding, adoption, or artificial insemination services, counseling, or rental of bedrooms. There have been no claims of a right to simply refuse to deal with gay people."[57]

Those three sentences shatter the strongest case for SOGI laws. Amid several years of fierce debates and intense media attention, all but one of the refusals we've seen that SOGI laws would target have involved vendors opposed to serving same-sex weddings, and professionals and nonprofits convinced that children ought to have a mother and father, that marriage unites husband and wife, or that sex is for marriage. They don't involve people or organizations treating LGBT people differently just for being LGBT. So the strongest grounds for enacting SOGI laws—denials of housing, or employment, or medical care—are mercifully rare to vanishing.

So are denials in public accommodations. Even if the occasional mom-and-pop bed and breakfast were to turn some away, beneath the public radar, this would hardly diminish a single person or couple's range of opportunities for room or board or entertainment. We find no evidence of refusals by a single hotel chain of the sort that you could find at any exit off any highway. Or by a single major restaurant. Or by a single major employer. In fact, the Human Rights Campaign—the nation's premier LGBT advocacy group—reports that 89 percent of Fortune 500 companies have policies against considering sexual orientation in employment decisions.[58] And "median LGBT household income is $61,500 vs. $50,000 for the average American household," according to Prudential.[59] As we detail in our reply essay, U.S. tax returns show that same-sex couples—gay and lesbian, with and without children—enjoy even more dramatic income advantages over their opposite-sex counterparts.

In addition, even those few businesses that base decisions on what we'll show below are honest and honorable grounds— moral and religious convictions about marriage and sex—are paying a price in the market. They lose customers and some of the best employees. Progressive outlets like the Center for American Progress admit that market forces are already squeezing those who dissent: "Businesses that discriminate based on a host of job-irrelevant characteristics, including sexual orientation ... put themselves at a competitive disadvantage compared to businesses that evaluate individuals based solely on their qualifications and capacity to contribute."[60]

So there is no strong evidence—and some evidence against the idea—that discrimination keeps LGBT people out of markets for goods or services, professions, or income brackets. Maybe some providers going unnoticed by professional or social media are turning LGBT people away just for being LGBT. But even if such refusals ever clustered, it's hard to imagine a sector of commerce or a region of the United States where media coverage wouldn't provide a remedy swift and decisive enough to restore access in days. Think of the example made of the pizzeria in small-town Indiana when protests and boycotts forced it to shut down for several months. The local news had simply reported that—when pressed with a hypothetical—its owners said not that they wouldn't serve LGBT people or couples but that they would—if ever *actually* pressed—decline to cater gay weddings (with *pizza!*).[61] This example and others like it highlight a final and related point: The LGBT community's political influence is meaningful and growing.

Indeed, progressives like Koppelman have noted that gathering cultural pressures put cracks in the case for coercion: "With respect to the religious condemnation of homosexuality, this marginalization is already taking place. But that does not mean that the conservatives need to be punished or driven out of the marketplace. There remains room for the kind of cold respect that toleration among exclusivist religions entails."[62]

Bigotry against LGBT people has not vanished. As with any minority, it exists. As with other forms of contempt, our communities must fight it at every turn. But it doesn't seem to have worked the systematic material harms that would justify legal coercion. As for abuses that remain, media, markets and culture are driving them ever more to the margins. Where we can leave these more efficient forces to do the job, we should.

As we see it, this leaves two other possible defenses of SOGI laws. First, proponents may argue there are still less tangible, *social* harms to fight. And second, they might still want to try to fight even material harms, on the theory that we have nothing to lose, and might have *something* to gain: maybe the paucity of evidence proves only that material harms aren't egregious. We now turn to these concerns.

In the next section, we'll argue that the social effects targeted today by SOGI law advocates are ones that an open society can't afford to fight. And in the section following that, we'll show that passing SOGI laws absent serious need wouldn't simply cover society's bases. It would curtail basic goods and civil liberties to little benefit. More than inefficient, that is unjust.

3.7.2 Social or Dignitary Harms and Cultural Forces

To take the first point first: Given how sparse the evidence is for material harms, we suspect that SOGI law advocates are mainly concerned to fight what they see as the harmful social meaning of certain interactions. But as we've just seen, almost all the interactions discussed involve refusals based on traditional moral convictions about sex and marriage. And even if those convictions are false and offensive, that alone isn't the kind of social harm that could justify coercion in a society hoping to remain free, dynamic, and open to reform.

So if we're going to suppress conscientious refusals to facilitate same-sex weddings, it can't be because they convey the idea that same-sex sexual relationships are nonmarital or immoral. Again, rejecting that idea as deeply offensive isn't enough. Worse than offensive, the ideas conveyed must unfairly impugn a group's abilities, character, proper social status, or moral worth, eroding the social conditions for flourishing that law must preserve. To require anything less egregious before punishing actions for their social meaning would be to slide into punishing ideological dissent. It would be stultifying.

When it comes to social meaning, then, the question is how reasonable observers would interpret the conscience claims discussed here—by far the cases most often used to justify SOGI laws. Can they only be read as stemming from unfair assumptions about LGBT people's abilities or proper social status or worth? Or are there reasonable alternative readings? As we argued above, two guides to answering that question are the intellectual history of the ideas behind those refusals and patterns in the refusals themselves. We consider each in the next two subsections. As we'll see, the refusals debated in these culture wars don't have social meaning of the sort the law can curb. And even if they did, cultural forces are diminishing them on their own.

3.7.2.1 Social Meaning: Patterns in Today's Refusals

Moral conservatism about marriage and sex is often compared to Jim Crow ideology. But the forms of refusal that each involves couldn't differ more sharply. Jim Crow was about legally mandated segregation—about avoiding contact on socially equal terms with certain patrons, by refusing them any service. Today's complicity claims are about denying certain requests—whoever comes in to make them—while avoiding contact with no one. They are not about doctors' refusals to serve women, or florists' refusals to serve gay people, but about refusals to *perform abortions* or *celebrate weddings*. Allowing enough of these refusals to dominate a local market might have material effects, but it would not inflict the dignitary harm rightly targeted by the Civil Rights Act.

The point isn't that current refusals focus on particular actions, whereas Jim Crow focused on groups of people. Sure, Jim Crow supporters could have said they loved the sinner and hated the sin—that they liked blacks but not common use of water fountains. But their *further* reason for opposing the latter was to avoid mingling with African Americans on equal terms. That's why, for one thing, opposition wasn't limited to water fountains but covered every square inch of the outside world. An evangelical's reason for refusing to bake same-sex wedding cakes is manifestly *not* to avoid contact with gay people on equal terms. It's to avoid complicity in what she considers one distortion of marriage among others.

It isn't that status-based distinctions are always invidious, while conduct-based ones never are. Neither of these positions is right. To see if a distinction is invidious—rooted in contempt, or at least likely to breed it—look at the reasoning behind it. That can often be gleaned from broader patterns in the behavior of the people making the distinction. We elaborate on these points here using less politically fraught examples. The resulting analysis will dramatize the difference in kind between Jim Crow and moral conservatism about marriage and sex. It will show the unreasonableness of assuming that the latter generally springs from demeaning ideas about LGBT people. So it will show the unfairness of punishing related conscientious refusals on account of their social meaning alone.

Law is about social effects, but start with a single case. A Jewish musician performs at weddings but declines a Catholic one. Does she discriminate based on conduct? Or status? Is she acting invidiously? It depends on her reasoning—on the ideas and attitudes driving her policy.

If her reason for refusing a Catholic couple's request is to avoid entering houses of worship devoted to other gods, in order to avoid sacrilege, then *the couple's being Catholic* need not be the basis of a single step in her reasoning. She simply objects to one kind of conduct (her own entering a church) based on her objection to another kind (the worship of other gods). Her distinctions are about conduct all the way down. She isn't discriminating based on the couple's status (Catholicism) because their being Catholic plays no part in her reasoning. Indeed, she would have the same response if the couple were agnostics having the ceremony in a Catholic church simply to please their parents.

But even some status-based distinctions could be innocent. Say a photographer turns down Catholic weddings because she has promised her best friend that his would be the first Catholic wedding she served. Then all her refusals in the meantime would be status-based—she would be rebuffing couples because they're Catholics—but morally benign. On the other hand, if she turned Catholics away because she thought it beneath the dignity of Protestants like herself to mingle with them, that conduct-based distinction would be invidious *in itself*. It would rest *directly* on an unfair idea about social status: Catholics belong on a lower rung. For as we've argued, the idea that some should be marginalized (where in fact there's no good reason to shun them) *just is* one of the attitudes the state should contain. It wouldn't matter if our photographer held that belief about Catholics not out of personal animus but because she was taught that God commanded the separation of the two denominations, much as the trial court in *Loving v. Virginia* wrote that God wanted the races apart. For it would still be the kind of belief that would, if it spread, harm a group's social and material prospects unfairly (assuming, of course, that Catholics don't deserve to be shunned).

So status and conduct aren't well defined, and they don't matter per se. Conduct-based distinctions (like opposition to mingling) can be invidious, and status-based ones can be benign. In general, though, invidious distinctions are what we might call "status-*focused*," because they always have *some* foundation in ideas or attitudes about a group: unfair and socially debilitating assumptions about the group's abilities, habits, actions, proper social status, or moral worth. When those are the underlying motives, the resulting discrimination is invidious. But distinctions premised on morals that are simply false or offensive don't work the kind of dignitary harm that law can safely fight.

Thus we come to a difference in kind between the humiliation of being denied a seat at the table of public life and the pain of sitting by people who oppose decisions you prize. The first, rooted in others' contempt and ramifying into wider exclusions and harms, must be avoided. The second, stemming from others' consciences, is unavoidable in free societies and even good for reform. Somewhere behind the first you'll find unfair, socially debilitating ideas about a group. Behind the second lie—at worst—false and offensive moral views about actions (that needn't themselves rest on contempt). The second we shouldn't punish. Whatever material harms we fight, we should brook no freestanding right not to be offended.

Where do the refusals discussed in this book fall? Could they be motivated by anything besides unfair and debilitating assumptions about LGBT people? That depends partly on patterns in the claimants' actions. The refusals of the bakers and photographers, charities and universities discussed here have nothing like the sweep or shape of racist practices. They don't span every domain but focus on marriage and sex. Within that domain, they're about avoiding complicity with certain choices, not contact with groups. Thus, Barronelle Stutzman, who refused to arrange wedding flowers for her client of ten years, clearly didn't think gay people vicious, incompetent, or unproductive. (Her business and livelihood depended on them as customers and employees.) She didn't think they mattered less or deserved shunning. (She employed them and served them faithfully as clients, denying them no other product.) Patterns in her behavior make nonsense of all these interpretations.

Indeed, her and the other refusals debated here needn't involve reasoning—or thus discriminating—based on orientation or gender identity at all. They rest on the beliefs that marriage is the one-flesh union that only man and woman can form, that sexual activity belongs in marriage, that biological sex is to be embraced or that motherhood and fatherhood are essential. Those beliefs make no reference to LGBT people one way or another. So the refusals they inspire *need* not involve SOGI-based discrimination at all, invidious or not. Unless, of course, those beliefs always rest on *further* ideas or attitudes that *are* about LGBT people. We'll consider that next.

3.7.2.2 *The History of Traditional Convictions on Sex and Marriage*

As we've seen, the structure of moral conservatives' complicity claims makes it unfair—absent more details about particular cases—to read into them socially debilitating ideas about a group. Now we'll see that the history of the ideas behind those conscience claims only confirms that impression. We'll again use Jim Crow as a contrast—not because it's the only kind of discrimination worth banning, but because it's an especially lucid case study in how history shapes social meaning.

Interracial marriage bans, to which traditional views of sex and marriage are often compared, never arose until colonial America. English common law, which the United States inherited, imposed no barriers to interracial marriage.[63] Antimiscegenation statutes, first appearing in Maryland in 1661, were the result of African slavery.[64] And since then, they've existed *only* in societies with a race-based caste system. Thus Harvard historian Nancy Cott: "It is important to retrieve the singularity of the racial basis for these laws. Ever since ancient Rome, class-stratified and estate-based societies had instituted laws against intermarriage between individuals of unequal social or civil status, with the aim of preserving the integrity of the ruling class. . . . But the English colonies stand out as the first secular authorities to nullify and criminalize intermarriage on the basis of race or color designations."[65] This history proves that antimiscegenation laws were part of an effort to hold one race in economic and political servitude. They were openly premised on the idea that contact with African Americans on an equal plane was wrong. That idea itself—not to mention its usual premises about blacks' moral status or habits or abilities—is of the essence of bigotry. Actions based on it clearly contribute to the culture of contempt that law rightly aims to fight.

The convictions behind today's conscience claims could not be a more vivid contrast. First, they sprang up in too many times and places to be attributable to any one religion. Indeed, as one historian observes, "marriage, as the socially recognized linking of a specific man to a specific woman and her offspring, can be found in all societies."[66]

History also proves that these convictions weren't born of ignorance of same-sex desire or hostility to same-sex relations. They prevailed in societies spanning the spectrum of attitudes on both—including some favorable toward same-sex relations and others lacking anything like our concept of gay identity as marking a class of people.

Thus, in ancient Greece and Rome, same-sex relations were common and drew no general popular scorn. And yet Plato approved of laws encouraging people to "couple, male and female, and lovingly pair together, and live the rest of their lives" together.[67] Aristotle located the foundation of political order in "the family group," by which he "mean[t] the nuclear family."[68] In his view, indeed, "between man and wife friendship seems to exist by nature," and their conjugal union has primacy even over political union.[69] Plutarch wrote of marriage as "a union of life between man and woman for the delights of love and the begetting of children."[70] He considered marriage a distinct form of friendship, specially embodied in the "physical union" of intercourse.[71] And for Musonius Rufus, the first-century Roman Stoic, a "husband and wife" should "come together for the purpose of making a life in common and of procreating children, and furthermore of regarding all things in common between them . . . even their own bodies."[72]

Again, none of these thinkers was in touch with Abrahamic religions, or ignorant of same-sex sexual relations, or biased against the latter by popular culture. They and other great teachers—of both East and West, from Augustine, Aquinas, Maimonides, and al-Farabi to Luther and Calvin, Locke and Kant, Gandhi and King—simply had honest, reasoned beliefs about the distinct value of male-female bonds.

This reflection on the past sheds light on the present. Today's moral conservatism isn't isolated. It didn't sprout overnight, fully formed, in recently poisoned soil. It grew organically out of millennia-old religious and moral traditions that taught the distinct value of male-female union; of mothers and fathers; of joining man and woman as one flesh, and generations as one family.[73] Social conservatives today are shaped by those traditions: be it the classical Western legal-philosophical traditions stretching from Plato to our own day; or the Muslim tradition, or the Jewish or Christian traditions. If history makes it impossible to see these intellectual streams as having their source in bigotry, it makes it unfair to assume that those they nourish are bigots. So it's wrong to coerce them just for the social meaning of their conscientious choices.

Some critics say that while it might have been possible for Aristotle or Kant or Gandhi to hold such views without animus, it isn't for us, knowing what we do now about sexuality. Not so. These traditions teach that there is distinct value in the kind of one-flesh union that only man and woman can form, and in the kinship ties that such union offers children. Those ideals don't hang precariously on empirical assumptions about sexual orientation. Nor does the recent social trend toward a more flexible, marriage-as-simple-companionship model make these ideals irrational to keep affirming. Nothing stops conservatives from also opposing this modern melting of marriage into general companionship that (they think) undermines valuable social purposes.

Some interactions *are* driven by demeaning beliefs about LGBT people. Our point is that this isn't the only reasonable inference to draw about today's conscientious refusals. So absent material harms, as we've argued, it would be unfair to punish all who engage in them, where integrity is at stake. That would fine them for pursuing all the basic goods adequately. And it would do so to muffle a potential social meaning that could have been softened and ameliorated with less collateral damage, had we embraced the more charitable of the available views on what moves the Barronelle Stutzmans of the world.

Besides, even if you think the spread of moral conservatism a harm, powerful market and cultural forces are arrayed against it, just as we saw that they are reducing isolated denials of material goods. Public figures—even powerful Silicon Valley CEOs—are deprived of their jobs and denied their ticket to polite society when it emerges that they're conservative on marriage. Thus again Koppelman, who thinks moral conservatism about these matters false and harmful: "The reshaping of culture to marginalize anti-gay discrimination is inevitable. To say it again: The gay rights movement has won. It will not be stopped by a few exemptions. It should be magnanimous in victory."[74] In the 1960s no one could pen such a line about racism.

So we've taken the measure of the *need* for SOGI laws. Today's conscience claims don't work the systematic material harms that justify coercion, and cultural forces are fighting isolated cases. They're doing the same with social effects— even with the expression of putatively offensive moral ideas that it would be a mistake for law to count anyway. And patterns in today's conscience claims and their intellectual history show the unfairness of chalking them up to debilitating ideas about a group. That unfairness—plus the importance of integrity—makes it unjust to punish these claims based on social meaning alone. That would involve backsliding into Puritanism: cracking down on dissenters for daring to live their creed on hostile turf. Absent material or social harms of the sort that liberal societies can use the law to fight, SOGI laws fail the first prong of our test for antidiscrimination laws: the need isn't there.

3.7.3 Sexual Orientation and Gender Identity Laws: A Blunt Instrument with Heavy Costs

The SOGI bills proposed so far also flunk the second half of our test: they aren't drawn narrowly enough to avoid needless burdens on other interests. By defining SOGI-based discrimination too broadly, they target too many actions that don't inflict material and social harms. (More than "no LGBT people allowed" policies, they target refusals to support morally controversial actions in the realm of sex and marriage.) Moreover, they apply to many more domains and activities than the Civil Rights Act of 1964. Finally, both problems are compounded by SOGI bills' stinginess about exemptions, which causes them to tax our civil liberties of conscience and religion—and even speech—without good cause.

First, many SOGI provisions' expansive definitions of discrimination, as applied, would threaten privacy and speech and even professional freedoms. Thus, several states and several healthcare providers recently sued over an HHS mandate that would require healthcare plans to cover sex-reassignment therapies and certain physicians to provide them.[75] And in May 2016, the Obama administration's Department of Justice and Department of Education determined that separate bathrooms for biological males and females (even where transgender persons are offered single-occupancy bathrooms) also violate antidiscrimination law.[76]

One example of the harms to free speech comes courtesy of the New York City Commission on Human Rights, which has threatened to fine employers up to $250,000 for not referring to employees by their chosen pronoun—including pronouns like "ze" and "hir" that pack morally and politically controversial assumptions about the body, gender, and sex.[77] As UCLA law professor Eugene Volokh explains, this would require "employers and businesses to prevent [the use of unwanted pronouns] by *co-workers and patrons* and not just by themselves or their own employees."[78]

That breadth is no aberration and no surprise. It flows from how SOGI laws, as applied, conceive of discrimination. They don't simply prevent people from turning LGBT people away because of their sexual desires or gender identity ("no LGBT people allowed"). They're also applied to require others' support for morally controversial choices. They mean to go after conscience-based refusals to *support or facilitate certain actions*—same-sex relationships and marriages, and repudiations of biological sex.

These costs are all multiplied by the vast territory of the laws that impose them. Take the Equality Act,[79] the centerpiece of the Human Rights Campaign's Beyond Marriage Equality Initiative.[80] It would add "sexual orientation" and "gender identity" to virtually all federal civil rights laws covering race—"Public Accommodations, Education, Federal Financial Assistance, Employment, Housing, Credit, and Federal Jury Service"[81]—and expand them beyond their current reach. It is also *explicitly* designed to shrink religious liberty protections.[82]

And it would stretch the scope of "public accommodations" quite far. The Civil Rights Act of 1964—which had to integrate half the continental United States after centuries of abuses—only covered entities like hotels, restaurants, theaters, and gas stations. The Equality Act would cover almost every business serving the public.[83]

Likewise, a 2014 SOGI law passed by the Houston City Council—but later voted down by Houstonians—would have covered "every business with a physical location in the city, whether wholesale or retail, which is open to the general public and offers for compensation any product, service, or facility."[84]

No inch of the public square would have been spared its costs to conscience, pluralism, and speech.

Finally, these bills are tightfisted about exemptions. The Equality Act makes no provisions for religious liberty. It would drop even the meager religious liberty protections offered in earlier federal SOGI bills. And it goes out of its way to ensure that marriage-traditionalists sued under it cannot invoke RFRA as a defense—a defense that would only give them the benefit of a day in court and a balancing test.[85]

Thus, SOGI laws are unlike other status protections. The need for them hasn't been established, unless we count goals that a liberal society has no business using coercion to achieve. They regulate commercial decisions best handled by private actors, and educational decisions best handled by parents and teachers. They endanger religious liberty and privacy, professional freedom and speech. Indeed, national SOGI bills seem targeted to do so.

3.7.4 Sexual Orientation and Gender Identity Laws: Definitions and Exemptions

Suppose we're wrong about whether the need for SOGI laws is great enough, or the costs low enough, to justify them. Suppose that, as an empirical matter, SOGI laws are needed to secure for LGBT people real opportunities to meet basic needs; participate in the market for other goods and services; gain social and political influence; and live and move in a social milieu that doesn't see them as incompetent, or think their interests less important.

Nonetheless, the law would need to define unlawful SOGI-based discrimination to target decisions based simply on a person's being gay, lesbian, bisexual, or transgender—and not those based on moral ideals regarding sex, marriage, and parenting. (We discuss above and in our rebuttal why this conception of

202 | DEBATING RELIGIOUS LIBERTY AND DISCRIMINATION

SOGI discrimination is most appropriate and best parallels protections given to religion, for example.) We'd have equally good reasons to grant conscience-based exemptions for hospitals and other charities, educational institutions, wedding and relationship professionals, and the like. Those definitions and exemptions would be justified for the simple reason that the goals of SOGI laws just mentioned—the most appropriate goals for law—would be served either way. So these measures would promote the good of integrity without serious public costs.

We can put this point in terms of what we identified above as the four premises needed to justify coercing private parties without exemptions: that the belief behind a certain kind of refusal is false, that refusals of this sort harm a public interest, that laws are needed to cure that harm, and that they can do so only if they brook no exceptions. Our point here is that even if you think the first three conditions have been met for SOGI laws, you can agree that the fourth has not been. The goals of SOGI laws don't require compliance even against conscience.

First, as we've just shown, it is reasonable and natural to interpret the conscience claims of hospitals and charities, educators, wedding vendors, and counselors as efforts to avoid complicity with choices to which these actors have moral or religious objections. The social message sent by those refusals is *not* that LGBT people matter less or should be shunned. If those were these actors' motivations, their refusals would be much wider, for one thing. Nor is the LGBT community's competence being questioned. It isn't that educational institutions with religious codes of conduct for students and teachers think LGBT people worse at learning or teaching. Catholic adoption agencies refusing to place children with same-sex couples are not acting on the assumption that LGBT individuals are bad at parenting but on the very different idea that the best father (gay or straight) can't provide the distinctive benefits of a mother (gay or straight), and vice versa.

Finally, given the small numbers of these refusals, the growing social and market pressures to diminish their number over time, a surfeit of other venues, and the failure of motivated and focused media outlets and advocacy groups to prove otherwise, there's absolutely no reason to think that granting these conscience claims would deny LGBT people access to basic goods or services or income brackets. In thick markets, LGBT people will be denied goods or services, jobs, or housing only if discrimination is common enough to pass a tipping point. Beneath that point, a few actors' choices to discriminate *will not contribute at all* to the kind of *exclusion* that law may fight.

Koppelman, who now supports SOGI laws, says that he has "worked very hard to create a regime in which it's safe to be gay" and for similar reasons "would also like that regime to be one that's safe for religious dissenters."[86] We think that the Koppelmans of the world could also support exemptions or accommodations from those laws, for moral and religious dissent by the parties whose liberties we've defended here.

3.8 SEXUAL ORIENTATION AND GENDER IDENTITY LAWS: A CHALLENGE TO SUPPORTERS

We close with a challenge. Here are two principles that we think uncontroversial:

1. Having decent opportunities for employment, housing, and essential services like healthcare ("the essentials") is *more* important than getting to avail yourself of the services of this or that *particular* wedding vendor, relationship professional, charity, or educational institution ("particular venues").

2. If a group lacks access to the essentials for reasons beyond its control, that's an injustice. If only the law can cure that injustice, then the law must do what it can, *as soon as it can.*

Our positions follow both principles. Again, if the LGBT community had essential needs that the law could best meet, we would think the law must act. We just believe that in the United States today, LGBT people aren't locked out of markets for goods or services or forms of employment.

But with this empirical point SOGI law supporters seem to *agree.* Their advocacy tells us that. If LGBT people were denied the essentials, advocates would look for the quickest way to provide them now, even if it meant waiting longer to coerce particular venues. They would opt for the most politically feasible solution that still secured the essentials. Yet despite decades of stalled proposals, they have never put forward the compromise measure that would do just that: one limited to banning decisions based simply on a person's sexual desires or gender identity (and not on morally controversial actions). Indeed, most advocates would find such a compromise offensive.

But it would punish decisions to fire a bus driver for her attraction to other women, or deny her a loan for identifying as transgender. At the same time, by leaving more room for pluralism, religion, and conscience than other SOGI bills, this compromise would draw wider support and be quicker to pass. So if LGBT people were being denied the essentials, justice would demand supporting it today, whatever your policy ambitions for tomorrow. It would be unfair to LGBT people to hold their most vital needs hostage until more sweeping bans could pass—potentially for many years.

Yet most SOGI law supporters *would* rather wait. Not a single bill (including the Utah SOGI law praised as the "Utah Compromise") has been crafted along these lines. Indeed, advocates are firmly opposed to compromising with dissenters *at all.* Take it from decades-long LGBT advocate Jonathan Rauch, in an October 2016 speech:

> Six years ago, in the prominent gay monthly the *Advocate*, I published an essay arguing for a conciliatory approach. "The smart approach," I said, "is to bend toward accommodation, not away from it, whenever we can live with the costs."
>
> I argued from legal strategy, saying that the First Amendment and religious liberty are bad issues to get on the wrong side of. I argued from political strategy, saying that reasonable accommodations will speed public acceptance of LGBT equality at an acceptable and rapidly declining cost to gay people. I argued above all from morality: "The real point of the gay rights movement is not just to secure equality for homosexuals; it is to maximize all Americans' freedom to be true to themselves—the freedom we were denied. The last thing a movement of former pariahs should seek is to inflict the same agony on someone else."
>
> For those reasons, I said, reasonable religious accommodations are something we should embrace as a cause, not resent as a concession.
>
> At the time, I got hearing. But that door, which was never more than just ajar, has closed. The strong consensus today in the LGBT world is that religious accommodations are a license to discriminate and are by their very nature a concession.[87]

The hardening of a *consensus* against compromise tells us something. Not that advocates don't care about meeting LGBT people's urgent needs, of course, but that many agree that those needs are already met: material harms just aren't there to make coercion urgent. Otherwise, advocates would be quick to enact this "compromise," which would really be a demand of justice by our lights and theirs.

The reason to hold out for wider bans, then, is less to empower some than to encumber others: to delegitimize those convictions and actions that it is gratuitous to crush.

But the ultimate source of this will to tame the moral heretic is not, we suspect, vindictiveness. It is fear: the authoritarian's fear that the dissident is a constant threat to justice and social order; the Rousseauian fear that "it is impossible to live at peace with those whom we regard as damned."[88] That fear made Rousseau yearn for one civil religion to bind us all to the state. It makes the New Puritans, like the originals, suspicious of rival religions and nervous of moral dissent. And it tempts the Puritans of every age to hoard freedom for themselves, to limit religious liberty to those beliefs already favored by the powerful, and so to make it pointless: a shield for the only side wielding a sword.

4

Reply to Anderson
and Girgis

JOHN CORVINO

■■■

I AM GRATEFUL TO RYAN T. Anderson and Sherif Girgis for their wide-ranging and thought-provoking essays.

Because they have the book's "last word," in what follows I both respond to their main essay, which precedes this section, and anticipate their reply, which follows. For space reasons I leave many points untouched. Sometimes I do so because we largely agree; sometimes I do so because explicating our disagreement would take considerable time, and other issues strike me as more pressing. I will focus on three broad areas of dispute: (1) moral and religious integrity, (2) limited government versus exemptions from laws, and (3) sexual orientation and gender identity discrimination.

Before addressing these, I want to do two things. First, I want to highlight some consensus. We agree, unsurprisingly, on the fundamental importance of religious liberty. We agree about the widespread human temptation to "create stable in-groups and out-groups, define a clan, and prefer it to others in systematically unjust ways,"[1] as they helpfully put it, and that this temptation often leads to religious persecution. We agree that burdens on religion therefore deserve heightened attention. Yet we also agree that when religious exercise undermines the common good, the law may constrain it. We agree that combatting unjust discrimination requires social and personal means as well as legal ones.

Moreover, we agree more about the federal RFRA than it may initially appear. For example, we agree that its protections should be expanded to cover comparable secular conscience claims—a significant and controversial point of consensus. And we might even agree that RFRA is too demanding as written: Anderson and Girgis say that they endorse it "as applied," and they acknowledge that its application has been "far less demanding" than what we normally associate with strict scrutiny (p. 242). But they stop short of calling for amending its terms. My own view is that, as much as possible, the law should say what it means, and vice versa. The alternative invites arbitrariness and abuse.[2]

Second, I want to make some very general remarks about issues that Anderson and Girgis cover at length but that I mention only in passing: private hospitals, charities, and educational institutions. My goal is not to decide these issues but to flag points for discussion elsewhere.

Virtually no one wants to force doctors to provide abortions against their convictions. Conflicts arise because in some (usually Catholic) hospitals, doctors who *do* want to provide certain procedures are not permitted to do so—or even to discuss them with the patient. Religious hospitals provide nearly 20 percent of hospital beds.[3] They are monopoly providers in some towns, and they benefit from significant public funding and tax exemptions. Their refusals mean that, for example, women who are admitted for an emergency C-section and want a tubal ligation must schedule a second, later surgery at a separate hospital, thereby increasing their risk—regardless of their doctor's willingness or medical judgment. They mean that rape victims are not told about emergency contraception during the short time-window in which such contraception is effective.[4] And they sometimes even mean that women are denied information about potentially life-saving treatment.[5] Religious liberty should never be a license for putting patients at risk.

Anderson and Girgis also mention a case in which a student was dismissed from a counseling training program for refusing to counsel a gay client.[6] But there are good reasons for the American Counseling Association's position that such refusals are "a clear and major violation of the 2005 ACA Code of Ethics."[7] A core value of the counseling profession is that referrals should be based on the client's needs and values, not the therapist's needs and values.

The case of adoption service agencies is complicated. We all want policies that will place as many children as possible in good homes. I believe that goal would be best achieved if religious adoption agencies would refrain from discriminating on the basis of sexual orientation. Unfortunately, several Catholic adoption agencies have closed their doors rather than comply with antidiscrimination guidelines—with the unfortunate result that fewer agencies are working to place children. Thus, as an empirical matter, such guidelines may make the best the enemy of the good.[8]

Finally, regarding schools: Legally, I have no problem with schools' choosing an explicitly religious character and then requiring commitment to it as a condition for admission or hiring. But there's a difference between granting that freedom and granting the significant tax benefits and other subsidies that come with 501(c)(3) status. It's fine to let "Notre Dame be Catholic, and Wheaton be Evangelical, and Zaytuna be Muslim, and Yeshiva be Jewish," as my counterpoint authors advocate (p. 116); it's even fine (legally) to let Bob Jones University be segregationist Christian. Whether the rest of us should continue to subsidize them when they refuse to comply with antidiscrimination law is a different matter.

The questions motivating this book are difficult and complex. It's tempting to imagine that one's preferred answers all fall neatly out of simple overarching theories. But I am skeptical of tidy system-building—where the apparent coherence often results less from principled consistency than from mental gerrymandering—and my focus here is correspondingly modest. Let us turn now to some key disagreements.

4.1 MORAL AND RELIGIOUS INTEGRITY

Anderson and Girgis describe the good of moral and religious integrity as "harmony ... within the self, and ... between the self and the transcendent." You achieve it by "trying to harmonize your choices, actions, and expressions with your moral convictions: your best judgments about what morality requires," and "with whatever ultimate source of meaning there might be" (pp. 125, 131).

All of this sounds wonderful in the abstract: Shouldn't everyone be in favor of harmonizing choices, actions, and expressions with convictions about what God and morality require?

The answer is that it depends upon the *content* of those convictions. To take an extreme example: if your convictions require throwing virgins into volcanoes, you would be better off *not* harmonizing your actions with them. (So would the virgins.) Reflective disequilibrium can be a good thing.

For a more contemporary example, recall Justice of the Peace Keith Bardwell, with his "piles and piles of black friends." When for years he declined to marry interracial couples, he was harmonizing his "choices, actions and expressions with

[his] moral convictions." He had integrity, as my counterpoint authors define it. But his convictions were bad ones, and everyone would have been better off had he failed to execute them.

My counterpoint authors agree—to a point. Certainly, they agree that *the world* is better off when moral agents fail at throwing virgins into volcanoes or at thwarting interracial marriages. Yet they appear to deny that *these agents* are better off when they fail, claiming that such failures could make the agents "deficient" in integrity. That's because Anderson and Girgis treat integrity—in the sense of harmonizing conviction and action—as a basic good. (Of course, all three of us think that it's better for agents to have the right convictions in the first place, but that's not always an option.)

Let me be clear: I am not suggesting that integrity has value "only when the underlying belief is true" (p. 259). Rather, my claim is that integrity—in their specific sense of harmony between belief and action—may lack value when the underlying belief is *badly* wrong. And one way to determine when the belief is badly wrong is its tendency to cause harm to others. In such cases, it is not sufficient simply to weigh the value of the integrity against the value of preventing the harm, as Anderson and Girgis propose, for it is not clear that the integrity (again, in the formal sense of harmony) deserves any "weight" at all. Bardwell's case makes this point clear, and one only needs a single counterexample to disprove the philosophical claim that integrity/harmony is a *basic* good.

So of course I wouldn't advocate forcing a Jew to eat pork, or a capital-punishment opponent to give a fatal injection, to take Anderson and Girgis's examples (p. 259). But that's very different from the question of whether we harm Bardwell by forcing him to choose between being a justice of the peace and being able to avoid marrying interracial couples. To that question, Anderson and Girgis answer yes; I answer no.

But suppose they are correct. Suppose we grant that there is always *some* good when individuals—even Bardwell—harmonize their actions with their moral convictions. My main difference with Anderson and Girgis concerns what happens next. For even if it is good for Bardwell to achieve such harmony, *it does not follow that the rest of us should make it easy for him to do so.* The blurring of this distinction—between what the religious claimant should do and what everyone else should do—is a pervasive problem in their discussion.

The problem is not merely that the claimant's actions might create third-party burdens—although that's important. It's also that, in addition to caring about people's internal harmony, we should also care about their getting things right. Some views are truly bad enough that they deserve repudiation rather than accommodation.

To see why, return to Bardwell. Recall that he did not actually thwart anybody's marriage: He referred interracial couples to nearby officiants. The third-party burdens he created were minimal—certainly more minimal than in the Kim Davis case. It was only when his refusals became public that he was pressured to do his job or resign.

At that moment, there were three ways for Bardwell to maintain harmony between conviction and action. He could change his convictions. He could resign (as he did), thus removing the conflict. Or he could be granted an accommodation and be allowed to keep discriminating. Of these, the third seems the least desirable alternative. Yet it's the one that Anderson and Girgis consistently reach for in such cases. The result is integrity on the cheap. According to their view, anytime a law burdens the "fragile" good of integrity, we must weigh that burden against third-party burdens. But that approach cannot explain why Bardwell should be denied an accommodation, given the easy availability of alternate officiants.

Anderson and Girgis repeatedly claim that we shouldn't penalize people for exercising their religious and moral convictions. But their use of words like "penalize," "punish," and "force" is misleading. Medieval Catholic Church inquisitors wanted to force people to violate their moral and religious convictions, literally, on pain of torture and death. So do some totalitarian states today. By contrast, telling people that *if* they want to be clerks, they can't substitute their own understanding of marriage for the state's, or that if they want the business benefits of incorporation, they have to comply with antidiscrimination laws, doesn't *force* them. It constrains their choices, certainly, but all laws do that.

But doesn't my view require some people to "pay more" for the good of integrity? Yes, but that's not a special problem for integrity. A law imposing tariffs on long-distance calls may make some people pay more for the good of friendship, if their friends happen to live overseas. A law prohibiting people from running in the park after midnight may make some people pay more for the good of health, if their work schedule makes that the only reasonable time for them to run, and their only alternative is a pricey gym membership. Laws generate burdens, and these burdens may vary depending on citizens' particular circumstances. But it's tendentious to characterize these laws as "fining" people for pursuing the relevant goods.

Anderson and Girgis also mischaracterize the Kim Davis case and dodge the hard questions raised by it. (Davis changed her stance multiple times, as I explained in my main essay.) They emphasize the "win-win" solution of removing the clerk's name from the form, allowing Davis to keep her job and same-sex couples to receive their licenses. At the time *Obergefell* was decided, however, that option wasn't available without calling a special session of the legislature. More important, there's a difference between setting things up in advance so as to minimize potential conflicts for clerks and responding after the fact when clerks publicly deny the legitimacy of laws they are sworn to uphold—especially when they do so for reasons that the majority recognize as discriminatory.[9]

We can make the problem clearer by looking at some additional cases. Consider the following characters, some of whom you'll recall from earlier:

1. Keith Bardwell, who opposes interracial marriage. Suppose he works as a Kentucky clerk, and he requests the "win-win" solution of eliminating the clerk's name from marriage licenses. Should we accommodate him?

Same question for:

2. Mr. Burqa, who opposes issuing marriage licenses for women who enter the courthouse unveiled
3. Ms. Ingroup, who opposes interfaith marriages
4. Ms. Lifelong, who opposes remarriage after divorce
5. Mr. Dawkins-Hitchens, who opposes issuing marriage licenses for people known to be religious; he believes that religion is morally pernicious and he doesn't want to encourage religious people to procreate

It would be as easy to accommodate these clerks as to accommodate Davis. Should we? Anderson and Girgis believe that the answer to that question depends only upon whether we can do so without causing anyone "embarrassment or delay" (p. 254). I disagree.

In the end, Anderson and Girgis allow no room for the distinction between respecting integrity and abetting bad reasons. Although it is often desirable to let people "do their own thing," accommodation cases are never merely about letting people do their own thing: They're also about how the rest of us do "our thing" when coordinating for common purposes. And religious conservatives are not the only ones who worry about complicity.

Anderson and Girgis's argument also rests on an important theological assumption. They argue that "a person is better off for having performed sincere religious acts even when they rest on false premises" (p. 143). But the truth of this claim depends on the nature of God, and how eager God is to punish those who worship false gods.

While Anderson and Girgis's tolerant spirit is admirable, it is far from universal. True, the quest for harmony with the divine has inspired believers, as Anderson and Girgis say, to raise a temple to Ishtar or the sun god, to pay homage to Aten or Brahma, to search and to protest and to preach. But it has also inspired them to fly planes into buildings, to wage murderous Crusades, to drown and to slaughter and to burn. As Notre Dame philosophy professor Gary Gutting explains: "The potential for intolerance lies in the logic of religions like Christianity and Islam that say their teaching derive from a divine revelation. For them, the truth that God has revealed is the most important truth there is; therefore, denying or doubting this truth is extremely dangerous, both for nonbelievers, who lack this essential truth, and for believers, who may well be misled by the denials and doubts of nonbelievers. Given these assumptions, it's easy to conclude that even extreme steps are warranted to eliminate nonbelief."[10]

To be clear: Anderson and Girgis do not advocate such extreme steps. But the quest for harmony with the divine is as logically compatible with them as with the far more tolerant posture we all espouse.

4.2 LIMITED GOVERNMENT VERSUS EXEMPTIONS FROM LAWS

Another concern is that Anderson and Girgis vacillate between arguing for exemptions from laws and arguing for more limited government generally—that is, for fewer or more narrowly drawn laws. It's possible to endorse both. But it is important to face squarely what exemptions do: They tell a certain group of citizens that they don't have to follow the same rules as everyone else.

The problem here is the one identified by Justice Scalia in *Smith*, citing *Reynolds*: If the law's authority were to vary based on the diverse moral and religious commitments of citizens, then all persons could become a law unto themselves. Would Anderson and Girgis have supported a religious exemption for George Reynolds, who felt duty-bound to take multiple wives and whose integrity was burdened by antipolygamy laws? They never say.

Anderson and Girgis's tendency to vacillate between arguing against laws and arguing for exemptions from them is most pronounced when they discuss the HHS contraception mandate and sexual orientation and gender identity antidiscrimination laws. In each case, they believe that the law is unjustified. They thus hold that *no one* should be bound by it. Given that assumption, it obviously follows that *no one with religious objections* should be bound by it. But a convincing case for *exemptions* must take a different route: It must assume (if only for the sake of argument) that a law is justified, and then explain why certain citizens, and only those citizens, should not be bound by it.

In making such an argument, one needs to grapple with the "Swiss cheese" objection: the idea that poking the law full of holes undermines both its efficacy and its authority. Anderson and Girgis respond by noting that RFRA, which has been in effect since 1993, has managed to do its job without the sky falling. I have several rejoinders.

First, just a few years after it was passed, RFRA was struck down as applied to the states.[11] Limiting RFRA to federal law blunts some of its risks, which have resurfaced with recent state RFRAs—sometimes proposed with the clear objective of overruling duly passed local antidiscrimination ordinances.[12]

Second, as virtually everyone agrees (including Anderson and Girgis), most judges have applied RFRA in a manner much weaker than its explicit terms. My argument calls for bringing those terms in line with that reasonable application.

Third, one of my main concerns about RFRA was that it favored religious citizens over their secular counterparts. If we extend it to cover secular conscience claims (as all three of us favor) without also refining its explicit terms (as I favor), the potential for abuse will grow considerably.

Fourth and finally, the "Swiss cheese" worry is not the same as a "sky falling" worry. Justice Scalia was a smart man. When he warned about "court[ing] anarchy," he was not so much predicting chaos as making a plea for legal consistency. The objection is one of principle as much as prudence.

For illustration, consider *Hobby Lobby*. If we exempt the Greens because of their sincere religious objections to certain contraceptives, what is our *principled reason* for not providing the same accommodation to Jehovah's Witness business owners who don't want to provide insurance that covers blood transfusions, or Scientologists who don't want to provide mental health care? What about business owners with religious objections to vaccines? Anesthesia? Antidepressants?[13] How many holes are too many? And if the difference consists in the fact that the Supreme Court majority is more comfortable with evangelical Christian scruples than with those of Jehovah's Witnesses or Scientologists, the religious privilege problem returns.

One begins to wonder whether poking holes is part of the point: Social conservatives have made no secret of their distaste for Obamacare. As the head of Eden Foods, which brought a RFRA suit against the mandate, revealingly put it, "I don't care if the federal government is telling me to buy my employees Jack Daniel's or birth control. What gives them the right to tell me that I have to do that? That's my issue, that's what I object to, and that's the beginning and end of the story."[14] This is precisely the sort of abuse of RFRA that critics worry about.

In their Reply Anderson and Girgis note that the HHS mandate already includes secular exemptions. They fail to mention that these exceptions stem largely from grandfathered plans, which are gradually disappearing.[15] In any case, there's a significant difference between granting exemptions to a finite, dwindling group of employers during a transition period and granting exemptions to any employer who might ever raise a religiously framed objection, in perpetuity.

A related worry is that of burden shifting. It's true that some religious exemptions have long shifted burdens, the prime example being conscientious objection in wartime—which, I have argued, is a unique case. And it's also true, as Anderson and Girgis note, that the important question is less about whether burdens are "shifted" than about whether in the end they are distributed fairly. But the cost of third-party burdens must be weighed, and that cost is growing under today's complicity-based claims.[16]

From a legal perspective, the status quo matters. As Justice Scalia has correctly observed, "when the State makes a public benefit generally available, that benefit becomes part of the baseline against which burdens on religion are measured."[17] The baseline, in other words, is *equal treatment under the law.*

By analogy, consider minimum wage laws. They burden employers. And some have sought exemptions from them on religious grounds.[18] But there's a difference between arguing against minimum wage laws because of the general burden they place and arguing that minimum wage laws should stand, but not apply to employers who happen to raise religious scruples. Such exemptions take the general burden and redistribute it, shifting it in a way that impacts both competitors (who lack the exemption) and employees (who are paid less). Throughout their essay, Anderson and Girgis obscure this difference.

One last point on exemptions: I'm glad that Anderson and Girgis support extending religious conscience exemptions to secular conscience claims. This would be a significant change from current policy. The law favors currently religious objectors over their secular counterparts on a host of matters, from regulations on dress and grooming to zoning ordinances, insurance coverage, compulsory education, vaccines, and even child-abuse reporting requirements. Among other problems, such religious privilege tempts social conservatives into framing objections to progressive legislation in religious terms, even when doing so is an obvious stretch.

For an example, take the recent spate of "bathroom bills," which require people to use public restrooms that match the gender on their birth certificate. One reason I spent no time discussing these bills is that they strike me as having virtually nothing to do with religious liberty. Proponents have typically framed them as being about children's safety, despite the fact that they contribute nothing to that goal: After all, if sexual predators are not deterred by already existing laws against sexual assault, they're certainly not going to be deterred by "bathroom bills." Meanwhile, such legislation does pose a real threat to transgender people, who are frequently the targets of violence, and who, like everyone else, are simply looking for safe and comfortable restrooms.[19]

But now, in addition to this fearmongering about children's safety, proponents are framing the issue in terms of religious liberty and our "God-given nature" as male or female. Such framing reinforces the worry that virtually anything—even telling other people where they must relieve themselves—can be stretched into a religious liberty claim when doing so is politically convenient.

4.3 SEXUAL ORIENTATION AND GENDER IDENTITY DISCRIMINATION

Not surprisingly, our greatest differences concern sexual orientation and gender identity discrimination: what constitutes it, how pervasive it is, and what the law should do about it. Here I discuss some specific disputes.

4.3.1 Do Wedding Service Refusals Constitute Sexual Orientation Discrimination?

Anderson and Girgis argue that refusing to sell items for same-sex weddings is not sexual orientation discrimination. "'Discriminating' based on X," they say, "means taking X as a reason for treating someone differently" (p. 249). When bakers refuse to sell a cake for a lesbian wedding, however, their opposition is not to the customer's orientation but to her nonconjugal relationship. So if a heterosexual mother came in to buy a cake for her daughter's lesbian wedding, the bakers would still refuse. But if the lesbian daughter came in to buy a birthday cake, they would serve her.

It is easy to see how badly wrong their reasoning is by plugging in a different trait: race. Imagine a baker who refuses to provide cakes for interracial weddings. Suppose that if the bride's white mother-in-law came in to order the cake, and the baker knew it was for an interracial wedding, he would still refuse. But if the daughter came in to buy a birthday cake, he would serve her. From Anderson and Girgis's logic, it follows that this baker is not engaged in racial discrimination. Neither was Keith Bardwell, as long as he was willing to provide other services for his "piles and piles of black friends." This conclusion is absurd.

The problem is that Anderson and Girgis assume that in order to discriminate on the basis of a trait, one must discriminate in the face of *any manifestation* of that trait. But that's not even true with respect to racial discrimination. The racists of the Old South interacted with blacks in various and sometimes intimate ways, even employing them as wet nurses. The idea wasn't to avoid blacks entirely but to keep them "in their place."

It is not surprising that efforts to keep gay, lesbian, and bisexual people in their place arise in the wedding context. Sexual orientation is a relational property; it's about the sex or gender of the people with whom you have relationships or desire to have relationships. It manifests itself in the context of those relationships, and unless it manifests itself, would-be discriminators can't target it. That explains why the Toledo, Ohio, baker had no problem selling a birthday cake to a lesbian customer—*until* she went on the customer's Facebook page and realized that the cake was for the customer's female partner.[20] At that point the baker canceled the order. According to Anderson and Girgis's view, she should be permitted to do so, provided that her objection is to the nonconjugal nature of their relationship.

But is such discrimination *invidious* discrimination? Anderson and Girgis insist that it is not, because the baker's "reason for refusing to bake same-sex wedding cakes is manifestly *not* to avoid contact with gay people on equal terms" (p. 191). But that's a strange claim, given that the bakers are refusing to sell gay people *the very same items* they sell to other customers. They do so precisely because they judge same-sex relationships to be morally inferior. Like Anderson and Girgis, they believe that such relationships aren't real marriages and that they are unworthy of the same rights and privileges as heterosexual relationships.[21] If this isn't "avoid[ing] contact with gay people on equal terms," I'm not sure what is.

Anderson and Girgis refer to my discussion of anti-LGBT discrimination as "conceptually slopp[y]" (p. 250). But I distinguish carefully between neutral and moralized senses of "discrimination" and inform readers that I'll be using the moralized sense—*just as they do* (p. 71, 164). I then explain the historical context that makes it reasonable for people to interpret differential treatment of LGBT people as being part of a larger system of subordination. I'm not surprised that my counterpoint authors see things differently, but for them to suggest that I don't do the work is itself sloppy.

It's true that in this book I am less interested in making the case for sexual orientation and gender identity antidiscrimination laws than in making the case against religious exemptions to them. Others have made the positive case at considerable length elsewhere—including Andrew Koppelman, whom Anderson and Girgis cite over and over while downplaying the fact that he has long supported such laws.[22] In any case, there is a substantial literature demonstrating not only the harms of anti-LGBT discrimination but also the effectiveness of antidiscrimination law in ameliorating it.[23]

Unsurprisingly, Anderson and Girgis don't acknowledge the material and dignitary harms caused by the exclusion from legal marriage: They support that exclusion. They have denounced the U.S. Supreme Court's *Obergefell* decision, which recognizes same-sex couples' right to marry as a matter of equal treatment under law.[24] Some of their colleagues have even urged officeholders to disregard *Obergefell* as binding precedent, comparing it to the atrocious *Dred Scott* decision, which prohibited Congress from banning slavery.[25] Elsewhere I have argued at length that their case against same-sex marriage fails; I encourage interested readers to review those arguments.[26]

Moreover, for all their talk of liberty, Anderson and Girgis never acknowledge, much less repudiate, the laws criminalizing same-sex relations in parts of the United States until as recently as 2004. These laws had devastating consequences—affecting job prospects, child custody, police relations, military discharges, and more. Many of Anderson and Girgis's colleagues endorsed such laws; some still do.[27]

Anderson and Girgis also mostly ignore my discussion of Pastor Kevin Swanson's rhetoric of antigay disgust. Swanson makes explicit what regularly occurs as subtext: the message that gays are spiritually infected and infectious. That message does tremendous psychological harm to LGBT people, especially LGBT youth.[28] It reinforces the debilitating isolation of the closet. And it helps explain why even something as seemingly innocuous as being turned away from a bakery might cause Rachel Bowman-Cryer to doubt that she was "supposed to love or be loved, have a family or go to heaven."[29]

To their credit, Anderson and Girgis concede that sexual orientation and gender identity are "irrelevant to a host of transactions . . . So it is unjust for people to take them into account in public life, or to shun others for them in private life. Abuses of both sorts—by relatives and friends, colleagues and neighbors and governments—have left deep scars, and made scapegoats and second-class citizens of many" (p. 184–5). Yet they inexplicably fail to connect the dots between these abuses and the reasonableness of antidiscrimination protections. They also completely ignore the ways in which existing law, as well as beliefs about the law, have contributed to shaping this more tolerant culture. Precisely because anti-LGBT discrimination is illegal in some places, many people mistakenly believe it to be illegal everywhere—and act accordingly.[30] As Anderson and Girgis have acknowledged elsewhere, the law is a powerful teacher.[31]

4.3.2 Animus and Social Meanings

Anderson and Girgis draw a sharp contrast between racial discrimination and anti-LGBT discrimination. On their telling, race discriminators are hateful people, motivated by animus, who want to avoid contact with blacks and other racial minorities, whereas sexual orientation and gender identity "discriminators" are conscientious people, motivated by moral principle, who want merely to avoid complicity in actions that violate their beliefs. (I'm using "discriminator" in the morally neutral sense here and throughout this section.)

This description is misleading twice over. Both race discriminators and sexual orientation and gender identity discriminators are a mixed bunch. As has been shown, many race discriminators have acted out of sincere moral and religious convictions. And not all sexual orientation and gender identity discriminators are gracious figures like my counterpoint authors. Quite the contrary: I have a stack of recent hate mail on my desk maligning gays as "pedophiles" and telling me that "fags" should "die of AIDS." One need not attend Swanson's National Religious Liberty Conference to hear self-identified Christians expressing anti-LGBT animus in truly nasty terms. Just go to my YouTube page. Here's a typical recent comment:

> Faggots are a hideous abomination, always were, always will be. Dress it up all you like, make it palatable as possible for this current "touchy-feely," safe-space generation; convince them all that nearby friends and relatives are all harboring gay thoughts for each other and that all of this is natural . . . then do me a solid and go read about Sodom and Gomorrah. Then go read about Jesus Christ. He said to love everyone, but never once denied that there'd be consequences for being an unnatural freak. This social acceptance of perversion will pass, and the latent backlash will be hideous.[32]

Refusals of service happen within a social context. Religious conservatives have made clear their beliefs that same-sex relationships are "unnatural" and "an abomination"; that gays should remain in the closet; that we should be denied the legal right to marry; and that homosexual conduct should maybe even be recriminalized. Against this backdrop, it is not difficult to understand why same-sex couples perceive invidious discrimination when told that they cannot purchase the very same items that their heterosexual fellow citizens do.

Anderson and Girgis argue that traditional marriage norms were not born of animus. Even if correct, that argument is entirely beside the point, for at least two reasons.

First, the relevant question is not about the *origins* of these norms but about the *maintaining* of them: One can hold (as I do) that marriage norms originally had little to do with LGBT people, but that retaining them today requires negligent disregard for our needs and interests.

Second, and equally important, discriminatory acts need not be rooted in animus in order to be harmful. As has been shown, discrimination often results from sheer ignorance of the ways in which one's actions affect others.

Consider again Bob Jones University: Maybe its admissions officers hated blacks. Maybe they loved blacks but honestly believed their founder's interpretation of scripture. Maybe they had a quirky aesthetic preference for couples with consistent skin tones, much like those who argued against integrating the Rockettes on the grounds that black dancers would spoil the "look of precision."[33] The government is not really in a position to know how they reasoned, and for the purpose of applying antidiscrimination law, it doesn't need to know: What matters are the effects. (Interestingly, my counterpoint authors recognize the weight of "same effects" when discussing integrity, but refuse to acknowledge it when discussing sexual orientation and gender identity discrimination [p. 241].) It bears repeating that the ultimate objective of antidiscrimination law is not to punish haters (not all discriminators are haters) but to ensure equal access in the public sphere.

This is not to say that discriminators' reasons aren't relevant at all, at any stage. They are relevant to how we *morally* evaluate such cases. They are also relevant contextually: The fact that such discrimination has been rooted in animus in the past makes it more likely that it will contribute to social harm in the present, whether intentionally or not.

4.3.3 The Analogy to Speech; the Analogies to Killing

Anderson and Girgis ask: "Why accept immense dignitary harms to make room for free speech, but not for freedoms of conscience and religion, where the dignitary harms are often lighter anyway? Why the double standard of counting dignitary harm (*in addition to* material harms) against conscience claims, but *not at all* against speech? This is a challenge to which progressives have no response" (p. 172).

I have two responses, both of which show that there is no double standard. First, Anderson and Girgis get the relevant distinction wrong. It is not between freedom of speech and freedom of conscience/religion but between freedom of speech and freedom of *action*. The Kleins of Sweet Cakes engaged in both, and both were an expression of religious conscience. It was their refusal of service, however—their action, not their speech—that triggered government sanction. The right question to ask, then, is why count dignitary harm against freedom of *action* (religious or otherwise) but not against freedom of speech (religious or otherwise)? The answer to that question is that in general, actions pose greater risks than speech. Although it's strictly false that "sticks and stones may break my bones, but names will never hurt me," the adage captures a point that most everyone understands. The speech/action distinction is thus a reasonable if necessarily imperfect place to draw a legal line with respect to dignitary harms.

Second, for both speech and religious exercise, one must distinguish between direct burdens and incidental ones. I am as against direct burdens on religious freedom as I am against direct burdens on freedom of speech, with only rare exceptions (involving speech or religious exercise that poses immediate bodily danger). Indirect burdens are quite another matter. A law requiring the Kleins not to discriminate on the basis of sexual orientation burdens their religion in the same way that a law prohibiting obscene signage limits their free speech: indirectly, as an effect of neutral, generally applicable laws.

Anderson and Girgis repeatedly analogize sexual orientation and gender identity antidiscrimination laws with forcing prolife doctors to perform abortions or executions, or forcing pacifist citizens to go to war. The issues are not remotely comparable. First, those who oppose abortion, execution, and war believe them to involve *killing*. Not all complicity claims are created equal, and part of what makes them unequal is the gravity of the subject matter. Second, antidiscrimination law doesn't force anyone into a same-sex marriage against their will; it simply places constraints on what they may do when they enter the commercial sphere. As I've argued, jumbling together such disparate claims ultimately erodes support for religious exemptions in cases that truly merit them.

4.3.4 Fair Weather Libertarianism

Anderson and Girgis repeatedly stress that they are not libertarians. But they certainly sound libertarian whenever they discuss sexual orientation and gender identity antidiscrimination laws.

Helpfully, they explicate their standard for when antidiscrimination laws are justified. They claim that

> a group faces (a) *material* harms of the sort that justifies anti-discrimination law when private discrimination against it is so pervasive that (i) it can't meet *basic needs* for housing, lodging, loans, jobs, education, healthcare, and the like; (ii) it's excluded

from the *markets* for other goods and services; or (iii) its *social mobility* or *political influence* is seriously curtailed. . . . [b] Social harms that also justify antidiscrimination laws . . . consist of cultural ideas and attitudes unfairly impugning a group's abilities, actions, character, proper social status, or moral worth. Call these ideas and attitudes—even when the person acting on them isn't hateful himself—"contempt." As social contempt for a group metastasizes, others find it harmful, dangerous, socially improper, or wrong to deal with the group on equal terms. That's why the state has reason to fight social contempt, by curbing conduct whose social meaning fosters it (p. 180).

I have two reactions. One is that, in explaining social harm or contempt, Anderson and Girgis have done a decent job of describing the way in which LGBT people are often treated: having our moral worth impugned, being smeared as threats to children, making it seem "harmful, dangerous, socially improper, or wrong to deal with [us] on socially equal terms." And these problems in turn explain why, in certain markets and jurisdictions, our social mobility and political influence are indeed seriously curtailed. Remember, the reason that sexual orientation and gender identity are not covered in federal and many state antidiscrimination statutes is not because anti-LGBT discrimination hasn't been widespread but because until recently it was accepted as a matter of course.

The second and more important reaction is to wonder which *existing* antidiscrimination protections, if any, would survive Anderson and Girgis's standards. Certainly, discrimination against blacks during the civil rights era merited legal intervention. But one wonders whether racial discrimination in public accommodations *currently* meets Anderson and Girgis's threshold, given the political and social advances of the last few decades.

Even more, one wonders about protections for religion, sex, national origin, age, marital status, disability, veteran status, and so forth. It is by no means clear that discrimination on the basis of each of those traits is so pervasive that the corresponding groups can't meet "basic needs for housing, lodging, loans, jobs, education, healthcare, and the like" or are widely regarded with contempt.

Take religion: Do Anderson and Girgis think that it should be legal to fire someone because she is Catholic (assuming that the job is not religious in nature)? Or to refuse to rent to Catholics, or to sell them off-the-shelf items?

In their reply, they are noncommittal: "Bans on religious discrimination ... were enacted to fight anti-Semitism and anti-Catholicism. We suspect that neither problem would be pervasive enough today to lock Jews or Catholics out of markets. Does this justify now repealing bans on religious discrimination in employment or accommodations? That depends on whether doing so would allow, say, exclusion of Muslims to surge; or whether the message sent by repealing (as opposed to never enacting) these laws might do its own social harm. Our test for antidiscrimination laws ... allows no easy slide from SOGI to religion or any other classification" (p. 246). In other words, protections for Catholics should be left in place, but LGBT people are out of luck.

Do not let the focus on bakers and florists obscure this point: It is currently legal in most states to fire people for being lesbian, gay, bisexual, or transgender; to refuse to rent them apartments or hotel rooms; even to refuse to tow their cars or repair their furnaces. Should this change? Anderson and Girgis argue that it should not.

4.3.5 Their Challenge

And yet, in a parting nod to compromise, Anderson and Girgis offer a challenge to sexual orientation and gender identity law supporters, asking us to endorse a bill "limited to banning decisions based simply on a person's sexual desires or gender identity (and not on morally controversial actions)" (p. 204). Such a bill would "punish decisions to fire a bus driver for her attraction to other women, or deny her a loan for identifying as transgender," but not decisions to discriminate on the basis of objections to same-sex marriage (p. 204).

This concluding section is simply strange. If their point is to show that sexual orientation and gender identity antidiscrimination law supporters disagree with their proposed exemptions, then the section is unnecessary: I've already acknowledged that I disagree with their proposed exemptions, and I spent an entire section of my essay (section 4, "Discrimination and the Law") explaining why. If their point is, as they say, to show that we are more interested in sending a message about the harmfulness of anti-LGBT views than in protecting people's urgent material interests, then they're invoking a false dilemma: We are interested in both. And if their point is to offer a compromise, then they should stop being coy: Now is the time to tell us whether they support *any* sexual orientation and gender identity antidiscrimination protections, including the limited bill that they sketch here. That's how compromise works: One side makes a proposal; the other makes a counterproposal; and we try to meet in the middle.

But Anderson and Girgis don't make a counterproposal. Instead, they suggest that we sexual orientation and gender identity law supporters should be making proposals that are weaker than those we actually believe in. They do so immediately after making it clear that, given their assessment of the current need, they have no intention of supporting any such proposals. That's not offering a compromise; it's inviting us to negotiate against ourselves.

As to why more LGBT rights organizations are not offering watered-down proposals for the sake of quickly securing the most urgent protections: That's a complicated question of political strategy. Such organizations have likely calculated that they have a shot at full-fledged protections in jurisdictions where they're likely to secure any protections at all, and that the best way to secure the core protections is to aim high and let the chips fall where they may. That said, LGBT rights organizations and other sexual orientation and gender identity law supporters have in fact supported proposals with broad exemptions. The "Utah Compromise" is a prime example: Utah passed a law that prohibits discrimination on the basis of sexual orientation and gender identity in employment and housing—but not public accommodations—and that contains broad exemptions for religious organizations, schools, and hospitals. It was endorsed by the Human Rights Campaign, Equality Utah, and the ACLU of Utah, among other progressive organizations.[34] So Anderson and Girgis's challenge is based on a false premise.

4.4 CONCLUSION: DOUBLE STANDARDS AND THE PURITAN MISTAKE

Before concluding, I want to summarize my position. Unfortunately, only a distorted version of it appears in Anderson and Girgis's rebuttal.

I support heightened scrutiny for laws that burden religion. I think the best reason for that scrutiny is to promote inclusion, given how religion has historically been a site of conflict. In particular, religion has often led in-groups to discriminate against out-groups—sometimes deliberately, but often unwittingly. For that reason, I'm skeptical of exemptions that create systematic third-party burdens, especially burdens for other out-groups. I thus oppose most exemptions from duly passed antidiscrimination legislation—my starkest contrast with Anderson and Girgis. I would retain RFRA, but I would modify it to make it more equitable, bringing its terms in line with how judges have usually applied it and extending its exemptions to comparable secular conscience claims.

Parts of my essay involve "thinking out loud," and that process can occasionally be messy. I tried to provide sufficient detail, without pretending that these puzzles are easier than they actually are. As is apparent in my counterpoint authors' rebuttal, however, much of this detail is lost on them.

When I call for a principled legal consistency, they describe me as imagining that the sky is falling. When I object to a lesbian's being turned away from a public business after being told that she cannot purchase the same items as her heterosexual fellow citizens, they claim that I object to "offensive remarks." When I make a nuanced argument about how celebration involves expressing something, they read me as collapsing conscience and speech. When I grant that even good laws can have unpalatable consequences when overzealously applied, they suggest that I support laws in response to "phantom threats." And when I acknowledge that, notwithstanding the ground we've covered, there are many worthwhile issues remaining to discuss, they criticize me for evasiveness. Such rhetorical moves do little to promote the productive ongoing conversation that all three of us desire.

Let me close with a final thought experiment.

Two casually dressed women enter a roadside motel. "We would like a room," one says, catching the attention of the desk clerk.

"Excellent. We have vacancies!" he responds. "One bed or two?"

"Two," the woman responds, and the desk clerk reaches for a key. As he turns to hand it to her, he notices the Virgin Mary pendant around the second woman's neck.

"Are you Catholics?" he asks, frowning.

"Yes," the first woman responds, puzzled. "We both are."

"I'm sorry," the clerk responds. "We do not rent to your kind around here."

"Excuse me?"

"Catholicism is idolatry," the man continues. "Read the Ten Commandments. We only rent to real Christians."

Discrimination on the basis of religion is against the law everywhere in the United States, as it should be. This innkeeper—call him Mr. Antipapist—is acting illegally.

Should Mr. Antipapist's refusal be illegal? Or do laws requiring him to serve Catholics constitute a "new Puritanism," by "coerc[ing] conscientious dissenters to live by the majority's views"? After all, Catholics are not "locked out of markets for goods or services": There are other motels, as well as strong market incentives for them to rent to all.

What about laws that prohibit Mr. Antipapist from firing Catholics, or from refusing to lease apartments to them—not because he harbors animus but because he doesn't want to contribute to the spread of "idolatry"? Do those laws constitute "progressive Puritanism," in Anderson and Girgis's view?

Anderson and Girgis criticize me for claiming that Mississippi's FADA—which they support—committed the Puritan mistake. They argue: "Puritans persecuted people who believed and lived differently. First Amendment Defense Acts coerce no one, and could only prevent government from coercing citizens—from waging a campaign of *progressive* Puritanism against those who believe and live differently" (p. 240).

Anderson and Girgis can sustain this criticism only by ignoring half of my argument. The problem with Mississippi's FADA is not that it offered protection for same-sex marriage opponents. The problem (among others) is that it offered protection for same-sex marriage opponents, *while offering none for same-sex marriage supporters, let alone LGBT people.* To borrow an apt turn of phrase from Walter Olson of the libertarian Cato Institute, this "isn't really an accommodation law. It's an our-guys-win law."[35]

Anderson and Girgis retort that there's "nothing scandalous about protections for particular views at odds with those on which the government acts" (p. 239). But "the government" is not a monolithic entity. Kentucky clerk Kim Davis is "the government." Alabama judge Roy is "the government." Given the political landscape, which views on marriage are most likely to need protection in Mississippi?

In the introduction, we described a 1922 Oregon law requiring children to attend public schools. It was ostensibly aimed at promoting shared American values. But that wasn't the real aim: The real aim was to undermine recent Catholic immigrants.[36]

Too many "religious liberty" measures today commit the same error. Although they dress themselves up in the language of freedom, they're not really about freedom: They're about signaling disapproval for certain forms of life. Their proponents want freedom for themselves that they proudly oppose for LGBT citizens: the freedom to marry, the freedom to express views about marriage without "discriminatory action" by government, and the freedom to enter the commercial sphere without threat of discrimination. It's a double standard.

To the extent that exemptions abet this double standard, they are not "win-win" solutions. They are a betrayal of our commitment to equal justice under law.

5

Reply to Corvino

RYAN T. ANDERSON AND SHERIF GIRGIS

∎∎∎

THIS BOOK'S GOAL HAS BEEN to develop and test against each other two approaches to cultural clashes post-*Obergefell*. Corvino's approach has been dialectical: addressing just a few conflicts, considering just a few proposals, and developing just enough theory to pick among the proposals he considers on the conflicts he addresses. We've tried to build up general principles to address the range of the challenges in a unified way. Each approach has its benefits and risks. We picked ours in the hope that by tackling the full spectrum of these conflicts, we would be likelier to address the toughest cases for us; that by tracing the theoretical building blocks of our proposals, we could ensure they fit together; that by hauling them away from the partisan fray for calmer examination and more general defense, we could make it easier for the persuaded to apply them elsewhere—and easier for critics to pick them apart. These are doubly important goals for a policy debate, since fairness requires the law to be ever more the working out of a consistent set of principles. No doubt we've had varying degrees of success meeting all these goals, and critics will help us correct and refine.

So has Corvino, whose contribution is—like its author—sophisticated, civil, and well-informed. Engaged as we are by what he says, however, we see missed opportunities in what he omits—especially in his decision not to address many of the conflicts prompting this book.

Thus, he asserts in passing that "virtually no one" wants to force prolifers to perform abortions, but that consensus crumbles as we write: the prominent journal *Bioethics* just published an article by a University of Oxford scholar titled "Doctors Have No Right to Refuse Medical Assistance in Dying, Abortion or Contraception."[1] What would Corvino's approach commit him (or anyone) to holding on this issue? He doesn't say—or say enough to enable us to say. Corvino says "there are good reasons" for basing counseling referrals on the client's needs, not the therapist's. But he never says what those reasons are, or why they don't bid respect for *both* sets of needs. He would prefer that Catholic adoption agencies stopped "discriminating on the basis of sexual orientation," but begs the question of whether preferring homes with a father and mother is orientation-based discrimination. He supports gender identity antidiscrimination laws but is silent on whether they should force doctors to do sex-reassignment surgeries. He would leave religious schools generally free but avers that whether we "should continue to subsidize them . . . is a different matter." Yet he doesn't offer his own view of that matter—despite its potentially fatal consequences for thousands of schools; despite the United States' stunning admission, in oral argument for *Obergefell*, that it was "going to be an issue."

In a book on religious liberty and discrimination, Corvino offers no general case for enacting SOGI antidiscrimination laws, no account of what qualifies as discrimination based on gender identity, no word on whether there should be exemptions for anyone but custom-service providers, and no more general principle on exemptions to point toward an answer. Finally, without more on the theoretical foundations of the proposals he does make, it is harder to know whether they cohere (as we argue his assumptions on freedoms of religion and speech do not), or whether they might have other, less palatable consequences (as we argue of his working conception of discrimination). So it's hard to judge whether his preferred policies apply the same principles consistently, as legal systems should aspire to do. Indeed, Corvino's concern about the risks of a "Swiss cheese" surface of legal rules tells more powerfully against a Swiss cheese body of principles shaping law at its core—and thus against his essay's methodology. We say this not to "criticize [Corvino] for evasiveness" or to engage in "rhetorical moves," as he charges. We say it because these gaps lighten the argumentative burden for his general approach to these issues, so they are relevant to judging which of our approaches is more compelling overall. And judging that is the point of this book.

Nevertheless, Corvino's essay reveals some agreement. We agree that conscientious objections deserve protection whether their roots are religious or secular. We agree that freedoms of conscience and religion can require exemptions from good law—but only where granting them won't undermine justice or the public good. We agree that minorities sometimes need legal protection against the harms of private discrimination—but that there is no right not to be offended. We agree that holding traditional views on sexuality doesn't make you a bigot—but that anti-LGBT bigotry is real. We agree that the law shouldn't force custom-service providers to celebrate choices that conflict with their beliefs—but not because commercial freedom is an absolute value or because the state should limit itself to fighting force and fraud.

Here we focus on our differences. First, Corvino is skeptical of legislation we support because he finds himself increasingly uneasy about religious exemptions, and worried about religious privilege. Second, he thinks that those acting on traditional views of sexuality discriminate based on SOGI and should be penalized for it. Third, he doubts that what we call moral and religious integrity has value in itself.

We will suggest he is led to these conclusions by a distorted view of the social and legal landscape. Where exemptions give believers an equal shot at living with integrity, Corvino sees favoritism. Where statutes give the occasional religious liberty claimant her day in court, he sees a teeming mass of claims about to choke the workings of government. Where a sprawling body of regulations sits, rife with exemptions for everyday secular purposes, Corvino sees a system of laws so necessary in its details that religious exemptions might be ruinous. In conservative professionals facing steep fines on conscience, Corvino sees new Puritans; and in their bureaucratic harassers, he sees freedom fighters. Down the path to exemptions he sees a slippery slope; when society doesn't tumble, he imagines it stopped by legal barriers that aren't there, because they aren't needed. And at the horizon—where others search for harmony with the transcendent, their path cleared by freedoms of conscience and religion—he sees at best a socially useful mirage.

5.1 LEGISLATION AND EXEMPTIONS

Corvino criticizes FADA in passing and RFRA at great length—but his objections to both cut against one another, and against points made throughout his essay.

5.1.1 First Amendment Defense Acts

The First Amendment Defense Act would prevent government from disadvantaging people or organizations for their

convictions on marriage when it comes to granting or denying tax-status, accreditation, licensing, and the like. Corvino's
criticisms of the bill go awry from the start. Its definition of
governmental "discriminatory action" is limited to tax penalties, but he reads it as referring to *any* penalty. He lists nine
applications of the bill; six are misreadings. Thus, it expressly
says it cannot override civil rights laws; and as revised, it would
"exempt . . . Federal employees" as they work, limit the "definition of 'discriminatory action'" (obviating most of Corvino's
concerns), and exempt "publicly traded for-profit entities."[2]

Having misread its details, Corvino suggests that a state
FADA violated the establishment clause.[3] But as law professor
Richard Epstein explains, that clause—meant to "knock down
state coercion for religion"—can't be used to invalidate "a statute whose whole purpose was to insulate private parties from
any form of coercion."[4]

The revised federal FADA protects the consciences of both
social progressives and conservatives against government discrimination. We support that breadth—as do major actors
opposed to *Obergefell*, including the Catholic bishops, the
Southern Baptists, and the Heritage Foundation. But there would
be nothing scandalous about protections for particular views at
odds with those on which the government acts. When the government takes Americans to war, exceptions cover pacifists.
When the government guarantees abortion, they cover prolifers.
These exemptions don't amount to establishments of any religion.
And neither would laws protecting dissenters after *Obergefell*.

More important, these legal details shift Corvino's attention from the more pressing normative and policy question:
should institutions get anything like FADA's protections?
Should government yank religious universities' nonprofit tax
status or federal student aid for their refusal to hew to the
state's new view of marriage?

The First Amendment Defense Act enshrines the opposite of the Puritan mistake. Puritans persecuted people who believed and lived differently. First Amendment Defense Acts coerce no one, and could only prevent government from coercing citizens—from waging a campaign of *progressive* Puritanism against those who believe and live differently. Yet it is the dissenters seeking a peaceful settlement whom Corvino calls Puritans here.

5.1.2 The Religious Freedom Restoration Act and Religion's Pervasiveness

The specificity Corvino finds so lamentable in FADA is the answer to his mirror-image objection to RFRA: that its wide exemptions cut a slippery slope toward anarchy. Corvino worries that: (1) what counts as "religion" under RFRA is "expansive and expanding"; (2) RFRA is "too demanding"; and (3) claims made under it today impose "greater third-party burdens" than before. Each worry is unwarranted.

The first is puzzling. He notes there are thousands of denominations. So what? Yes, as he observes, believers needn't prove their religious beliefs *true* to win legal protection. But who would change that? He says religious liberty today—more than letting people "do their own thing"—increasingly affects "how the rest of us do 'our thing' when coordinating for common purposes." But accommodations are *always* from laws meant to coordinate our actions together—by definition.

His main fear is that in a world of diverse religions shaping every domain of life, RFRA's exemptions spell anarchy. But with twenty-three years of RFRAs to produce anarchy, Corvino can only reach for a single, "not entirely hypothetical" case of people objecting to time zone changes, as well as "satirical 'Pastafarians'" just trying to make a point. (When objectors have to tug at the sky to convince you it's falling, their case is weak.) He later retreats to worrying less about chaos than "legal consistency." But to say that exemptions provide different rules for some cases is to say that exemptions exempt.

Corvino's appeal to Justice Scalia misses his point: Scalia allowed exemptions crafted by legislatures, and only denied that the Constitution *required* them. There would be anarchy if people sought freedom from every restriction that ever imposed on anything they might do with religious intent. But they don't, and our framework shows why they shouldn't. A law merits extra scrutiny when it penalizes you for the chance to pursue basic goods adequately—as it does regarding integrity when it puts a high price on keeping a clean conscience. But that never happens when the law leaves you *affordable alternatives* for living by your convictions. Again, even if you feel duty-bound to attend church on time, speeding laws don't force you to pay to obey conscience since they leave you a cheap alternative: leaving home earlier.

And indeed, in that kind of case, people don't bring RFRA claims, nor would the law honor them. *That* is why the sky remains intact. People tend to bring claims just when our theory urges: when the law penalizes them for living by their convictions, as it did by requiring the Hahns and Greens in *Hobby Lobby* to lose millions, or their business.

Corvino says it's tendentious to call this an effective fine on conscience. But it has the same effects. To adapt to *Hobby Lobby* an earlier example, imagine a law saying: "Every citizen must now facilitate the use of abortifacients as follows. . . . Those who refuse will have their business fined or confiscated, if they own one; or be barred from opening one up, if they don't." That is clearly a fine on conscience, but it does only what the HHS mandate does. And both are *designed* to do so. The penalty of giving up your business or huge sums flows *entirely from the HHS mandate's terms*, as with any law imposing a fine. And it leaves prolifers stuck. They can't make up for the hit to their integrity (or their money, or livelihood) by switching their convictions on abortion, or working harder to live by their other beliefs. Even then, RFRA offers them no automatic exemption, only a balancing test. And it is when that test is satisfied that exemptions will restore fairness, as Corvino agrees they ought—and not "religious privilege," as he claims they often do.

5.1.3 *Hobby Lobby* and the Religious Freedom Restoration Act's Demandingness

Corvino also considers that test—"strict scrutiny"—too favorable to religious liberty. But scholars across the spectrum agree that as applied, it is far less demanding than tests going by that name in other fields of law.[5] Our view on its proper substance flows from our basic norm of political morality: the state must protect the conditions under which all have a chance to pursue the basic goods adequately, without needless penalty.

This suggests the following standard. In any exemption dispute, consider (1) those who claim an exemption from the law, and (2) those whom the law is meant to help. Would a certain result protect adequate access to all the basic goods for both? If so, the law should opt for it. If not, it should rule for the side with more to lose on that score.

Thus, in *Hobby Lobby*, HHS raised the cost to prolifers of pursuing the basic good of integrity. They could pay millions in fines, or give up any business they had built. Whereas allowing them not to cover merely the insurance of just four of several contraceptives would hardly make an appreciable difference to their employees. It certainly wouldn't deprive them of adequate access to a basic good. For these reasons, Hobby

Lobby should have won even under Corvino's preferred, intermediate level of scrutiny.

Moreover, his discussion of the case is distorted by extraordinary optimism about our legal system. Exemptions should be rare, he says, because we should pass coercive laws only for the best reasons. Yes, but we don't. With the growth of the administrative state, coercive rules don't have to walk the veto-ridden path by which bills become laws. Empowered by sweeping mandates from Congress and enormous deference from courts, agencies pass enough regulations that by 2014, extant federal agency rules alone took up 175,496 pages.[6] In such a regime, exemptions from this or that rule are hardly detectable. The mandate in *Hobby Lobby* itself had *secular* exemptions, with no sunset clause, covering a third of the country: 100 million Americans.[7] If corporations can be exempted for convenience, so can Hobby Lobby and its owners, for the sake of conscience.

With Hobby Lobby's claim, as elsewhere, Corvino passes judgment on whether the beliefs seeking relief are true, noting that "the mainstream medical community denies that these drugs are abortifacients." But Hobby Lobby's owners don't object to whatever subset of lethal treatments we happen to label "abortifacient." They object to causing the death of embryonic human beings—which the FDA says these drugs can do.[8]

Discussing the "least restrictive means" prong of the *Hobby Lobby* decision, Corvino writes: "RFRA only requires that there is a less restrictive alternative *possible*, not that it actually be offered." But if it isn't, that is hardly the religious claimant's fault. Prior to 2012, no one thought employers duty-bound to provide cost-free coverage of potentially life-ending contraceptives. After *Hobby Lobby*, it was HHS that *chose* not to restore that coverage to the company's employees. Both points suggest that applying the mandate to Hobby Lobby wasn't needed to serve compelling interests after all.

5.1.4 The Religious Freedom Restoration Act and Third-Party Harms

This leaves Corvino's final worry: that today's RFRA claims differ from the "familiar religious-liberty claims" of yore because they involve objections to being made complicit in others' choices—objections that the law would shift harm onto third parties by honoring. But shifting burdens isn't new. As law professor Thomas Berg explains, clergy-penitent privilege shifts harms from the penitent to the crime victim denied potentially useful testimony; the *Sherbert* decision shifted harms from the fired employee to her former employer (now subject to higher unemployment taxes).[9] And exemptions from the draft, which Corvino supports, shift the very heaviest burden imaginable.

Moreover, as the Supreme Court has noted, if third-party burdens could always defeat religious liberty claims, then by simply "framing any . . . regulation as benefiting a third party," the government could "turn all regulations into entitlements" allowing no exemptions.[10] So it tells us nothing to ask which shifted a burden—a complicity-based exemption, or the regulation. Both always do. The question is: Which shift was fair? The answer will depend not on what our policy happens to be but on what it should be. Not from any given party's self-interested perspective but objectively. It will depend on each option's spread of burdens and benefits, but not on whether either option caused a *shift*.

We've argued that RFRA helps restore a just order, by restoring a fair chance for believers to pursue basic goods adequately, without keeping others from doing the same. It's tendentious to respond that its exemptions would "impose" traditionalists' values on others. We'd never say that with other civil liberties.

Suppose it was your *free speech* right to protest the Iraq war that burdened others. Let's say it dredged up traumatic memories in veterans' families. Would anyone say that your protesting "imposed" your antiwar views on those so burdened? Would anyone say that enforcing your freedom violated those families' right to freedom of belief about the issues of the day? Of course not. Then why should the side effects of your exercise of *religious* freedom effectively "impose your religion" on those affected—or undermine their own freedom of religion?

"Imposing values" suggests coercing others to follow them. It steals its rhetorical force from the wrong of doing *that*. But Hobby Lobby—and conservative bakers and charities—*coerce no one into doing anything*. Nor would granting requests that pass RFRA's test impose steep costs on others' pursuit of basic goods. Against these points there is something decidedly Orwellian about seeing the actual coercion of traditionalist consciences as the neutral, freedom-loving baseline.

5.2 DISCRIMINATION

Corvino offers little argument for a major source of these conflicts, SOGI laws; and no principle for telling what should qualify as SOGI discrimination. His defense is surprising: "[I]n this book, I am less interested in making the case for SOGI antidiscrimination laws than in making the case against religious exemptions to them." That's not how we expected that sentence to end. In a book on religious liberty and discrimination, Corvino can't assume that his opponents discriminate, much less that they do enough harm to justify sweeping legal coercion. He owes readers arguments.

Remarkably, though Corvino says almost nothing to justify SOGI laws, he accuses *us* of conflating that issue with the question of whether to grant religious exemptions from them.

He manages to sustain this objection (which the reader can test, by flipping back a few pages) only by writing as if two-thirds of our opening essay didn't exist.

We offered a six-part account of when antidiscrimination laws are justified, and then applied it to SOGI. We proposed a four-part test for telling when exemptions may be granted from any such law (which Corvino says nothing to undermine—because he says nothing about it at all). And *then* we put them together. Assuming that the conditions justifying SOGI laws obtained, we showed how exemptions would leave intact their best goals. Corvino, having accused us of conflating these two issues, offers no rival account on the first and says little or nothing on our arguments on either.

By failing to appreciate this framework's relevance to our policy views, Corvino enfeebles his attempt to draw from the latter surprising or absurd results. Consider his closing question: whether our view that current social conditions don't justify SOGI laws would entail the same of bans on religious discrimination. The latter were enacted to fight anti-Semitism and anti-Catholicism. We suspect neither problem would be pervasive enough today to lock Jews or Catholics out of markets. Does this justify now repealing bans on religious discrimination in employment or accommodations? That depends on whether doing so would allow, say, exclusion of Muslims to surge; or whether the message sent by repealing (as opposed to never enacting) these laws might do its own social harm. Our test for antidiscrimination laws requires data and reflection on six questions, and allows no easy slide from SOGI to religion or any other classification.

There is, though, a vital difference between SOGI and every other protected status, and it's what most concerns us. Laws against religious discrimination aren't used to harass and penalize the Human Rights Campaign or Planned Parenthood. Catholics don't sue these groups for religious discrimination as they live out their principles in hiring and operations. But SOGI laws sure are used to punish organizations for living by *their* missions all the time. The double standard Corvino detects runs in the other direction.

5.2.1 Race Analogies

The SOGI-race analogy is overdone. Corvino agrees that "reductio ad interracial"–style objections are often unfair. It's rash to say that support for separate male and female showers entails accepting separate bathrooms for whites and blacks: that depends on whether sex matters more for physical privacy than race. The Civil Rights Act of 1964 didn't prohibit restaurants from excluding women, but that doesn't make it incoherent for banning exclusion of blacks: in accommodations, racial discrimination was far more stubborn and pervasive. As we showed, policy conclusions on these matters hang on many empirical as well as moral premises, which might look different case-to-case.

Corvino does fault conservatives for drawing a contrast between conduct and status. Yet we argued that (apart from material harms that can flow from even innocent distinctions) it *can* be invidious to make distinctions based on conduct, not simply status. Whether a distinction is invidious—rooted in harmful attitudes or ideas about a group and so likely to spread contempt—depends not on whether it's conduct- or status-based but on the reasoning behind it. Invidious distinctions are rooted in unfair, socially debilitating attitudes or ideas about people's worth, proper social status, abilities, or actions.

By this standard, bans on interracial marriage were paradigms of invidious discrimination. To be sure, they were about conduct—intermarrying. Historically, as we showed, the deeper premises were beliefs about African Americans, especially their supposed incompetence and threat to whites (especially women). Did some people believe that blacks belonged apart and at the margins based simply on a sincere conviction that God willed the separation of races—and not on any deeper belief about blacks per se? Well, even if some did, their first belief itself—about blacks' properly separate social status—*just is* one of the forms of contempt we've specified. That it's rooted in other premises not focused on blacks wouldn't change that.

For all these reasons, contra Corvino, our analysis explains why a baker refusing to bake for an interracial wedding discriminates by race, whoever comes to place the order. She declines based on a view about interracial marriage that in turn rests on ideas about a group defined in racial terms: African Americans. That is what makes her refusal a case of race-based discrimination (even in the neutral sense); what makes it *invidious* is the fact that those ideas about African Americans are unfair and socially debilitating.

Some people's refusals to bake for gay weddings might be ill-motivated—Corvino cites Pastor Swanson, based on facts specific to him. But we showed that it's *unfair to assume* that actions based on traditional sex ethics are premised on ideas harmful to gay people. Indeed, refusals to bake needn't be based on beliefs or attitudes about LGBT people, good *or* bad; they needn't be discrimination based on orientation at all.

Corvino begs to differ: "This objection overlooks the way in which some actions are constitutive of identity. It's like saying, 'I'm not discriminating against *Catholics*, I'm just discriminating against people who attend Catholic mass.'" This misses the mark, as we illustrated in our main essay with our example of the Jewish musician. It also has surprising results. Consider a government official who says: "In fining or shutting down bakeries that refuse gay weddings, I'm not discriminating against *Catholics*, I'm just discriminating against people who have Catholic moral beliefs about marriage." Catholics' beliefs and actions flow out of their religious identity. Does this mean that the SOGI policies Corvino supports would have the government discriminate based on religion, in violation of its own laws? Did Mozilla Firefox violate federal law by discriminating against Brendan Eich based on his religion, when it pushed him out for his religiously inspired view of marriage?

Corvino's analysis supports the Colorado Civil Rights Commission's finding that a baker declining to bake same-sex wedding cakes discriminated based on orientation (thus meriting crippling fines)—after all, as Corvino says, gay marriage flows out of gay identity. But consider the Commission's ruling when others refused to bake cakes with Bible verses saying God loves sinners and gay sex is sinful. Did it say they discriminated based on religion, since Christian messages flow out of Christian identity? No. As a Colorado court noted, "the bakeries did not refuse the patron's request because of his creed, but rather because of the offensive nature of the requested message"; so their decisions weren't based on "the patron's religion."[11] But if that is true, then the Christian baker's refusal to affirm a "requested message" about marriage didn't discriminate based on orientation. Corvino faults us for not noting that the progressive bakeries were willing to sell off-the-shelf items. But so was the Christian baker. The point remains: if the latter discriminated based on orientation, the former did based on religion.

The Commission, like Corvino, has a double standard for what constitutes discrimination. Its second analysis was right: "discriminating" based on X, in the neutral sense, means taking X as a reason for treating someone differently. Invidiousness involves discriminating in a way that discounts the interests of people with that trait, or credits unfair beliefs about them, to their social detriment. Refusals to serve interracial weddings were premised on the fact that one partner was black. People objected to interracial marriage because they objected to mixing with blacks, based on their beliefs about blacks' "tendencies" or "proper status." The evangelical refuses to bake for a same-sex wedding because she objects to same-sex marriage, based on her belief that *it isn't marital* (along with many other relationships—sexual and not, dyadic and larger, same- and opposite-sex), according to her religion. Nowhere need her reasoning refer to the partners' sexual orientation—or any ideas or attitudes about LGBT people, good or bad. Her choice might yet be unjustified or burdensome or worth coercing. But before assessing that, it's important to get the classification right.

Why? Because Corvino's approach conflates two stages of analysis: whether someone took a certain trait into account in reasoning about how to treat others, and whether her actions wronged people marked by that trait (e.g., whether she denied patrons a wedding cake because of their sexual orientation, and whether that denial wronged gay people). Corvino's approach isn't just conceptually sloppier. It makes his job easier. It leaves no room for asking whether there is, in any given case, a meaningful difference between beliefs about people with a certain trait and beliefs about associated actions. It gives Corvino a shortcut to the conclusion that the refusals discussed here contribute to dignitary harm—that it's reasonable to interpret them as focused on a certain group, and reflective of harmful attitudes or beliefs about them.

But it's an open question—and one's concept of "discrimination" should leave entirely open—whether it's fair to read the belief that, for example, nonconjugal sex is immoral as supported by the idea that gay people count for less. To show that requires argument, which we've challenged Corvino to offer. He has made his job on this score easier by simply *collapsing* invidious, status-focused distinctions into ones based on associated actions—by dissolving the question he has refused squarely to address.

Lastly, Corvino says that Christian bakers deny to gay people "the very same items" they would sell to others, and that this counts as "avoiding contact with gay people on equal terms."

That is an astonishing claim with absurd results. A baker refuses to sell an off-the-shelf cake for a banquet celebrating Benjamin Netanyahu's service as Israeli prime minister, out of objections to his (and Israel's) policies. Is the baker an anti-Semite? Say she refuses the very same cake to a group of Christian pastors meeting to celebrate their victory on California Proposition 8, which enshrined traditional marriage. Is she "avoiding contact with [Christians] on equal terms"? These questions answer themselves.

5.2.2 About That Cake

When Corvino finally turns to a concrete example of what he considers SOGI discrimination in the marketplace, his policy conclusions prove a bad fit with his own instincts.

Corvino retells the story of Rachel and Laurel Bowman-Cryer and their successful $135,000 lawsuit against Aaron and Melissa Klein. He recounts that Rachel and her mother left the Kleins' store after Aaron declined to bake a same-sex wedding cake. When Rachel's mother returned to tell Aaron what she thought of his views, he quoted the Bible in a way that deeply offended her. That offense makes this incident the most useful for Corvino's view. But Corvino wouldn't ban offensive speech. So his focus on this incident only serves to highlight that speech often does more emotional harm than conscience.

As we have noted, progressives apply a double standard in treating offensiveness and emotional pain as reasons to override conscience and religion, but not free speech. Corvino replies that the real divide is between action and speech. Actions do more harm than speech, so we restrict only freedom of action. But that's false. The law restricts some speech, too—like incitement to violence. In short, we all agree the state should sometimes limit religion *and* speech to curb *concrete* harms. The question is why we should *further* limit religious liberty based on dignitary harms—given that we refuse to limit *speech* on that basis *at all*. Why the double standard of counting dignitary harms against religion but never speech? Corvino has completely sidestepped *that* question, and it has no answer. He also notes that with both religion and speech, he opposes direct burdens but allows some incidental ones. Again, that doesn't show why incidental burdens should be imposed on religion, but not on speech, for the sake of reducing dignitary harm.

In fact, Corvino wouldn't even ban the Kleins' refusal to bake custom cakes, since they involve speech and artistic expression. But to protect conscience only where it overlaps with speech and expression is to let conscience drop out of the picture. The same collapse of moral or religious objections into merely expressive ones occurs when Corvino repeatedly misreads the concerns of such wedding professionals. At first he quibbles with their views on complicity: "Normally, one is complicit in something by causally contributing to it or failing to prevent it when one ought to have done so," whereas in these cases "marriage happens with or without cake."

But people reasonably worry about complicity even when the objectionable action would happen without them. To dramatize the point, think of a physician who refuses in conscience to assist at an execution, knowing that it'll happen either way. The concern of professionals discussed here is not that they would be causing a wedding, but that they would be forced to participate in or help celebrate it.

Still second-guessing the claimant, Corvino dismisses this concern, too. He points out that allowing the Kleins to post a sign indicating their objections, while forcing them to bake, would give them distance from any "celebratory message." Here again, he collapses their conscience claim into a category with which he is evidently more at ease: speech. But their concern—like the progressive physician's and the pacifist's—is not simply that others might mistake their true beliefs; it's that participating itself violates their convictions. Corvino's view about what their conscience *should* tell them about complicity doesn't change what it actually says. He notes that abortion and capital punishment are much more serious matters than sexuality and marriage. That is right and irrelevant. Our analogy is meant to show that complicity is about more than sending the wrong message—that you can't always cancel it by announcing your objections. This point has nothing to do with the gravity of the action to which one objects.

In fact, this is all a distraction. Under RFRA-like regimes, the Kleins' case could be resolved without relying at all on the concept of complicity, as we argued in discussing the Little Sisters case. All a court would need to know is whether the Kleins believed it sinful—a violation of their religion—to bake the cake. The court would then pick up where the Kleins' conscience left off. The question for the court would be whether fining people hundreds of thousands of dollars for avoiding what they think sinful is a "substantial burden" on their religion. The only sensible answer is yes. The last question to ask is whether forcing the Kleins to violate their conscience was the least restrictive means to a compelling public interest. The answer to that is pretty clear, too.

5.2.3 Parade of Horribles

At several points, Corvino says that our principles would lead to absurdity. In each case, the parade of horribles is a phantom. Sometimes he thinks that only certain legal barriers would keep back the parade—and some of those walls are phantoms, too. No one notices their absence because they aren't needed: most awful discrimination is contained by some mix of culture and commercial incentive.

Thus, our essay argues that county clerks should be free to recuse themselves from issuing marriage licenses against their conscience so long as they cause no one embarrassment or delay. Corvino raises the cases of Mr. Bardwell, Ms. Ingroup, Ms. Lifelong, Mr. Burqa, and Mr. Dawkins-Hitchens. But the North Carolina law we held up as an example *already* allows recusals in these cases—without harm to anyone. Thus, a federal judge just dismissed a lawsuit against that law brought by gay and inter-racial couples, ruling that it caused them no cognizable injury.[12] And note that Corvino's preferred custom-product exemption would apply to bakeries run by the same characters driving his objections to our view.

Occasionally, Corvino sees that the slopes aren't so slip-pery. Writing elsewhere on a proposal to allow businesses to post signs indicating objections to same-sex sexual relation-ships, he pointed out that "businesses are currently allowed to make such postings, and hardly any do."[13] The same goes for most of the forms of discrimination we would all con-sider heinous. The federal Civil Rights Act of 1964 doesn't apply to bakeries. Yet racial discrimination isn't rampant at Dunkin' Donuts, not least because all incentives are aligned against it. Federal law allows restaurants of any size to refuse to admit women. It allows theaters and stadiums to turn away Democrats just for being Democrats. And yet culture and commerce prevent these and other forms of discrimination, without any help from the law.

But while Corvino wants to pass certain laws to meet phantom threats, he laments some of the real-world effects those laws have, once passed. Speaking of Barronelle Stutzman, the florist fined for declining to make floral arrangements for the wedding of a gay man she had served for years, Corvino says her state's antidiscrimination laws are "good laws" but that "there were better ways to handle this situation." That reply would work if Stutzman's case—a refusal to serve a same-sex wedding, on grounds of conscience—were an aberration. But as we'll see, it is a *central target* of SOGI laws for businesses.

REPLY TO CORVINO | **255**

Corvino cannot object to this use of these laws, establish no serious alternative need to justify having them, and then insist that having them is essential.

Corvino notes our agreement that sexual desire is irrelevant to a host of market transactions (and therefore unjust to consider in deciding how to treat someone), but says we "fail to connect the dots" between the injustice of such refusals and the need for certain SOGI laws. But we would support legal remedies precisely where discrimination is pervasive enough to make a concrete difference to LGBT people's access to markets for labor or essential services, so long as the law defined "discrimination" to target identified harms, and not the reasonable policies of schools, charities, and wedding professionals. So we aren't being "coy," as he says. We devote thousands of words to specifying what we oppose and why—and what we'd support, based on what sort of empirical evidence.

Corvino says SOGI laws are less about cakes than "access to employment, housing, and basic goods and services." We agree that these essential needs, if unmet, would require a policy response. We simply think those needs *are* met—and that most SOGI law supporters agree. As evidence, we cited the fact that SOGI advocates would refuse an offer to immediately pass bills targeted to securing those essentials, if that meant having to wait longer for the chance to punish and delegitimize the views of people like Barronelle Stutzman and organizations like Catholic Charities. (They wouldn't hold out for wider bans tomorrow if they really thought LGBT people were being denied essentials today.) Corvino admits as much when he says candidly that our challenge asks progressives to "negotiate against [them]selves."

He answers that challenge by pointing to SOGI law advocates' support for the "Utah Compromise." But first, that law didn't define SOGI discrimination as we've argued one should in order to target essential LGBT needs without cutting into other interests; it relied on exemptions. Second, reactions even to those exemptions beautifully illustrate our point. In *Slate*, three law professors who advocate for SOGI laws said that the Utah's law's "troubling exemptions" made it a terrible "model for the nation."[14] The LGBT editor of *ThinkProgress* denounced it as a "Dangerous LGBT Trojan Horse" because its exemptions "actually directly contradict the intention of the legislation by allowing for discrimination."[15] Translation: The "intention" of SOGI laws is to punish entities that serve all comers but live by dissenting views on marriage and childrearing. But if you have any last doubts, recall the 2016 speech by LGBT advocate Jonathan Rauch: "I said reasonable religious accommodations are something we should embrace as a cause, not resent as a concession. At the time, I got hearing. But that door, which was never more than just ajar, has closed. The strong consensus today in the LGBT world is that religious accommodations are a license to discriminate and are by their very nature a concession."[16] So the point of our challenge to SOGI supporters, though lost on Corvino, has already been conceded by Rauch and exemplified, he laments, by the "consensus" of his allies.

5.2.4 Beyond Cakes

Corvino's affirmative argument that SOGI laws are needed for access to essentials rests on a few data points—on self-reported experiences of discrimination, on a straight–gay pay gap, and on a 1.5 percent higher poverty rate for lesbian couples. He offers not a word on what drives these numbers or whether they're shrinking even without the law.

Indeed, his evidence may be outdated—all coming before the two Supreme Court rulings on marriage. Today, insofar as there is a gay–straight pay gap, evidence suggests it goes *the other way*. An August 2016 report from the U.S. Treasury—based on tax returns, not self-reports of discrimination—shows opposite-sex couples earning on average $113,115, compared to $123,995 for lesbian couples and $175,590 for gay male couples. For couples with children, the gap is even more dramatic: $104,475 for opposite-sex couples, but $130,865 for lesbian couples, and $274,855 for gay couples.[17]

But even taken at face value, Corvino's bullet points alone don't justify legal coercion. It's as if, to justify coercing law-school admissions offices, we cited data showing that lawyers were disproportionately Democrats—without asking what drove the gap, whether markets and culture might close it more efficiently, what *sort* of policy could do the job if not, and at what collateral cost. We address each of these issues in the SOGI context. Corvino catapults over them all to conclude that SOGI laws should coerce private actors; forbid distinctions based on moral convictions about marriage, sex, and bodily integrity as much as demeaning ideas about LGBT people; and apply to schools, charities, professionals, and civil servants with only the narrowest exceptions. Indeed, on schools and charities, two of the four flashpoints we discuss at length, he says almost nothing, and nowhere faces up to how they'd fare under policies he favors. All while admitting that the traditional views he thinks harmful to LGBT people are fast receding on their own. When corporate giants like the NBA, the NCAA, the NFL, Apple, Salesforce, Delta, and the Coca-Cola Company threaten to boycott states over laws merely giving believers their day in court, it's hard to see the case for coercing them to achieve progressives' social goals. We didn't just say so, but offered analyses that Corvino excuses himself from addressing by rebutting libertarian ideas we already reject.

5.2.5 Kim Davis

Corvino accuses Kim Davis of repeating the Puritan mistake. But as he later acknowledges, she asked lawmakers—*before* the

U.S. Supreme Court's ruling on marriage—to find a way to respect clerks' consciences *and* guarantee any eligible couple a license without inconvenience or delay. Corvino confesses it's "hard to argue with" this win-win—later granted by another governor—"but not impossible." He "worr[ies] about the message" it sends. But the government's message on marriage is clear; that's why the conflict exists. The only message sent by accommodations is that conscience also matters.

Here as elsewhere, Corvino would protect only convictions that pass his own tests for rigor. He accuses Davis of getting her religion wrong by "selectively cit[ing] the Bible." Corvino, a former Catholic, reaches what we as practicing Catholics think a sound reading of the Bible. But alas, Protestants aren't Catholics. That doesn't make them hypocrites.[18] If religious liberty were only the liberty to act on beliefs that outsiders considered reasonable for you to hold, it wouldn't do much.

5.3 MORAL AND RELIGIOUS INTEGRITY

5.3.1 Integrity

We are puzzled by which rationales for "singling out" religion Corvino engages. He says little about our main rationale, while devoting considerable space to rebutting the idea that religion is a proxy for especially deep commitments—an odd choice, since it originated among academic *opponents* of giving religion special treatment.[19] Corvino ends up saying that the "best reason" to protect religious liberty is to watch for laws that "squeeze[] minorities." Would he really be quicker to grant Amish conscience claims than evangelical ones? Would he sooner exempt from zoning laws the Quaker meetinghouse than the synagogue? If he doesn't accept these implications of his primary rationale for religious liberty, why not?

Our own rationale centers on the fact that religion and moral integrity are basic goods, to which the state denies citizens adequate access when it coerces conscience, which it shouldn't do needlessly. Corvino demurs: from the fact that it's good for people to harmonize actions with moral convictions, he says, "it does not follow that the rest of us should make it easy for [them] to do so." Agreed. It only follows that others have *a* reason to do so. We say that other considerations can override the reason to help a person live by integrity, and even that it can require us to pass laws that keep him from doing so. This hardly shows that integrity (even for mistaken beliefs) counts for nothing. You needn't agree with our conclusions about the value of integrity to see that Corvino's objections are simply targeting a different view.

He continues: "In addition to caring about people's internal harmony, we should also care about their getting things right." Agreed again: You're better off in *one* respect when you align your actions with your convictions (compared to not doing so). You're better off still when you align your actions and your convictions both with the truth. (Indeed, sometimes acting with integrity based on faulty views may be worse for your life overall.) It's just that, when you've tried your best to discern the truth but remain in error, that superior realization of integrity will be inaccessible then and there (though superior for you all the same).

Then does integrity not matter in itself? Might integrity be a part of your flourishing only when the underlying belief is true? This view is woefully inadequate. Imagine a Jew forced to eat pork, or a death penalty opponent forced to do the injecting. She will feel violated. Suppose you yourself are a Gentile, or a supporter of capital punishment. Should your only concern be that this sordid episode might have upset the person's feelings?

Has she not been otherwise harmed? If so, then integrity matters in itself—even if Jews are mistaken about pork; even if capital punishment is just; and even if, as we argued, aligning actions *and* beliefs with the truth is better still.

Corvino tries to split the difference. He thinks living by erroneous beliefs has inherent value, but only if the beliefs aren't *too* badly off. How would he measure your belief's distance from the truth? And how far can it veer before living by it plummets from being inherently enriching for you, to being worthless? The more natural view here, by far, is that living even by mistaken beliefs makes you better off in one way, even if it creates other harms.

5.3.2 God

Corvino never engages our parallel argument on the value of *religious* integrity (nor even mentions the second reason we offer for religious freedom: its fostering of other civil liberties and civil society). He repeatedly misunderstands our argument about religion as a *basic* good (of *intrinsic* value) as if it were about religion's instrumental benefits: "There is no doubt that religion does all of these things, and does them well." This allows him to treat the harmful consequences it has had as points against our main argument. (As for those harms, we repeatedly say that religious liberty is both limited and justified by justice and the common good.) Earlier we saw that Corvino could only appreciate religious conscience by collapsing it into speech and expression. Now we see that he can only understand religion's value in terms of its *instrumental* purposes.

He isn't alone. Many scholars today are liable—against the classical liberal tradition—to deny religious liberty protection where it doesn't overlap with other values. Maybe they see no transcendent being to achieve harmony *with*, no basic good to protect. For the secularist, this whole realm of human pursuit is based on delusion, and valuable only instrumentally—and only if its benefits outweigh its costs.

Given these intellectual causes of religious liberty's collapse, we should say a word on theism. In an academic culture for which atheism is the default, it's easy to forget that it has been history's greatest thinkers who have offered the most salient arguments for God's existence. Most begin from ordinary experiences and observations and reason up to a higher cause. That's the approach of Plato in the *Laws* and Aristotle in the *Metaphysics* and countless others across two and a half millennia.

One approach is the cosmological argument,[20] which begins with the insight that this world cannot account for itself. It's contingent. It could have not been. The point isn't simply that the Big Bang might never have gone off. Even if the universe were eternal, the question would remain of *why* there was something all along, rather than nothing at all. The second step is to notice that reason demands explanations except where it shows that none is possible. So it leads us here to a reality that explains the whole natural (contingent) world—but which can't be just another thing within it.

In this way, reasoned reflection points to the existence of something that needs no explanation but explains the existence of all contingent reality. It leads us to a necessary being: one that *had* to exist, so that no further explanation of its existence is possible (or, thus, rationally compelled). A being that—unlike everything in our experience—exists by its essence, lacking all trace of mere potential. But because that being is necessary while the world it causes is contingent, the causal link between them must itself be contingent. It must have been possible for the necessary being *not* to give rise to the contingent world. And yet its causing or not can't be determined by anything outside it, since it is after all the cause of everything else. So: the necessary being ultimately responsible for the existence of all things must be free, and therefore capable of harmony with other free beings.

So it is that for Aquinas, religion is a *natural* human good, available to all, and a duty owed by all to the creator. As if to illustrate the point, the pagan Cicero long before him wrote of religion as the homage paid to "a superior nature that men call divine."

Indeed, as Aquinas saw, arguments for the God sustaining us in existence double as arguments for divine worship and obedience as matters of justice. For they show that in the very deepest sense, we depend on God, who quite literally made us who we are. On top of it all, then, protecting religious liberty enables us to fulfill a duty of justice.

Thus does one of the founding era's arguments for this civil liberty, from Washington and Madison on down, find support in the perennial philosophy of the West. And it was that philosophy, with its tendency to point to a source of meaning beyond itself, and a source of moral limits beyond the state, that led to the idea of religious liberty, and the flowering of civil society, and the articulation and defense of the other civil liberties that shield us all, individuals and communities, from the state's besetting temptation to commit the Puritan mistake.

ACKNOWLEDGMENTS

FROM ALL THE AUTHORS

We wish to extend our sincere gratitude to Peter Ohlin and the superb staff at Oxford University Press, as well as to anonymous reviewers.

This book benefited from three workshops while in progress, and we would like to thank the participants, many of whom offered detailed comments on drafts:

At Wayne State University, with support from the College of Liberal Arts and Sciences and the Office of the Vice President for Research: Jonathan Cottrell, Joseph Dunne, Ryan Fanselow, Cody Gomez, Eric Hiddleston, Katherine Kim, Timothy Kirschenheiter, Andrew Koppelman, Christopher Lund, Mark Navin, Brad Roth, Bruce Russell, Michael Weber, and Kevin Vallier.

At Princeton University, with support from the James Madison Program: Stephanos Bibas, Matt Franck, Robert P. George, Marci Hamilton, Daniel Mark, Matt O'Brien, Karen Rupprecht,

David Skeel, and R. J. Snell. Dwight Newman provided additional comments, though unable to attend the workshop.

At the Heritage Foundation: Stephanie Barclay, David Boaz, Rebecca Kukla, Meghan Page, Christen Price, Mark Rienzi, Gene Schaerr, and Tim Schultz.

FROM JOHN CORVINO

I want to thank to Ryan T. Anderson and Sherif Girgis for agreeing to this project, and for their perseverance, graciousness, and intellectual rigor throughout.

I learned a great deal from my students at Wayne State University in seminars I conducted on this topic in the fall of 2014, the fall of 2015, and the fall of 2016. I am also grateful to audiences at the University of Colorado, Boulder, the University of Missouri–Kansas City, the University of Texas at Austin, Georgetown University, Wayne State University's Humanities Center and Center for the Study of Citizenship, and the University of Leuven, for helpful discussion of material that eventually found its way into the book.

In addition to the various workshop participants mentioned above—several of whom (especially Andy Koppelman) provided ongoing discussion long after the workshops were over—I would like to thank the following: John Adentire, Matthew Lee Anderson, David Blankenhorn, David Boonin, Amir Brown, Dale Carpenter, Sewell Chan, Greta Christina, Robin Dembroff, Maggie Gallagher, Arthur A. Gianelli, Jeremy Hooper, Timothy Hulsey, Dan Johnson, David Link, Lawrence B. Lombard, Simon Căbulea May, Judi O'Kelley, David Lat, Douglas Laycock, Brian Leiter, Kyle Luebke, Stephen Macedo, Clancy Martin, Carlos Maza, Martha Nussbaum, Walter Olson, Michael Perry, Jonathan Rauch, Frank Ravitch, Soraya (Layla)

Saatchi, Justin Sledge, Tara Smith, Mark Joseph Stern, Adam Teicholz, Jonah Wacholder, Lori Watson, Josh Wilburn, Robin Fretwell Wilson, Evan Wolfson, and Robert J. Yanal. Some commented on particular arguments or sections; others read the full manuscript, sometimes in multiple iterations; all made the book, and my thinking, better than it would otherwise have been. Of course, the errors remaining are mine.

I am indebted to Thomas Wood for invaluable research assistance over the last year, with additional assistance from Joseph Dunne. I am constantly indebted to my colleagues in the Wayne State University Philosophy Department for providing me with a lively, rigorous, and collegial working environment.

Finally, my gratitude to my friends, my family, and especially my husband, Mark, for their patience as I buried myself in this project.

FROM RYAN T. ANDERSON AND SHERIF GIRGIS

Above all we wish to thank John Corvino, who for years has been a friend and brilliant sparring partner—and each thanks in part to the other.

We're also grateful to several people who offered helpful feedback on arguments or drafts, including Matt Bowman, Justin Dyer, Ben Eidelson, Rick Garnett, Gabrielle Girgis, John Inazu, and Phillip Munoz. Special thanks, too, to workshop participants who took the trouble to follow up with more insights, heaping favor upon favor: Andy Koppelman, Mark Rienzi, Tim Schultz, and Kevin Vallier.

Thanks to the Heritage Foundation for allowing Anderson to take some time for the book; and to Alliance Defending Freedom and the Becket Fund for Religious Liberty for the generous help and support of their staff, and for their important work on these causes.

We also thank Jennifer Marshall and Roger Severino, Anderson's bosses; Melody Wood, his excellent research assistant; and John Malcolm (head of the Heritage Foundation's legal department) and Matthew Kacsmaryk (of First Liberty Institute) for their help on legal matters.

NOTES

Chapter 1

1. See Evan Wolfson, "What's Next in the Fight for Gay Equality?," *New York Times*, June 26, 2015, http://www.nytimes.com/2015/06/27/opinion/evan-wolfson-whats-next-in-the-fight-for-gay-equality.html?_r=1.
2. See Ryan T. Anderson, *Truth Overruled: The Future of Marriage and Religious Freedom* (Washington, DC: Regnery, 2015).
3. The key portion reads: "No one may, in public places, wear clothing that is designed to conceal the face," but the intended target of the law is clear from its legislative history. See SAS v. France, no. 43835/11, dec. 01/07/2014, 36 BHRC 617.
4. Church of Lukumi Babalu Aye v. Hialeah, 508 U.S. 520 (1993).
5. Church of Lukumi Babalu Aye v. Hialeah, 508 U.S. 520 (1993).
6. Pierce v. Society of Sisters, 268 U.S. 510–1925.
7. Worthington Chauncey Ford, ed., *Journals of the Continental Congress, 1774–1779*, vol. 5 (Washington: U.S. Government Printing Office, 1906), 189.
8. Quoted in Mark Hall, "Religious Accommodations and the Common Good," Heritage Foundation, Backgrounder #3058, October 26, 2015, n. 28, http://www.heritage.org/research/reports/2015/10/religious-accommodations-and-the-common-good#_ftn28.

9. Hall, "Religious Accommodations and the Common Good," n. 30, http://www.heritage.org/research/reports/2015/10/religious-accommodations-and-the-common-good#_ftn30.
10. Reynolds v. United States, 98 U.S. 145 (1879).
11. Reynolds v. United States, 98 U.S. 145, 162 (1879).
12. Reynolds v. United States, 98 U.S. 145, 162 (1879).
13. Sherbert v. Verner, 374 U.S. 398 (1963).
14. Wisconsin v. Yoder, 406 U.S. 205 (1972).
15. Sherbert v. Verner, 374 U.S. 398, 401 (1963).
16. Sherbert v. Verner, 374 U.S. 398, 404 (1963).
17. United States v. Lee, 455 U.S. 252, 257–58 (1982).
18. McDaniel v. Paty, 435 U.S. 618 (1978).
19. Employment Division, Department of Human Resources of Oregon v. Smith, 494 U.S. 872 (1990).
20. See Nussbaum, *Liberty of Conscience: In Defense of America's Tradition of Religious Equality* (New York: Basic Books, 2010), 149–50.
21. *Employment Div., Dept. of Human Resources of Ore. v. Smith*, 494 U.S. 872, 880 (1990) (internal citations omitted).
22. *Employment Div., Dept. of Human Resources of Ore. v. Smith*, 494 U.S. 872, 885 (1990) (internal citations omitted).
23. Peter Steinfels, "Clinton Signs Law Protecting Religious Practices," *New York Times*, November 17, 1993, http://www.nytimes.com/1993/11/17/us/clinton-signs-law-protecting-religious-practices.html.
24. http://www.presidency.ucsb.edu/ws/index.php?pid=46124&st=religious+freedom+restoration+act&st1.
25. City of Boerne v. Flores, 521 US 507 (1997).
26. See Ryan T. Anderson, *Truth Overruled: The Future of Marriage and Religious Freedom* (Washington, DC: Regnery, 2015), 115–16.
27. See Anderson, *Truth Overruled*, 116–17, citing Douglas Laycock.

Chapter 2

1. For background to the case, see Sarah Barringer Gordon, *The Mormon Question: Polygamy and Constitutional Conflict in Nineteenth-Century America*, 1st new ed. (Chapel Hill, NC: University of North Carolina Press, 2002), 114–32.

2. Gordon, *Mormon Question*, 114.
3. Reynolds v. United States, 98 U.S. 145, 162 (1879).
4. Reynolds, 98 U.S. 145, 166–67 (1879).
5. For contemporary criticisms of antipolygamy laws, see Richard A. Vazquez, "The Practice of Polygamy: Legitimate Free Exercise of Religion or Legitimate Public Menace—Revisiting Reynolds in Light of Modern Constitutional Jurisprudence Note," *New York University Journal of Legislation and Public Policy* 5 (2001): 225–54. I have previously expressed doubts about the wisdom of legalizing polygamy, although I am currently agnostic on the question. See John Corvino, "Homosexuality and the PIB Argument," *Ethics* 115, no. 3 (2005): 501–34, doi:10.1086/428456; John Corvino and Maggie Gallagher, *Debating Same-Sex Marriage* (New York: Oxford University Press, 2012).
6. Obergefell v. Hodges, 135 S. Ct. 2071 (2015).
7. "Kim Davis Denied Marriage Licenses for Her Friends," *ABC News*, September 23, 2015, http://abcnews.go.com/US/kentucky-clerk-kim-davis-denied-marriage-licenses-friends/story?id=33939041.
8. Alan Blinder and Richard Pérez-peña, "Kentucky Clerk Denies Same-Sex Marriage Licenses, Defying Court," *New York Times*, September 1, 2015, http://www.nytimes.com/2015/09/02/us/same-sex-marriage-kentucky-kim-davis.html.
9. Tony Lee, "Mike Huckabee: We Must Stand with Kim Davis against 'Criminalization of Christianity,'" *Breitbart*, September 7, 2015, http://www.breitbart.com/big-government/2015/09/07/mike-huckabee-we-must-stand-with-kim-davis-against-criminalization-of-christianity/, accessed July 10, 2016.
10. Of course, there were subquestions in that debate too, and some of them were quite nuanced and difficult. But the main question was clear and simple, unlike here.
11. Eugene Volokh explains the ins and outs of the case in Volokh, "When Does Your Religion Legally Excuse You from Doing Part of Your Job?," September 4, 2015, https://www.washingtonpost.com/news/volokh-conspiracy/wp/2015/09/04/when-does-your-religion-legally-excuse-you-from-doing-part-of-your-job/?utm_term=.027ee99f3822.
12. Volokh, "When Does Your Religion Excuse?"
13. Wisconsin v. Yoder, 406 U.S. 205 (1972).

14. Aleksandra Sandstrom, "Nearly All States Allow Religious Exemptions for Vaccinations," *Pew Research Center*, July 16, 2015, http://www.pewresearch.org/fact-tank/2015/07/16/nearly-all-states-allow-religious-exemptions-for-vaccinations/. In forty-six states, the exemptions are religion-specific; in Minnesota they are broader, thus including nonreligious exemptions. I'm indebted to Mark Navin for discussion on this point.

15. Burwell v. Hobby Lobby Stores, Inc., 134 S. Ct. 2751 (2014).

16. See, for example, The Jesus Center v. Farmington Hills Zoning Board of Appeals, 544 N. W. 2d 698 (Mich. Ct. App. 1996). Although *Boerne v. Flores* ruled that RFRA, the law under which this case was decided, was not applicable to the states, RLUIPA effectively revived such application of RFRA. See 42 U.S.C. § 2000cc et seq. (2000).

17. U.S. Department of Health and Human Services, "Clergy as Mandatory Reporters of Child Abuse and Neglect," Children's Bureau, 2015, Child Welfare Information Gateway, 3, https://www.childwelfare.gov/pubPDFs/clergymandated.pdf.

18. For an argument to this effect, see Richard A. Vazquez, "The Practice of Polygamy: Legitimate Free Exercise of Religion or Legitimate Public Menace—Revisiting Reynolds in Light of Modern Constitutional Jurisprudence Note," *New York University Journal of Legislation and Public Policy* 5 (2002): 225–54.

19. Douglas Laycock, "Religious Liberty as Liberty," *Journal of Contemporary Legal Issues* 7, no. 2 (1996): 313–56.

20. See John Corvino, *What's Wrong with Homosexuality?* (Oxford: Oxford University Press, 2013), chap. 2.

21. Torcaso v. Watkins, 367 U.S. 488 (1961). Note that similar requirements remain on the books in a handful of states but are considered unenforceable after *Torcaso*.

22. Everson v. Board of Ed. of Ewing, 330 U.S. 1, 16 (1947).

23. Engel v. Vitale, 370 U.S. 421 (1962) and Abington School Dist. v. Schempp, 374 US 203 (1962).

24. Campbell Robertson, "Roy Moore, Alabama Chief Justice, Suspended over Gay Marriage Order," *New York Times*, October 1, 2016, http://www.nytimes.com/2016/10/01/us/roy-moore-alabama-chief-justice.html?_r=0.

25. Heather Long, "The Sunday Blues: Some US States Don't Seem to Realize Prohibition Is Over," *Guardian*, March 3, 2013, sec. "Comment Is Free," http://www.theguardian.com/commentis-free/2013/mar/03/no-sunday-alcohol-sales-states-prohibition.

26. Jamie LaReau, "The Battle over Sunday Sales," *Automotive News*, May 3, 2015, http://www.autonews.com/article/20150503/RETAIL07/304279869/the-battle-over-sunday-sales.

27. "Code of the Borough of Paramus, NJ," https://law.resource.org/pub/us/code/city/nj/Paramus.html#8544536, accessed July 10, 2016.

28. J. B. MacKinnon, "America's Last Ban on Sunday Shopping," *New Yorker*, February 7, 2015, http://www.newyorker.com/business/currency/americas-last-ban-sunday-shopping.

29. Ira C. Lupu and Robert W. Tuttle, *Secular Government, Religious People* (Grand Rapids, MI: Eerdmans, 2014), 191–92; Braunfeld v. Brown, 366 U.S. 599 (1961).

30. As Justice Douglas wrote in his dissent to *McGowan v. Maryland*, one of the "blue laws" cases: "No matter how much is written, no matter what is said, the parentage of these laws is the Fourth Commandment, and they serve and satisfy the religious predispositions of our Christian communities." McGowan v. Maryland, 366 U.S. 420, 572–73 (1961), 366.

31. The Court actually cites the "pure minded women" phrase from the lower court's ruling and rejects *Reynolds*'s contention that it is prejudicial. See Reynolds v. United States, 98 U.S. 145, 168 (1879).

32. *Reynolds*, 98 U.S. 145, 167 (1879).

33. Sherbert v. Verner, 374 U.S. 398 (1963).

34. Sherbert v. Verner, 374 U.S. 398, 404 (1963), 374.

35. See for example p. 140 in this volume.

36. Sherbert v. Verner, 374 U.S. 398, 416 (1963).

37. Sherbert v. Verner, 374 U.S. 398, 406 (1963).

38. Unfortunately, Brennan identifies this argument as merely a secondary point: "The unconstitutionality of the disqualification of the sabbatarian is thus *compounded by* the religious discrimination which South Carolina's general statutory scheme necessarily effects" (emphasis added). Sherbert v. Verner, 374 U.S. 398, 406 (1963).

39. Ira Lupu and Robert Tuttle have made a similar point. See *Secular Government, Religious People*, esp. 191–92.
40. Sherbert v. Verner, 374 U.S. 398, 413 (1963).
41. Employment Div., Dept. of Human Resources of Ore. v. Smith, 494 U.S. 872 (1990).
42. Employment Div., Dept. of Human Resources of Ore. v. Smith, 494 U.S. 872 (1990).
43. Employment Div., Dept. of Human Resources of Ore. v. Smith, 494 U.S. 872 (1990) (internal citations omitted).
44. For more on this legislative approach, see Marci A. Hamilton, "The Case for Evidence-Based Free Exercise Accommodation: Why the Religious Freedom Restoration Act Is Bad Public Policy," *Harvard Law & Policy Review* 9, no. 13 (2015).
45. Oregon Revised Statutes 475.752(4).
46. Phillip Gunn et al., H.B. 1523 Protecting Freedom of Conscience from Government Discrimination Act, 2016, https://legiscan.com/MS/text/HB1523/id/1382645.
47. Phillip Gunn et al., H.B. 1523 Protecting Freedom of Conscience from Government Discrimination Act, 2016. https://legiscan.com/MS/text/HB1523/id/1382645.
48. Barber v. Bryant, No. 16-CV-417-CWR-LRA, 16-CV-442-CWR-LRA (S.D. Miss. June 30, 2016).
49. *Religious Liberty and H.R. 2802, the First Amendment Defense Act (FADA), Hearing on H.R. 2802, Committee on Oversight and Government Reform.* 114th U.S. Congress, House of Representatives. July 12, 2016. Testimony of Professor Katherine Franke. https://oversight.house.gov/wp-content/uploads/2016/07/2016-07-12-Franke-Columbia-Law-Testimony.pdf (internal citations omitted).
50. *Religious Liberty and H.R. 2802*, 2.
51. *Religious Liberty and H.R. 2802*, 2.
52. *Religious Liberty and H.R. 2802*, 2.
53. *Religious Liberty and H.R. 2802*, 2–3.
54. *Religious Liberty and H.R. 2802*, 3.
55. *Religious Liberty and H.R. 2802*, 3.
56. *Religious Liberty and H.R. 2802*, 3.
57. *Religious Liberty and H.R. 2802*, 3.
58. *Religious Liberty and H.R. 2802*, 3.

59. FADA § 6(3)(D).

60. Samuel Smith, "FRC Withdraws Support for Bill to Protect Gay Marriage Opponents' Religious Freedom after It's Weakened in Congress," *Christian Post*, July 15, 2016, http://www.christianpost.com/news/frc-withdraws-support-bill-gay-marriage-opponents-religious-freedom-congress-fada-166504/.

61. "Hobby Lobby Stores on the Forbes America's Largest Private Companies List," *Forbes*, http://www.forbes.com/companies/hobby-lobby-stores/, accessed September 22, 2016.

62. "Our Story," Hobby Lobby, http://www.hobbylobby.com/about-us/our-story, accessed July 10, 2016.

63. Cathy Lynn Grossman, "What's Abortifacient? Disputes over Birth Control Fuel Obamacare Fight," *Washington Post*, January 28, 2014, https://perma-archives.org/warc/P767-8SPN/http://www.washingtonpost.com/national/religion/whats-abortifacient-disputes-over-birth-control-fuel-obamacare-fight/2014/01/28/61f080be-886a-11e3-a760-a86415d0944d_story.html, accessed July 10, 2016.

64. Jamie Mason, "What an Abortifacient Is—and What It Isn't," *National Catholic Reporter*, February 20, 2012, https://www.ncronline.org/blogs/grace-margins/what-abortifacient-and-what-it-isnt, accessed July 10, 2016.

65. Stephanie Pappas, "Fact Check: Yes, Pregnancy Can Kill," *Live Science*, October 19, 2012, http://www.livescience.com/24127-fact-check-walsh-pregnancy-can-kill.html, accessed July 10, 2016.

66. Burwell v. Hobby Lobby Stores, Inc., 134 S. Ct. 2751, 2763 (2014).

67. The phrase was coined by Gerald Gunther, "Foreword: In Search of Evolving Doctrine on a Changing Court: A Model for a Newer Equal Protection," *Harvard Law Review* 86 (1972): 1–48.

68. Employment Div., Dept. of Human Resources of Ore. v. Smith, 494 U.S. 872, 888 (1990) (internal citations omitted).

69. See Lupu, "*Hobby Lobby* and the Dubious Enterprise of Religious Exemptions," *Harvard Women's Law Journal* 38, no. 2012 (2015): 84, esp. 54; Hamilton, "The Case for Evidence-Based Free Exercise Accommodation."

70. City of Boerne v. Flores, 521 U.S. 507 (1997).

71. Burwell v. Hobby Lobby Stores, Inc., 2014, 134 S. Ct. 2751, 2761 (2014), 134.

72. Andrew Koppelman and Frederick M. Gedicks, "Is Hobby Lobby Worse for Religious Liberty than Smith?," *University of St. Thomas Journal of Law and Public Policy* (Minnesota) 9 (2014): 223, 234; William P. Marshall, "Bad Statutes Make Bad Law: Burwell v Hobby Lobby," *Supreme Court Review* 2014, no. 1 (2014): 71, 118; Noah Marks, "Least Restrictive Means: Burwell v. Hobby Lobby," *Harvard Law Policy Review Online* 9 (2015): 19.

73. Koppelman and Gedicks, "Is Hobby Lobby Worse for Religious Liberty than Smith?," 223; Marshall, "Bad Statutes Make Bad Law," 71, 118; Noah Marks, "Least Restrictive Means: Burwell v. Hobby Lobby." *Harvard Law Policy Review Online* 9 (2015): 19.

74. On this point see Koppelman and Gedicks, "Is Hobby Lobby Worse for Religious Liberty than Smith?," especially n. 40 and accompanying text.

75. Burwell v. Hobby Lobby Stores, Inc., 134 S. Ct. 2751, 2763 (2014).

76. Burwell v. Hobby Lobby Stores, Inc., 134 S. Ct. 2751, 2798–99 (2014).

77. Wheaton College v. Burwell, 134 S. Ct. 2806 (2014). For helpful discussion, see Dahlia Lithwick, Sonja West, and Aisha Harris, "Quick Change Justice," *Slate*, July 4, 2014, http://www.slate.com/articles/news_and_politics/jurisprudence/2014/07/wheaton_college_injunction_the_supreme_court_just_sneakily_reversed_itself.html.

78. Wheaton College v. Burwell, 134 S. Ct. 2806, 2808 (2014), 134.

79. Linda Greenhouse, "A Religion Case Too Far for the Supreme Court?," *New York Times*, July 23, 2015, http://www.nytimes.com/2015/07/23/opinion/linda-greenhouse-religion-case-too-far-for-the-supreme-court.html.

80. I might have a different view if Hobby Lobby had an explicitly sectarian character, like a religious bookstore or kosher supermarket, and made that character clear to prospective employees.

81. Burwell v. Hobby Lobby Stores, Inc., 134 S. Ct. 2751, 2795–96 (2014). "By law, no religion-based criterion can restrict the work force of for-profit corporations.... The distinction between a community made up of believers in the same religion and one embracing persons of diverse beliefs, clear as it is, constantly escapes the Court's attention."

82. Koppelman and Gedicks, "Is Hobby Lobby Worse for Religious Liberty than Smith?"

83. Alissa J. Rubin, "French 'Burkini' Bans Provoke Backlash as Armed Police Confront Beachgoers," *New York Times*, August 24, 2016, http://www.nytimes.com/2016/08/25/world/europe/france-burkini.html?_r=0.

84. Douglas NeJaime and Reva B. Siegel, "Conscience Wars: Complicity-Based Conscience Claims in Religion and Politics," *Yale Law Journal* 124 (2015): 2516–91.

85. United States v. Lee, 455 U.S. 252, 261 (1982).

86. Adam Liptak, "Supreme Court Says Kentucky Clerk Must Let Gay Couples Marry," *New York Times*, August 31, 2015, http://www.nytimes.com/2015/09/01/us/supreme-court-says-kentucky-clerk-must-let-gay-couples-marry.html. See also Adam Beam, "Jailed Clerk's Attorney: Marriage Licenses for Gays Are Void," *Yahoo News*, September 4, 2015, http://news.yahoo.com/gay-couples-try-wed-defiant-clerk-sits-jail-082850785.html.

87. Ryan T. Anderson, "We Don't Need Kim Davis to Be in Jail," *New York Times*, September 7, 2015, http://www.nytimes.com/2015/09/07/opinion/we-dont-need-kim-davis-to-be-in-jail.html?_r=1.

88. Bowen v. Roy, 476 U.S. 693, 703 (1986).

89. Douglas Laycock, "The Religious Freedom Restoration Act," *Brigham Young University Law Review* (1993): 221, 229–30.

90. U.S. Equal Employment Opportunity Commission, "Questions and Answers about Religious Discrimination in the Workplace," January 31, 2011, http://www.eeoc.gov/policy/docs/qanda_religion.html.

91. Mormons actually differ on whether Kolob is a star or a planet, but most agree that it is the heavenly body closest to God's physical throne.

92. "Standard Time Zones in U.S. Mark 100 Years" (Associated Press), *New York Times*, November 20, 1983, http://www.nytimes.com/1983/11/20/us/standard-time-zones-in-us-mark-100-years.html.

93. Brian Handwerk, "Time to Move On? The Case against Daylight Saving Time," *National Geographic News*, November 1, 2013, http://news.nationalgeographic.com/news/2013/11/131101-when-does-daylight-savings-time-end-november-3-science/.

94. Brian Leiter, *Why Tolerate Religion?* (Princeton: Princeton University Press, 2013), 34.

95. Michael W. McConnell, "Why Protect Religious Freedom?," review of *Why Tolerate Religion?* by Brian Leiter, *Yale Law Journal* 123, no. 3 (December 2013): 770–811, http://www.yalelawjournal.org/review/why-protect-religious-freedom, accessed July 11, 2016. For a reply from Leiter, see Brian Leiter, "Why Tolerate Religion, Again? A Reply to Michael McConnell," SSRN scholarly paper (Rochester, NY: Social Science Research Network), May 8, 2016, http://papers.ssrn.com/abstract=2777208.

96. McConnell, "Why Protect Religious Freedom?"

97. Douglas Laycock, "The Religious Exemption Debate," *Rutgers Journal of Law and Religion* 11 (2009): 139, 171.

98. Employment Div., Dept. of Human Resources of Ore. v. Smith, 494 U.S. 872, 888 (1989).

99. For the pledge, see West Virginia Bd. of Ed. v. Barnette, 319 U.S. 624 (1943). For a particular example of criticizing the government ("Fuck the draft"), see Cohen v. California, 403 U.S. 15 (1971).

100. Christopher L. Eisgruber and Lawrence G. Sager, *Religious Freedom and the Constitution* (Cambridge, MA: Harvard University Press, 2007), 82.

101. I'm indebted to Karen Stohr for this example.

102. Marci A. Hamilton, "The Case for Evidence-Based Free Exercise Accommodation: Why the Religious Freedom Restoration Act Is Bad Public Policy," *Harvard Law Policy Review* 9, no. 13 (2015): 129–60, 131.

103. See Martha Nussbaum, *Liberty of Conscience: In Defense of America's Tradition of Religious Equality* (New York: Basic Books, 2010), 127–28.

104. I see these not as constituting strict necessary and sufficient conditions but as the grounds for a holistic assessment.

105. Kyle Glatz, "Why Are Sikhs Upset over New Motorcycle Helmet Law?," *World Religion News*, September 4, 2014, http://www.worldreligionnews.com/culture/sikhs-upset-new-motorcycle-helmet-law. Canada does not have a RFRA.

106. U.S. Equal Employment Opportunity Commission, "Questions and Answers about Religious Discrimination in the Workplace."

107. Nick Reid, "Signs for Jesus case against town of Pembroke to head to federal trial," *Concord Monitor*, February 16, 2016, http://www.concordmonitor.com/Archive/2016/02/signs4jesus-cm-021616.

108. Sherbert v. Verner, 374 U.S. 398, 416 (1963).

109. See Christopher Lund, "Religion Is Special Enough," *Virginia Law Review* 103 (forthcoming).

110. United States v. Seeger, 380 U.S. 163, 166 (1965).

111. Welsh v. United States, 398 U.S. 333, 340 (1970).

112. Employment Div., Dept. of Human Resources of Ore. v. Smith, 494 U.S. 872, 887 (1990).

113. I should note that some have argued that moral obligations make no sense without God: Even though atheists may *feel* moral obligation, there's no good reason for them to do so. For a statement of this position see George Mavrodes, "Religion and the Queerness of Morality," in *Rationality, Religious Belief, and Moral Commitment: New Essays in the Philosophy of Religion*, ed. Robert Audi and William Wainwright (Ithaca, NY: Cornell University Press, 1986). For a compelling reply (though written before Mavrodes's piece), see Kai Nielsen, "Ethics without Religion," *Ohio University Review* 6 (1964): 48–62.

114. Luke W. Galen, "Does Religious Belief Promote Prosociality? A Critical Examination," *Psychological Bulletin* 138, no. 5 (September 2012): 876–906, PsycARTICLES, EBSCOhost, accessed September 3, 2016.

115. See Nussbaum, *Liberty of Conscience*.

116. Simon Căbulea May, "Exemptions for Conscience," in *Religion in Liberal Political Philosophy*, ed. A. Bardon and C. Laborde (Oxford University Press, 2017), p. 196.

117. May calls him Chester.

118. May, "Exemptions for Conscience," p. 198.

119. One might try to argue, in an Aristotelian or virtue-ethics vein, that any claim is morally significant to the extent that it is important to someone's self-conception; I set that argument aside here. For a reply to this claim, see Susan Wolf, "Moral Saints," *Journal of Philosophy* 79, no. 8 (August 1982): 419–39.

120. Steven Weinberg, "A Designer Universe?," *PhysLink.com*, http://www.physlink.com/Education/essay_weinberg.cfm, accessed July 11, 2016.

121. Nussbaum, *Liberty of Conscience*, 116.
122. Laycock, "Religious Exemption Debate," 171.
123. For discussion of such difficulties, see Eisgruber and Sager, *Religious Freedom and the Constitution*.
124. Koppelman and Gedicks, "Is Hobby Lobby Worse for Religious Liberty Than Smith?"
125. Ryan T. Anderson, "We Don't Need Kim Davis to Be in Jail," *New York Times*, September 7, 2015, http://www.nytimes.com/2015/09/07/opinion/we-dont-need-kim-davis-to-be-in-jail.html?_r=1.
126. "Interracial Couple Denied Marriage License in Tangipahoa Parish" (Associated Press), *NOLA.com*, October 16, 2009, http://www.nola.com/crime/index.ssf/2009/10/interracial_couple_denied_marr.html, accessed July 11, 2016.
127. "Interracial Couple Denied Marriage License in Tangipahoa Parish" (Associated Press), *NOLA.com*, October 16, 2009, http://www.nola.com/crime/index.ssf/2009/10/interracial_couple_denied_marr.html, accessed July 11, 2016.
128. Bardwell's reason was not overtly religious; he claimed, rather, that such unions were bad for the resulting children, who might be rejected by both black and white society. But one need not look far to find religious objections to interracial relationships; I'll discuss some shortly.
129. Bob Jones Univ. v. United States, 461 U.S. 574, 580–81 (1983).
130. Loving v. Virginia, 388 U.S. 1 (1967).
131. From the university's website: "BJU's history has been chiefly characterized by striving to achieve those goals; but like any human institution, we have failures as well. For almost two centuries American Christianity, including BJU in its early stages, was characterized by the segregationist ethos of American culture. Consequently, for far too long, we allowed institutional policies regarding race to be shaped more directly by that ethos than by the principles and precepts of the Scriptures. We conformed to the culture rather than providing a clear Christian counterpoint to it. . . . In so doing, we failed to accurately represent the Lord and to fulfill the commandment to love others as ourselves. For these failures we are profoundly sorry. Though no known antagonism toward minorities or expressions of

racism on a personal level have ever been tolerated on our campus, we allowed institutional policies to remain in place that were racially hurtful." "Statement about Race at BJU," Bob Jones University, http://www.bju.edu/about/what-we-believe/race-statement.php, accessed July 11, 2016.

132. Jones, Bob, "Is Segregation Scriptural?," November 12, 2014, Sermons of Bob Jones: A Digital History Project, https://bobjonessermons.wordpress.com/sermons/is-segregation-scriptural/.

133. "Bob Jones University Apologizes for Its Racist Past," *Journal of Blacks in Higher Education*, December 26, 2016, http://www.jbhe.com/news_views/62_bobjones.html, accessed July 11, 2016.

134. Loving v. Virginia, 388 U.S. 1 (1967).

135. Kellan Howell, "Florida 'Muslim-Free' Gun Shop Owner Wins Discrimination Suit," *Washington Times*, November 28, 2016, http://www.washingtontimes.com/news/2015/nov/28/florida-muslim-free-gun-shop-owner-wins-discrimina/, accessed July 11, 2016.

136. Leigh Remizowski, "Teacher Who Was Fired after Fertility Treatments Sues Diocese," *CNN*, April 26, 2012, http://www.cnn.com/2012/04/26/us/indiana-in-vitro-lawsuit/index.html, accessed July 11, 2016.

137. Tresa Baldas, "Pediatrician Wouldn't Care for Baby with 2 Moms," *Detroit Free Press*, February 19, 2015, http://www.freep.com/story/news/local/michigan/macomb/2015/02/18/discrimination-birth/23640315/.

138. http://abcnews.go.com/US/nj-bridal-shop-refused-sell-wedding-dress-lesbian/story?id=14342333.

139. Amy Montgomery, "Same-Sex Couple Denied a Birthday Cake by Local Bakery," *13ABC*, July 7, 2016, http://www.13abc.com/content/news/Same-sex-couple-denied-a-birthday-cake-by-local-bakery-385783221.html, accessed July 12, 2016.

140. "Ohio Bakery: No Birthday Cakes For Gay Couples" (blog entry), Joe.My.God., July 7, 2016, http://www.joemygod.com/2016/07/07/ohio-bakery-no-birthday-cakes-for-gay-couples/, accessed July 12, 2016.

141. Benjamin Eidelson, *Discrimination and Disrespect* (Oxford: Oxford University Press, 2016), 16.

142. Girgis and Anderson add an additional criterion: that discrimination "involves mistreatment based on a stable, socially salient trait, around which *many* forms of arbitrary treatment have clustered." I'm not sure that I share their linguistic intuitions here—I think it's possible to discriminate, unjustly, for quirky reasons—but I don't think anything hangs on this difference between us.

143. I think this description may be somewhat misleading. If one spends a full day trying on wedding dresses and only then is told that one cannot buy one (on grounds of being a lesbian, or planning a same-sex wedding), one is certainly worse off than when one started.

144. For further discussion, see for example Leslie Meltzer Henry, "The Jurisprudence of Dignity," *University of Pennsylvania Law Review* 160, no. 1 (2011): 189–90. Henry actually distinguishes five different concepts of dignity employed in Supreme Court jurisprudence: institutional status, equality, liberty, personal integrity, and collective virtue.

145. Pablo Gilabert, "Human Rights, Human Dignity, and Power," in *Philosophical Foundations of Human Rights*, ed. Rowan Cruft, Matthew Liao, and Massimo Renzo (Oxford: Oxford University Press, 2015), 196–213.

146. Obergefell v. Hodges, 135 S. Ct. 2584, 2639 (2015).

147. Andrew Koppelman makes a similar point about anti-Semitic slurs. See Andrew Koppelman, "Gay Rights, Religious Accommodations, and the Purposes of Antidiscrimination Law," *Southern California Law Review* 88 (2015): 645.

148. I'm grateful to that British colleague, Jonathan Cottrell, for discussion on this point.

149. I'm indebted to Dan Johnson for helpful conversation on these points at John Corvino, "Rejoinder to Dan Johnson: A Plea for Distinctions," Partially Examined Life Philosophy Podcast, October 13, 2015, https://www.partiallyexaminedlife.com/2015/10/13/rejoinder-to-dan-johnson-a-plea-for-distinctions/.

150. For the current landscape, see Human Rights Campaign, "Maps of State Laws and Policies," http://www.hrc.org/state_maps, accessed September 28, 2016.

151. See Christy Mallory and Brad Sears, "Evidence of Employment Discrimination Based on Sexual Orientation and Gender Identity: An Analysis of Complaints Filed with State

Enforcement Agencies," Williams Institute, October 22, 2015, http://williamsinstitute.law.ucla.edu/research/workplace/ evidence-of-employment-discrimination-based-on-sexual-orientation-and-gender-identity-an-analysis-of-complaints-filed-with-state-enforcement-agencies/. See also Christy Mallory and Brad Sears, "Evidence of Housing Discrimination Based on Sexual Orientation and Gender Identity: An Analysis of Complaints Filed with State Enforcement Agencies, 2008–2014," Williams Institute, February 9, 2016, http://williamsinstitute.law.ucla. edu/research/workplace/evidence-of-housing-discrimination-based-on-sexual-orientation-and-gender-identity-an-analysis-of-complaints-filed-with-state-enforcement-agencies-2008-2014/, and Christy Mallory and Brad Sears, "Evidence of Discrimination in Public Accommodations Based on Sexual Orientation and Gender Identity: An Analysis of Complaints Filed with State Enforcement Agencies, 2008–2014," *Williams Institute*, February 16, 2016, http://williamsinstitute.law.ucla.edu/research/work-place/evidence-of-discrimination-in-public-accommodations-based-on-sexual-orientation-and-gender-identity-an-analysis-of-complaints-filed-with-state-enforcement-agencies-2008-2014/.

152. Thomas Harkin, "S. Rept. 113-105—The Employment Non-discrimination Act of 2013" (webpage), U.S. Senate, September 12, 2013, 15–17, https://www.congress.gov/113/crpt/srpt105/ CRPT-113srpt105.pdf.

153. Harkin, "S. Rept. 113-105," 17.

154. Harkin, "S. Rept. 113-105," 17.

155. Harkin, "S. Rept. 113-105," 15.

156. Harkin, "S. Rept. 113-105," 17.

157. I discuss some of these effects in Corvino and Gallagher, *Debating Same-Sex Marriage*; see, for example, 8–11.

158. For a detailed history, see Joyce Murdoch and Deb Price, *Courting Justice: Gay Men and Lesbians v. The Supreme Court* (New York: Basic Books, 2002).

159. Lawrence v. Texas, 539 U.S. 558 (2003).

160. Bowers v. Hardwick, 478 U.S. 186, 196–97 (1986).

161. The information that follows is taken from Klein, Melissa and Aaron dba Sweetcakes by Melissa, 34 BOLI 102 (2015), https://www.oregon.gov/boli/SiteAssets/pages/press/Sweet%20 Cakes%20FO.pdf.

162. Klein, Melissa and Aaron dba Sweetcakes by Melissa, 34 BOLI 102, 104 (2015), https://www.oregon.gov/boli/SiteAssets/pages/press/Sweet%20Cakes%20FO.pdf.
163. I address Leviticus and other Bible verses in Corvino, *What's Wrong with Homosexuality?*, chap. 2.
164. Klein, Melissa and Aaron dba Sweetcakes by Melissa, 34 BOLI 102, 105 (2015).
165. Andrew Koppelman, "A Zombie in the Supreme Court: The Elane Photography Cert Denial," *Alabama Civil Rights and Civil Liberties Law Review* 7 (2015): 77. The article is about the Elane Photography case, but the principle still applies.
166. Andrew Koppelman, "Why Discrimination against Lesbians and Gay Men Is Sex Discrimination," *New York University Law Review* 69 (1994): 197; Klein, Melissa and Aaron dba Sweetcakes by Melissa, 34 BOLI 102, 154 (2015), https://www.oregon.gov/boli/SiteAssets/pages/press/Sweet%20Cakes%20FO.pd.
167. Eugene Volokh, "No, the Oregon Bakers Weren't Fined for Publishing the Complainant's Home Address, or for Otherwise Publicizing the Complaint against Them," The Volokh Conspiracy, July 10, 2015, https://www.washingtonpost.com/news/volokh-conspiracy/wp/2015/07/10/no-the-oregon-bakers-werent-fined-for-publishing-the-complainants-home-address-or-for-otherwise-publicizing-the-complaint-against-them/.
168. Abby Ohlheiser, "This Colorado Baker Refused to Put an Anti-gay Message on Cakes. Now She Is Facing a Civil Rights Complaint," *Washington Post*, January 28, 2015, https://www.washingtonpost.com/news/post-nation/wp/2015/01/22/this-colorado-baker-refused-to-put-an-anti-gay-message-on-cakes-now-she-is-facing-a-civil-rights-complaint/?utm_term=.7e8c24f6fd12. This is the customer's recollection of the requested wording. The baker reported the request as "God hates gays."
169. This section grew out of my blog post " 'Bake Me a Cake': Three Paths for Balancing Liberty and Equality," What's Wrong?, October 15, 2015, https://whatswrongcvsp.com/2015/10/15/guest-post-from-john-corvino-bake-me-a-cake-three-paths-for-balancing-liberty-and-equality/. My views have changed since that piece.

170. Thomas Berg et al., "Statement of Law Professors on Religious Liberty Implications of Proposed Hawaii Marriage Equality Act of 2013" (blog entry), Mirror of Justice, 2013, http://mirrorofjustice.blogs.com/files/hawaii-gaffney-et-al-testimony-full-final-28oct13-1.pdf.

171. Mary Anne Case, "Why Live-and-Let-Live Is Not a Viable Solution to the Difficult Problems of Religious Accommodation in the Age of Sexual Civil Rights," *Southern California Law Review* 88 (2015): 463–92.

172. Among standardly enumerated items in antidiscrimination law, age is an exception to this principle: One can and should refuse to sell alcohol to minors, for example. Many antidiscrimination laws that include age acknowledge this point. Oregon's law, for example, lists "age if the individual is of age, as described in this section, or older." In addition, by "very same item," I mean (what philosophers call) the same *type*, not the same *token*. If you sell the very same token to multiple customers, you are probably guilty of fraud.

173. The "Homosexuality is a detestable sin" customer lost his lawsuit against the Colorado bakery. See Alan Gathright and Eric Luphear, "Denver's Azucar Bakery Wins Right to Refuse to Make Anti-gay Cake," *7NEWS*, April 24, 2015, http://www.thedenverchannel.com/news/news-archive/archive-friday/denvers-azucar-bakery-wins-right-to-refuse-to-make-anti-gay-cake.

174. They mischaracterize it by failing to acknowledge that it did not involve refusal to sell the very same items to this customer that the baker sold to other customers: The baker was willing to sell the cake, and even provide the piping bag; she simply refused to provide the writing. My view would allow any baker to do that.

175. Not all custom work involves luxury items, of course. Imagine a person who designs prosthetics for a living—an occupation that certainly involves a considerable amount of artistry. If that person refused service to gays, or Muslims, or whoever, that would be far more concerning than denying custom cakes. But the case seems so unlikely—the homophobic prosthetic designer!—that I'm inclined not to worry about it, and to say that other considerations outweigh this hypothetical concern.

176. The objection was suggested to me by Lori Watson. And it's not far-fetched. See "Hindu Temples Deny Disabled People Entry," Damai Disabled Person Association Malaysia, February 7, 2012, http://damai.org.my/hindu-temples-deny-disabled-people-entry/.

177. Hosanna-Tabor Evangelical v. EEOC, 132 S. Ct. 694 (2011).

178. Eugene Volokh has argued that "to protect the church's right to discriminate in its choice of clergy, courts must abandon the notion that infringements of religious freedom are allowed so long as they pass strict scrutiny. In some situations, a court must hold—as lower courts generally do in clergy discrimination cases—that 'the inroad on religious liberty is too substantial to be permissible' even though the law is narrowly tailored to a compelling interest. What does the work here is not strict scrutiny, but an underlying theory of the autonomy of religious institutions." I think Volokh is right. See Eugene Volokh, "Freedom of Speech, Permissible Tailoring and Transcending Strict Scrutiny," *University of Pennsylvania Law Review* 144, no. 6 (1996): 2417–61, doi:10.2307/3312673.

179. In Dias v. Archdiocese of Cincinnati, No. 1: 11-CV-00251 (S.D. Ohio Mar. 29, 2012), the Catholic Church unsuccessfully claimed that its termination of a non-Catholic school technology officer for becoming pregnant out of wedlock was not discriminatory; by contrast, the music director for a church was found to be a "minister" despite having no liturgical responsibilities in Cannata v. Catholic Diocese of Austin 700 F. 3d 169 (Court of Appeals, 5th Circuit 2012); in addition, there is Henry v. Red Hill Evangelical Lutheran Church of Tustin, 201 Cal. App. 4th 1041 (Court of Appeal, 4th Appellate Dist., 3rd Div. 2011) where the exception was applied to the Catholic teacher/director of a Lutheran preschool because she led students in prayer.

180. See for example Andrew M. Koppelman, "Gay Rights, Religious Accommodations, and the Purposes of Antidiscrimination Law"; Douglas Laycock, afterword to *Same-Sex Marriage and Religious Liberty: Emerging Conflicts*, ed. Douglas Laycock, Jr., Anthony Picarello, and Robin Fretwell Wilson (Lanham, MD: Rowman and Littlefield, 2008), 198.

181. See Ken White, "Lawsplainer: So Are Those Christian Cake-Bakers in Oregon Unconstitutionally Gagged, or Not?," *Popehat*, July 8, 2015, https://popehat.com/2015/07/08/lawsplainer-so-are-those-christian-cake-bakers-in-oregon-unconstitutionally-gagged-or-not/.
182. Andrew Koppelman. "A Free Speech Response to the Gay Rights/Religious Liberty Conflict," *110 Northwestern University Law Review 1125*; Northwestern Public Law Research Paper No. 16-14, June 7, 2016, https://ssrn.com/abstract=2791641.
183. Elane Photography, LLC v. Willock, 309 P. 3d 53, 59 (N.M. 2013).
184. I'm indebted to Matthew Franck for discussion on this point.
185. Elane Photography, LLC v. Willock, 309 P. 3d 53-NM: Supreme Court 2013.
186. David E. Bernstein, "Context Matters: A Better Libertarian Approach to Antidiscrimination Law," *Cato Unbound*, June 16, 2010, http://www.cato-unbound.org/2010/06/16/david-e-bernstein/context-matters-better-libertarian-approach-antidiscrimination-law, accessed July 12, 2016.
187. Samuel R. Bagenstos, "The Unrelenting Libertarian Challenge to Public Accommodations Law," *Stanford Law Review* 66, no. 6 (2014): 1205–40.
188. Dale Miller, "Reluctant Florists, Same-Sex Weddings, and Mill's Doctrine of Liberty," *Public Affairs Quarterly*, 30, no. 4 (2016): 287–311, 302.
189. Burwell v. Hobby Lobby Stores, Inc., 2014, 134 S. Ct. 2751 (2014).
190. "Sexting Case Highlights Quandary over Child Porn Laws," *Chicago Tribune*, September 24, 2015, http://www.chicagotribune.com/news/nationworld/ct-sexting-teens-child-porn-laws-20150924-story.html.
191. Barronelle Stutzman, "Why a Friend Is Suing Me: The Arlene's Flowers Story," *Seattle Times*, November 9, 2015, http://www.seattletimes.com/opinion/why-a-good-friend-is-suing-me-the-arlenes-flowers-story/.
192. The most detailed philosophical treatment of which I'm aware is William M. Ramsey, "Bigotry and Religious Belief," *Pacific Philosophical Quarterly* 94, no. 2 (June 1, 2013): 125–51, doi:10.1111/j.1468-0114.2012.01448.x. Ramsey's own definition is "holding evaluative beliefs or other attitudes that are

(usually) negative and directed toward members of a group of persons where the property used for grouping fails to provide proper support for the negative evaluation" (141). I have some differences with Ramsey, discussion of which would take me too far afield here.

193. See Ramsey, "Bigotry and Religious Belief," 128.
194. Jennifer Steinhauer, Jonathan Martin, and David M. Herszenhorn, "Paul Ryan Calls Donald Trump's Attack on Judge 'Racist,' but Still Backs Him," *New York Times*, June 7, 2016, http://www.nytimes.com/2016/06/08/us/politics/paul-ryan-donald-trump-gonzalo-curiel.html.
195. Cited in E. J. Graff, *What Is Marriage For? The Strange Social History of Our Most Intimate Institution* (Boston: Beacon Press, 1999), 251–52.
196. For discussion, see Martha C. Nussbaum, *From Disgust to Humanity: Sexual Orientation and Constitutional Law*, 1st ed. (Oxford: Oxford University Press, 2010).
197. Sarah Jerde, "Anti-gay Pastor: If My Son Married a Man, I'd Spread Manure 'All over My Body'" (video), *TPM*, November 9, 2015. http://talkingpointsmemo.com/livewire/tea-party-pastor-same-sex-marriage, accessed July 12, 2016.
198. Katherine Stewart, "Ted Cruz and the Anti-gay Pastor," *New York Times*, November 16, 2015, http://www.nytimes.com/2015/11/16/opinion/campaign-stops/ted-cruz-and-the-anti-gay-pastor.html.
199. For the record, I am not among those who think opposition to homosexuality so obviously wrong as to not merit further discussion; indeed, much of my career has been spent engaging opponents of homosexuality. See, for example, John Corvino, *What's Wrong with Homosexuality?* Swanson's case is different, because his views are so ugly and extreme.
200. J. Bryan Lowder, "No, It's Not Too Soon to Condemn Public Figures for Being Anti-gay," *Slate*, April 7, 2014, http://www.slate.com/blogs/outward/2014/04/07/brenden_eich_s_mozilla_resignation_proves_gay_rights_are_no_longer_up_for.html.
201. J. Bryan Lowder, "Is Brendan Eich as Bigoted as Donald Sterling?," *Slate*, May 1, 2014, http://www.slate.com/blogs/

outward/2014/05/01/is_brendan_eich_as_bigoted_as_don-ald_sterling.html.

202. Brendan Eich, "Inclusiveness at Mozilla" (blog entry), *Brendan Eich*, March 26, 2014, https://brendaneich.com/2014/03/inclusiveness-at-mozilla/.

203. Mitchell Baker, "Brendan Eich Steps Down as Mozilla CEO" (blog entry), *Mozilla Blog*, April 3, 2014. https://blog.mozilla.org/blog/2014/04/03/brendan-eich-steps-down-as-mozilla-ceo/, accessed December 30, 2015.

204. "Gay and Lesbian Rights," *Gallup.com*, http://www.gallup.com/poll/1651/Gay-Lesbian-Rights.aspx, accessed December 30, 2015.

205. "Freedom to Marry, Freedom to Dissent: Why We Must Have Both," *RealClearPolitics*, April 22, 2014, http://www.realclear-politics.com/articles/2014/04/22/freedom_to_marry_free-dom_to_dissent_why_we_must_have_both_122376.html, accessed July 12, 2016. I did and still do have mixed feelings about the content of this letter, although I stand by its spirit.

206. This section borrows heavily from Corvino, *What's Wrong with Homosexuality?*, 118–20.

207. Loving v. Virginia, 388 U.S. 1 (1967); Lawrence v. Texas, 539 U.S. 558 (2003).

208. Paul McHugh and Gerard V. Bradley, "Sexual Orientation, Gender Identity, and Employment Law," *Public Discourse* July 25, 2013, http://www.thepublicdiscourse.com/2013/07/10636/.

209. Ryan T. Anderson, "Sexual Orientation and Gender Identity (SOGI) Laws Threaten Freedom," Heritage Foundation, November 30, 2015, http://www.heritage.org/research/reports/2015/11/sexual-orientation-and-gender-identity-sogi-laws-threaten-freedom.

210. Virginia law once defined anyone with "one-sixteenth or less of the blood of the American Indian" as a white person, in order "to recognize as an integral and honored part of the white race the descendants of John Rolfe and Pocahontas." See Loving v. Virginia, n. 4. And what are we to make of the well-documented history of immigrant groups now considered "white," such as the Irish, who were once considered nonwhite? Noel Ignatiev, *How the Irish Became White* (New York: Routledge, 2008).

211. Compare Laycock: "It is a risky step to interfere with the most intimate details of other people's lives while loudly claiming liberty for yourself." Douglas Laycock, "Religious Liberty and the Culture Wars," *University of Illinois Law Review* 2014 (2014): 839–80, 869.

212. Examples of conservative opposition to mosques abound in recent years: Laurie Goodstein, "Battles around Nation over Proposed Mosques," *New York Times*, August 7, 2010, sec. U.S., http://www.nytimes.com/2010/08/08/us/08mosque. html. Public Muslim prayer or calls to prayer are another recurring problem for American Muslims: David Zucchino, "At Duke, Many Criticize Decision Not to Broadcast Muslim Prayer Call," *Latimes.com*, January 16, 2015, http:// www.latimes.com/nation/la-na-duke-muslim-prayer-controversy-20150116-story.html; Mercedes White, "Muslim Students Struggle to Practice Faith in U.S. Schools, Seek Accommodation for Religion," *DeseretNews.com*, February 24, 2012, http://www.deseretnews.com/article/765554027/ Muslim-students-struggle-to-practice-faith-in-US-schools-seek-accommodation-for-religion.html?pg=all; John Leland, "Tension in a Michigan City over Muslims' Call to Prayer," *New York Times*, May 5, 2004. http://www.nytimes.com/2004/ 05/05/us/tension-in-a-michigan-city-over-muslims-call-to-prayer.html.

213. Travis Loller, "Kentucky Clerk Case Divides Religious Liberty Advocates," *Chicago Tribune*, September 14, 2015, http://www. chicagotribune.com/news/nationworld/sns-ap-us-rel--gay-marriage-kentucky-20150913-story.html.

Chapter 3

1. See, for example, the Universal Declaration of Human Rights and the Charter of Fundamental Rights of the European Union.

2. See Ryan T. Anderson, *Truth Overruled: The Future of Marriage and Religious Freedom* (Washington, DC: Regnery, 2015).

3. See Sarah Torre and Ryan T. Anderson, "Adoption, Foster Care, and Conscience Protections," Heritage Foundation *Backgrounder,*

no. 2869, January 15, 2014, http://www.heritage.org/research/reports/2014/01/adoption-foster-care-and-conscience-protection, and Anderson, *Truth Overruled*, 88–89.

4. Thomas C. Atwood, "Foster Care: Safety Net or Trap Door?," Heritage Foundation *Backgrounder*, no. 2535, March 25, 2011, 12, http://www.heritage.org/research/reports/2011/03/foster-care-safety-net-or-trap-door.

5. U.S. Department of Health and Human Services, Administration for Children and Families, "National Foster Care & Adoption Directory Search," Child Welfare Information Gateway, https://www.childwelfare.gov/nfcad/.

6. "Schulz, Craigen, Montague," YouTube video by Marriage Anti-Defamation Alliance, posted by NationForMarriage, December 15, 2011, http://marriageada.org/schulz-craigen-montague/.

7. "Tensions between Rights of Conscience and Civil Rights" (interview), Pew Forum, http://www.pewforum.org/2010/06/03/tensions-between-rights-of-conscience-and-civil-rights/, accessed October 4, 2016.

8. See Anderson, *Truth Overruled*, 92–104.

9. Pew Research Center, "Tensions between Rights of Conscience and Civil Rights," Pew Forum, June 3, 2010, http://www.pewforum.org/2010/06/03/tensions-between-rights-of-conscience-and-civil-rights/, accessed October 4, 2016.

10. Alice Lindstrom; Robert Davis, Plaintiffs-Appellees, v. Postmaster General, 781 F.2d 772 (1986), https://scholar.google.com/scholar_case?case=11303495795709437489.

11. Paul Byrne Haring, Plaintiff, v. W. Michael Blumenthal, Defendant, 471 F.Supp. 1172 (1979). http://law.justia.com/cases/federal/district-courts/FSupp/471/1172/1804986/.

12. Robin F. Wilson, "The Calculus of Accommodation: Contraception, Abortion, Same-Sex Marriage, and Other Clashes between Religion and the State," *Boston College Law Review* 53, no. 4 (September 2012): 1417–1513, at 1482.

13. McKenzie Romero, "Salt Lake Police Officer Says He Was 'Uncomfortable' with Parade Assignment," *Deseret News*, June 9, 2014, http://www.deseretnews.com/article/865604835/Salt-Lake-police-officer-says-he-was-uncomfortable-with-parade-assignment.html?pg=all, accessed October 4, 2016.

14. Ryan T. Anderson, "First Amendment Defense Act Protects Freedom and Pluralism after Marriage Redefinition," Heritage Foundation *Issue Brief,* no. 4490, November 25, 2015, http://www.heritage.org/research/reports/2015/11/first-amendment-defense-act-protects-freedom-and-pluralism-after-marriage-redefinition, accessed October 4, 2016.

15. Roger Severino, "Gov. Bryant Stands Up to Liberal Bullying, Signs Mississippi Religious Freedom Bill," *Daily Signal,* April 5, 2016, http://dailysignal.com/2016/04/05/gov-bryant-stands-up-to-liberal-bullying-and-enacts-mississippi-religious-freedom-bill/, accessed October 4, 2016.

16. John Finnis, *Natural Law and Natural Rights* (New York: Oxford University Press, 2011), 155.

17. Finnis, *Natural Law and Natural Rights,* 155.

18. Finnis, *Natural Law and Natural Rights,* 220–21.

19. For extended defenses of these civil liberties, see Robert P. George, *Making Men Moral: Civil Liberties and Public Morality* (New York: Oxford University Press, 1993), 192–208; 219–28. Portions of the next sections (on fragility and religious liberty generally, and on substantial burdens) are adapted from a forthcoming article by Sherif Girgis.

20. Caroline Mala Corbin, "Above the Law? The Constitutionality of the Ministerial Exemption from Antidiscrimination Law," *Fordham Law Review* 75, no. 4 (2007), 1975.

21. Ryan T. Anderson even wrote a dissertation titled "Neither Liberal nor Libertarian: A Natural Law Approach to Social Justice and Economic Rights."

22. See Paul VI, Declaration on the Relation of the Church to Non-Christian Religions, *Nostra aetate,* October 28, 1965, http://www.vatican.va/archive/hist_councils/ii_vatican_council/documents/vat-ii_decl_19651028_nostra-aetate_en.html, accessed October 4, 2016.

23. The argument in a nutshell is this: Religion, as a form of community, is built up by free and mutual acts of goodwill toward the other; by loving cooperation. Both goodwill and mutuality are present whenever someone makes good-faith efforts at harmony with the divine. In such cases, God and the believer each will the religious act for the sake of harmony with the other. The

believer wills that by hypothesis. But so does God, whom sound philosophical theism shows to be the ultimate cause of all positive contingent realities—of every created thing, insofar as it *is* (as opposed to evils, which are privations of what should be). As cause of the existence of human beings and of their honest religious efforts, God must be willing both, wherever both show up. So for a person to reach out to God in good faith is already for him to be cooperating with God's own will to support him in doing so. Thus, each party acts out of goodwill for the other, for the sake of harmony with the other. Genuine community is forged.

Of course, the more complete the believer's religion is, and the less alloyed it is by falsehoods, the more his religious acts are what they can be, and so the more perfectly they foster divine harmony. (Just as the more someone conscientiously acts in accordance with *true* moral principles, the more perfectly she realizes the good of integrity.) So we always have reason to pursue the truth more deeply and to purify our creed of error— another way that this view isn't relativistic. But if we have even a sliver of the truth about theology—even just the insight that it's worth trying to harmonize with the higher being, as anyone trying to do so must think—our efforts will realize the good of religion to *some* extent. So they deserve protection from attack.

A classical theist could hardly think that mistakes about the divine *generally* disable a person from realizing the good of religion. For almost every actual believer in history has had beliefs about God that contradict airtight classical theism (its doctrines on divine aseity, immutability, atemporality, ineffability, and so on). For realizing this basic good, then, perhaps it's enough to pursue a being under the guise of *at least one defining* feature of God (*e.g.*, the most perfectly one; the creator of all; the ultimate source of morality or value; the most transcendent reality). Maybe whenever someone *tries* to unite with a being so defined, she *succeeds* in achieving some harmony with the true God. In that case, even if the essence of the basic good of religion is harmony with the true God, period, you always realize it to *some* extent by seeking *what you take* to be the ultimate source of meaning, *vel cet.*

24. James Madison, "A Memorial and Remonstrance," letter to Honorable the General Assembly of the Commonwealth of Virginia, c. June 20, 1785, Founders Online, National Archives, http://founders.archives.gov/documents/Madison/01-08-02-0163, accessed October 4, 2016.

25. Madison, "A Memorial and Remonstrance."

26. Michael W. McConnell, Why Is Religious Liberty the "First Freedom"?, *Cardozo Law Review* 21 (2000): 1265.

27. Boy Scouts of America v. Dale, 530 U.S. 640, 647–48 (2000).

28. Brian Spegele, "China's Banned Churches Defy Regime, *Wall Street Journal,* July 28, 2011, www.wsj.com/articles/SB100014240 52702304567604576451913744126214, accessed October 4, 2016.

29. Brian J. Grim and Roger Finke, *The Price of Freedom Denied: Religious Persecution and Conflict in the Twenty-First Century* (New York: Cambridge University Press, 2011), 205.

30. See, for example, Thomas Aquinas, *Summa Theologiae* 1–2.96, articles 2 and 3. Within this moral theory, proponents are divided on whether pure paternalism is ever justified. See George, *Making Men Moral,* chap. 6 (describing debate with John Finnis on that question).

31. We owe this general argument to Eugene Volokh, "A Common-Law Model for Religious Exemptions," *UCLA Law Review* 46 (1999): 1465.

32. Volokh, "Common-Law Model for Religious Exemptions," 1599 n. 106.

33. *Hearings before the Subcommittee on Civil and Constitutional Rights of the Committee on the Judiciary, House of Representatives* (Washington, DC: U.S. Government Printing Office, 1993), https://www.justice.gov/sites/default/files/jmd/legacy/2014/07/13/hear-99-1992.pdf, accessed October 4, 2016, 63.

34. *Hearings before the Subcommittee on Civil and Constitutional Rights of the Committee on the Judiciary,* 80–81.

35. Plan B One-Step drug label, FDA.gov, Reference ID: 3329183, http://www.accessdata.fda.gov/drugsatfda_docs/label/2013/021998Orig1s003lbl.pdf, accessed September 30, 2016.

36. Our analysis here draws on J. M. Balkin, "The Constitution of Status," *Yale Law Journal* 106 (1997): 2313.

37. Douglas NeJaime and Reva B. Siegel, "Conscience Wars: Complicity-Based Conscience Claims in Religion and Politics," *Yale Law Journal* 124 (2015), 2516–2591, 2576.

38. See Andrew Koppelman, "A Free Speech Solution to the Gay Rights/Religious Liberty Conflict," September 15, 2015 (unpublished manuscript on file with author), 23: "Long before James Madison argued that democracy logically entailed the freedom to criticize incumbent officeholders, the principal focus of arguments against censorship was the prohibition of heresy and blasphemy. Free speech and freedom of religion weren't always in separate analytical silos."

39. Catholic Church, *Catechism of the Catholic Church: Revised in Accordance with the Official Latin Text Promulgated by Pope John Paul II,* 2nd ed. (Vatican City: Libreria Editrice Vaticana, 1997), 1324–25.

40. *See,* e.g., Dan Corner, "John 6:53 and the Catholic Holy Eucharist," Evangelical Outreach, http://www.evangelicaloutreach.org/communio.htm, accessed January 16, 2016, calling worship of the Eucharist "faulty worship in the form of *idolatry.*"

41. Thanks to Andy Koppelman for discussion on this point.

42. Ben Eidelson suggested this example.

43. Douglas Laycock, "Freedom of Speech That Is Both Religious and Political," *U.C. Davis Law Review* 29 (1996): 801–3.

44. Hurley v. Irish-American Gay, Lesbian and Bisexual Group of Boston, Inc. 515 U.S. 557 (1995), 573–74.

45. John Stuart Mill, *On Liberty* (1859), chap. 2.

46. West Virginia State Bd. of Educ. v. Barnette, 319 U.S. 624, 642 (1943).

47. Koppelman, "Free Speech Solution to the Gay Rights/Religious Liberty Conflict," quoting Jeremy Waldron, "Mill and the Value of Moral Distress," in *Liberal Rights: Collected Papers 1981–1991* (1993), 115, 120.

48. Bob Jones Univ. v. United States, 461 U.S. 574, 592 (1983).

49. Bob Jones Univ. v. United States, 461 U.S. 574, 592 (1983) (Powell, J., concurring).

50. Maureen E. Markey, "The Price of Landlord's 'Free' Exercise of Religion: Tenant's Right to Discrimination-Free Housing

and Privacy," *Fordham Urban Law Journal* 22, no. 3 (1994), http://ir.lawnet.fordham.edu/cgi/viewcontent.cgi?article= 1665&context=ul, accessed October 4, 2016.

51. Some states do ban private discrimination based on political affiliation.

52. Andrew Koppelman, "Gay Rights, Religious Accommodations, and the Purposes of Antidiscrimination Law," *Southern California Law Review 88* (February 16, 2014): 621, http://papers.ssrn.com/sol3/papers.cfm?abstract_id=2571058, accessed October 4, 2016.

53. Luis Garicano, Claire LeLarge, and John Van Reenen, "Firm Size Distortions and the Productivity Distribution: Evidence from France," National Bureau of Economic Research Working Paper no. 18841, February 2013, http://ideas.repec.org/p/nbr/nberwo/18841.html, accessed November 13, 2015.

54. See, e.g., Bruce Ackerman, *We the People,* vol. 3, *The Civil Rights Revolution* (Cambridge, MA: Harvard University Press, 2014), 142, 150. Portions of what follows are adapted from a forthcoming piece by Sherif Girgis.

55. Thanks to Ben Eidelson for discussion on this point.

56. Brief of Professors of History George Chauncey, Nancy F. Cott, et al., Lawrence v. Texas, 539 U.S. 558 (2003). See also George Chauncey, *Gay New York: Gender, Urban Culture, and the Making of the Gay Male World, 1890–1940* (1994): 173, 337.

57. Andrew Koppelman, "A Zombie in the Supreme Court: The Elane Photography Cert Denial," Northwestern Public Law research paper no. 14-27, June 17, 2014, 12–13, http://papers.ssrn.com/sol3/papers.cfm?abstract_id=2455848, accessed October 4, 2016.

58. Human Rights Campaign, "LGBT Equality at the Fortune 500," http://www.hrc.org/resources/entry/lgbt-equality-at-the-fortune-500, accessed October 4, 2016.

59. Prudential, "The LGBT Financial Experience," http://www.prudential.com/lgbt, accessed October 4, 2016.

60. Hans Bader, "Employment Non-discrimination Act Makes as Little Sense as Chemotherapy for a Cold," Competitive Enterprise Institute Open Market, June 13, 2012, http://www.openmarket.org/2012/06/13/employment-non-discrimination-act-makes-as-little-sense-as-chemotherapy-for-a-cold/, accessed November 13, 2015.

61. Madeline Buckley, "Threats Tied to RFRA Prompt Indiana Pizzeria to Close Its Doors," *IndyStar,* April 3, 2015, http://www.indystar.com/story/news/2015/04/02/threats-tied-rfra-prompt-indiana-pizzeria-close-doors/70847230/, accessed October 4, 2016,

62. Koppelman, "Zombie in the Supreme Court," 14.

63. Irving G. Tragen, "Statutory Prohibitions against Interracial Marriage," *California Law Review* 32, no. 3 (September 1944), http://scholarship.law.berkeley.edu/cgi/viewcontent.cgi?article=3614&context=californialawreview, accessed October 4, 2016. See also Francis Beckwith, "Interracial Marriage and Same-Sex Marriage," *Public Discourse*, May 21, 2010, http://www.thepublicdiscourse.com/2010/05/1324/, accessed October 4, 2016.

64. Beckwith, "Interracial Marriage and Same-Sex Marriage."

65. Nancy F. Cott, *Public Vows: A History of Marriage and the Nation* (Cambridge, MA: Harvard University Press, 2000), Kindle ed., location 483.

66. G. Robina Quale, *A History of Marriage Systems* (New York: Greenwood Press, 1988), 2.

67. Plato, *The Dialogues of Plato* (360 B.C.), trans. and ed. Benjamin Jowett (Oxford: Oxford University Press, 1953), vol. 4, 407.

68. Alberto Moffi, "Family and Property Law," in *Cambridge Companion to Ancient Greek Law,* ed. Michael Gagarin and David Cohen (2005), 254.

69. Aristotle, *Ethics*, in *The Complete Works of Aristotle*, ed. Jonathan Barnes (1836), vol. 2, rev. trans. (Oxford: Oxford University Press, 1984).

70. Plutarch, *Life of Solon*, in *Plutarch's Lives*, vol. 4, Loeb ed. (Cambridge, MA: Harvard University Press, 1961), 20.

71. Plutarch, *Erotikas,* Loeb ed. (Cambridge, MA: Harvard University Press, 1961), 769.

72. Musonius Rufus, *Discourses XIIIA*, in Cora E. Lutz (trans.), *Musonius Rufus "The Roman Socrates,"* Yale Classical Studies (1947), https://sites.google.com/site/thestoiclife/the_teachers/musonius-rufus/lectures/13-0.

73. For an extended philosophical and policy defense of these values, see Sherif Girgis, Ryan T. Anderson, and Robert P. George, *What*

Is Marriage? Man and Woman: A Defense (New York: Encounter Books, 2012).

74. Koppelman, "Gay Rights, Religious Accommodations, and the Purposes of Antidiscrimination Law," 628.

75. Ryan T. Anderson, "Obama Unilaterally Rewrites Law, Imposes Transgender Policy on Nation's Schools," *Daily Signal,* May 13, 2016, http://dailysignal.com/2016/05/13/new-obamacare-transgender-regulations-threaten-freedom-of-physicians/, accessed October 4, 2016.

76. Anderson, "Obama Unilaterally Rewrites Law, Imposes Transgender Policy on Nation's Schools."

77. Eugene Volokh, "You Can Be Fired for Not Calling People 'Ze' or 'Hir,' If That's the Pronoun They Demand That You Use," *Washington Post,* May 17, 2016, https://www.washingtonpost.com/news/volokh-conspiracy/wp/2016/05/17/you-can-be-fined-for-not-calling-people-ze-or-hir-if-thats-the-pronoun-they-demand-that-you-use/, accessed October 4, 2016.

78. Volokh, "You Can Be Fired for Not Calling People 'Ze' or 'Hir,' If That's the Pronoun They Demand That You Use."

79. Equality Act, S. 1858, 114th Cong., 1st sess., https://www.congress.gov/bill/114th-congress/senate-bill/1858/all-info, accessed November 13, 2015. The House version of the bill is H.R. 3185.

80. Human Rights Campaign, "Beyond Marriage Equality," http://www.hrc.org/campaigns/beyond-marriage-equality-a-blueprint-for-federal-non-discrimination-protect, accessed October 4, 2016.

81. Jeff Merkley, Tammy Baldwin, and Cory Booker, "The Equality Act" (fact sheet), U.S. Senate, 2015, 1, https://assets.documentcloud.org/documents/2170089/senate-equality-act-fact-sheet.pdf, accessed November 13, 2015.

82. Equality Act, S. 1858, 114th Cong., 1st Sess., https://www.congress.gov/bill/114th-congress/senate-bill/1858/all-info, accessed November 13, 2015. The House version of the bill is H.R. 3185.

83. Equality Act, S. 1858, 114th Cong., 1st Sess., 2, https://www.congress.gov/bill/114th-congress/senate-bill/1858/all-info, accessed November 13, 2015 (emphasis added).

84. Houston City Council, Ordinance No. 2014-530, May 28, 2014, Exhibit A, pp. 2–3, http://www.scribd.com/doc/228533432/

Equal-Rights-Ordinance, accessed November 13, 2015 (original emphasis).

85. Equality Act, S. 1858, 114th Cong., 1st Sess., https://www.congress.gov/bill/114th-congress/senate-bill/1858/all-info (accessed November 13, 2015). The House version of the bill is H.R. 3185.

86. Koppelman, "Gay Rights, Religious Accommodations, and the Purposes of Antidiscrimination Law," 621.

87. https://www.youtube.com/watch?v=3YezwtRX9XU.

88. Jean-Jacques Rousseau, *The Social Contract* (1762), trans. Maurice Cranston (London: Penguin, 1968), 122.

Chapter 4

1. Anderson and Girgis, p. 164 in this volume: hereafter cited parenthetically within the text.

2. For discussion, see Lupu, *"Hobby Lobby* and the Dubious Enterprise of Religious Exemptions," *Harvard Women's Law Journal* 38, no. 2012 (2015): 35–101; also Eisgruber and Sager, *Religious Freedom and the Constitution* (Cambridge, MA: Harvard University Press, 2007), chap. 3.

3. Debra B. Stulberg et al., "Religious Hospitals and Primary Care Physicians: Conflicts over Policies for Patient Care," *Journal of General Internal Medicine* 25, no. 7 (2010): 725–30, doi:10.1007/s11606-010-1329-6.

4. See Brownfield v. Daniel Freeman Marina Hosp., 208 Cal. App. 3d. 405, 409 (1989).

5. See American Civil Liberties Union, "Tamesha Means v. United States Conference of Catholic Bishops—Complaint," https://www.aclu.org/legal-document/tamesha-means-v-united-states-conference-catholic-bishops-complaint, accessed September 26, 2016. Means v. United States Conference of Catholic Bishops, unpublished, No. 15-1779 (6th Cir. 2016).

6. For discussion, see David M. Kaplan, "Ethical Implications of a Critical Legal Case for the Counseling Profession: Ward v. Wilbanks," *Journal of Counseling and Development* 92, no. 2 (2014): 142–46, doi:10.1002/j.1556-6676.2014.00140.x.

7. Kaplan, "Ethical Implications of a Critical Legal Case for the Counseling Profession," 143.

8. See Walter Olson, "Religious Agencies and Adoption: A Case for Pluralism," Cato at Liberty, July 2, 2015, http://www.cato.org/blog/religious-adoption-agencies-case-pluralism, for an argument to this effect.

9. It is worth noting that approval of same-sex marriage was dramatically higher when *Obergefell* was decided (60 percent) than approval of interracial marriage was when Bob Jones University's tax-exempt status was revoked (43 percent). See Gallup, "Gay and Lesbian Rights," *Gallup.com*; Gallup, "In U.S., 87% Approve of Black-White Marriage, vs. 4% in 1958," Gallup.com, http://www.gallup.com/poll/163697/approve-marriage-blacks-whites.aspx.

10. Gary Gutting, "How Religion Can Lead to Violence," *New York Times*, August 1, 2016, http://www.nytimes.com/2016/08/01/opinion/how-religion-can-lead-to-violence.html.

11. City of Boerne v. Flores, 521 U.S. 507 (1997).

12. Recall the discussion of Indiana's RFRA in the introduction. Even the federal RFRA is being interpreted as an exemption from antidiscrimination law in the wake of *Hobby Lobby*. See Mark Joseph Stern, "Federal Judge: Religious Liberty Includes a Right to Fire LGBTQ Employees," *Slate*, August 18, 2016, http://www.slate.com/blogs/outward/2016/08/18/federal_judge_uses_religious_liberty_to_legalize_anti_lgbtq_discrimination.html.

13. Justice Ginsburg mentions some of these in her dissent. Burwell v. Hobby Lobby Stores, Inc., 134 S. Ct. 2751, 2805 (2014).

14. Irin Carmon, "Birth Control, the Supreme Court and Me," MSNBC, November 25, 2013, http://www.msnbc.com/msnbc/birth-control-the-supreme-court-and-me.

15. For discussion see Ira C. Lupu, "Hobby Lobby and the Dubious Enterprise of Religious Exemptions," *Harvard Women's Law Journal* 38 (2015): 84.

16. Douglas NeJaime and Reva B. Siegel, "Conscience Wars: Complicity-Based Conscience Claims in Religion and Politics," *Yale Law Journal* 124 (2015): 2516–91.

17. Locke v. Davey, 540 U.S. 712, 726 (2003).

18. Tony and Susan Alamo Foundation v. Secretary of Labor, 471 U.S. 290 (1985).

19. In the past two years the Human Rights Campaign has logged almost forty American transgender people who have suffered violent deaths. Human Rights Campaign, "Violence against the Transgender Community in 2016," http://www.hrc.org/resources/violence-against-the-transgender-community-in-2016/, accessed September 19, 2016. The Anti-Violence Project reports that last year saw 1,253 incidents of hate violence against LGBTQ and HIV-affected people in eleven states. Anti-Violence Project, "2015 Report on Lesbian, Gay, Bisexual, Transgender, Queer, and HIV-Affected Hate Violence," AVP: The Anti-Violence Project, http://www.avp.org/resources/avp-resources/520, accessed September 19, 2016.

20. "Same-Sex Couple Denied a Birthday Cake by Local Bakery," *13ABC*, http://www.13abc.com/content/news/Same-sex-couple-denied-a-birthday-cake-by-local-bakery-385783221.html, accessed July 12, 2016.

21. See Sherif Girgis, Ryan T. Anderson, and Robert P. George, *What Is Marriage?: Man and Woman: A Defense* (New York: Encounter Books, 2012).

22. Moreover, Koppelman countenances only limited exemptions to such laws. See Koppelman, "Gay Rights, Religious Accommodations, and the Purposes of Antidiscrimination Law" (February 16, 2014), *Southern California Law Review* 88 (2015): 619, Northwestern Public Law research paper no. 15-11, Northwestern Law & Economics research paper no. 15-06, and Koppelman, "A Zombie in the Supreme Court," *Alabama Civil Rights & Civil Liberties Law Review* 7 (2015): 77. For an older but still illuminating book-length treatment, see Koppelman, *Antidiscrimination Law and Social Equality*, rev. ed. (New Haven, CT: Yale University Press, 1998).

23. For citations to numerous studies establishing such links, see Kamden Strunk, "LGBT Bias and Discrimination: Occurrence, Outcomes, and the Impact of Policy Change," ResearchGate, August 1, 2014, https://www.researchgate.net/publication/269277415_LGBT_bias_and_discrimination_Occurrence_outcomes_and_the_impact_of_policy_change. In addition: A study of three states concluded that "hate crime and employment non-discrimination laws that include sexual orientation reduce hate

crime incidence"; Levy and Levy, "When Love Meets Hate: The Relationship between State Policies on Gay and Lesbian Rights and Hate Crime Incidence," *Social Science Research*, doi:10.1016/j.ssresearch.2016.06.008, accessed September 28, 2016. A recent study of antitransgender discrimination found that "statewide nondiscrimination laws are associated with lower rates of perceived stigma at the community level, which, in turn, is associated with lower rates of discrimination, victimization, anxiety, and risk for attempted suicide." See Gleason et al., "Effects of State Nondiscrimination Laws on Transgender and Gender-Nonconforming Individuals' Perceived Community Stigma and Mental Health," *Journal of Gay and Lesbian Mental Health* 20, no. 4 (October 1, 2016): 350–62, doi:10.1080/19359705.2016.1207582. A study in Massachusetts concluded: "Discrimination in public accommodations is common and is associated with adverse health outcomes among transgender and gender-nonconforming adults in Massachusetts." See Reisner et al., "Legal Protections in Public Accommodations Settings: A Critical Public Health Issue for Transgender and Gender-Nonconforming People," *Milbank Quarterly* 93, no. 3 (September 1, 2015): 484–515, doi:10.1111/1468-0009.12127.

24. "Statement Calling for Constitutional Resistance to Obergefell v. Hodges," American Principles Project, October 8, 2015, https://americanprinciplesproject.org/founding-principles/statement-calling-for-constitutional-resistance-to-obergefell-v-hodges%e2%80%af/; Obergefell v. Hodges, 135 S. Ct. 2584 (2015); Ryan T. Anderson, *Truth Overruled: The Future of Marriage and Religious Freedom* (Washington, DC: Regnery, 2015).

25. "Statement Calling for Constitutional Resistance to Obergefell v. Hodges," American Principles Project, October 8, 2015, https://americanprinciplesproject.org/founding-principles/statement-calling-for-constitutional-resistance-to-obergefell-v-hodges%e2%80%af/. "After Obergefell: A First Things Symposium," *First Things*, June 27, 2015, https://www.firstthings.com/web-exclusives/2015/06/after-obergefell-a-first-things-symposium, accessed October 1, 2016.

26. For a critique of their view that can be easily accessed online, see Corvino, "What's Wrong with Gay Marriage?," *Philosopher's*

Magazine, January 25, 2015, http://www.philosophersmag.com/
index.php/tpm-mag-articles/11-essays/12-what-s-wrong-with-
gay-marriage, accessed October 2, 2016. For a more detailed treatment, see Corvino, "What Marriage Can Be," in *Justice Through
Diversity: A Philosophical and Theological Debate*, ed. Michael
J. Sweeney (Lanham, MD: Rowman and Littlefield, 2016), 285–
307. See also John Corvino, *What's Wrong with Homosexuality?*
(Oxford: Oxford University Press, 2013), chap. 4.

27. For example, Robert P. George, their coauthor of *What Is Marriage?*,
endorses them. See "Unnatural Law," *New Republic*, March 27,
2003, https://newrepublic.com/article/64542/unnatural-law.

28. Centers for Disease Control and Prevention, "LGBT Youth:
Lesbian, Gay, Bisexual, and Transgender Health," November
12, 2014, http://www.cdc.gov/lgbthealth/youth.htm, accessed
September 19, 2016.

29. Melissa Elaine Klein dba Sweetcakes by Melissa, 34 BOLI 102 (2015),
https://www.oregon.gov/boli/SiteAssets/pages/press/Sweet%20
Cakes%20FO.pdf.

30. Despite the fact that SOGI is not protected under federal law,
"eighty-seven percent of voters believe it is illegal under federal
law to fire someone for being gay and 78% believe it is illegal
under state law. Even in states without antidiscrimination laws,
75% of voters think it is illegal under state law to fire someone for being gay or lesbian." Human Rights Campaign, "New
HRC Poll Finds Vast Majority of Voters Support Employment
Antidiscrimination Laws," December 13, 2011, http://www.hrc.
org/press/new-hrc-poll-finds-vast-majority-of-voters-support-
employment-anti-discrimi/.

31. See Girgis, Anderson, and George, *What Is Marriage?*

32. John Corvino, *John Corvino—What's Morally Wrong with
Homosexuality?* (full DVD video), 2013, https://www.youtube.
com/watch?v=5iXA_0MED98&lc=z12ysvwqhrmfyzv1x22ou1p
ynwb5wd23k.

33. As the dance troupe's director, Violet Holmes, put it in the early
1980s: "One or two black girls in the line would definitely dis-
tract. You would lose the whole look of precision, which is the
hallmark of the Rockettes." The group was not integrated until
1987. See Bruce Lambert, "Rockettes and Race: Barrier Slips,"

New York Times, December 26, 1987, sec. N.Y./Region, http://www.nytimes.com/1987/12/26/nyregion/rockettes-and-race-barrier-slips.html.

34. Human Rights Campaign, http://www.hrc.org/blog/a-night-to-celebrate-in-utah.

35. Walter Olson, "Gay Marriage and Religious Rights: Say Nada to FADA," *Newsweek,* September 10, 2015, http://www.newsweek.com/gay-marriage-and-religious-rights-say-nada-fada-370860. Olson was writing about the original proposed federal FADA, not the Mississippi FADA, and his concerns were somewhat different from mine. But the description is apt in both cases.

36. Pierce v. Society of Sisters, 268 U.S. 510 (1925).

Chapter 5

1. Julian Savulescu and Udo Schuklenk, "Doctors Have No Right to Refuse Medical Assistance in Dying, Abortion or Contraception," *Bioethics,* 22 September, 2016, http://onlinelibrary.wiley.com/doi/10.1111/bioe.12288/full, accessed October 4, 2016.

2. U.S. Commission on Civil Rights, *Peaceful Coexistence: Reconciling Nondiscrimination Principles with Civil Liberties* (Washington, DC: September 2016), 151–52, http://www.usccr.gov/pubs/Peaceful-Coexistence-09-07-16.PDF, accessed September 30, 2016.

3. The federal FADA limits government action based on support for man-woman marriage *or* same-sex marriage. We support both bills.

4. Richard A. Epstein, "Religious Liberty under Siege In Mississippi," *Defining Ideas: A Hoover Institution Journal,* July 18, 2016, http://www.hoover.org/research/religious-liberty-under-siege-mississippi, accessed September 29, 2016.

5. Eugene Volokh, "A Common-Law Model for Religious Exemptions," *UCLA Law Review* 46 (1999): n. 106.

6. Clyde Wayne Crews, "New Data: Code of Federal Regulations Expanding, Faster Pace under Obama," Competitive Enterprise Institute, March 17, 2014, https://cei.org/blog/new-data-code-federal-regulations-expanding-faster-pace-under-obama, accessed September 30, 2016.

7. "Understanding Who Is Exempted from the HHS Mandate," Little Sisters of the Poor, http://thelittlesistersofthepoor.com/who-is-exempt-from/, accessed September 30, 2016.

8. "Plan B One-Step Drug Label," FDA.gov, Reference ID: 3329183, http://www.accessdata.fda.gov/drugsatfda_docs/label/2013/021998Orig1s003lbl.pdf, accessed September 30, 2016.

9. Thomas C. Berg, "Religious Accommodation and the Welfare State," *Harvard Journal of Law and Gender* 38 (2015): 103–151.

10. Burwell v. Hobby Lobby Stores, Inc., 134 S. Ct. 2751, 2805 (2014), 42.

11. David Harsanyi, "How a Cakemaker Became an Enemy of the State, *Federalist,* September 6, 2016, http://thefederalist.com/2016/09/06/how-a-cakemaker-became-an-enemy-of-the-state/, accessed September 29, 2016.

12. Gary D. Robertson, "Judge Dismisses Challenge to N. Carolina Gay-Marriage law," *Washington Post,* September 21, 2016, https://www.washingtonpost.com/national/judge-dismisses-challenge-to-n-carolina-gay-marriage-law/2016/09/21/0f23ab58-8016-11e6-ad0e-ab0d12c779b1_story.html, accessed September 29, 2016.

13. Corvino, " 'Bake Me a Cake': Three Paths for Balancing Liberty and Equality" (blog entry), What's Wrong?, October 15, 2015, https://whatswrongcvsp.com/2015/10/15/guest-post-from-john-corvino-bake-me-a-cake-three-paths-for-balancing-liberty-and-equality/.

14. "Utah 'Compromise' to Protect LGBT Citizens from Discrimination Is No Model for the Nation," *Slate,* March 18, 2015, http://www.slate.com/blogs/outward/2015/03/18/gay_rights_the_utah_compromise_is_no_model_for_the_nation.html.

15. Zack Ford, "The 'Utah Compromise' Is a Dangerous LGBT Trojan Horse," *ThinkProgress,* https://thinkprogress.org/the-utah-compromise-is-a-dangerous-lgbt-trojan-horse-db790ad3b69e#.4eose5vpx.

16. Kate Shellnutt, "Fairness for All: Evangelicals Explore Truce on LGBT and Religious Rights," *Christianity Today,* http://www.christianitytoday.com/ct/2016/december-web-only/fairness-for-all-evangelicals-explore-truce-lgbt-cccu-nae.html. https://www.youtube.com/watch?v=3YezwtRX9XU.

17. Robin Fisher, Geof Gee, and Adam Looney, "Joint Filing by Same-Sex Couples after Windsor: Characteristics of Married Tax

Filers in 2013 and 2014," Department of the Treasury Office of Tax Analysis working paper 108, August 2016, https://www.treasury.gov/resource-center/tax-policy/tax-analysis/Documents/WP-108.pdf, accessed September 30, 2016.

18. Russell Moore, "Is Divorce Equivalent to Homosexuality?," RussellMoore.com, September 25, 2016, http://www.russellmoore.com/2014/09/24/is-divorce-equivalent-to-homosexuality/, accessed September 29, 2016.

19. Christopher Eisgruber and Lawrence Sager, for example, argue that religion does *not* deserve special treatment as such precisely *because* it is one among many deep commitments.

20. We owe our presentation of this argument to Germain Grisez, *God? A Philosophical Preface to Faith* (South Bend, IN: St. Augustine's Press, 2005).

BIBLIOGRAPHY

Books and Periodicals

Ackerman, Bruce. *We The People.* Vol. 3. *The Civil Rights Revolution.* Cambridge, MA: Harvard University Press, 2014.

Adler, Jonathan, et al. "Freedom to Marry, Freedom to Dissent: Why We Must Have Both." *RealClearPolitics*, April 22, 2014. http://www.realclearpolitics.com/articles/2014/04/22/freedom_to_marry_freedom_to_dissent_why_we_must_have_both_122376.html. Accessed July 12, 2016.

American Civil Liberties Union. "Tamesha Means v. United States Conference of Catholic Bishops—Complaint." https://www.aclu.org/legal-document/tamesha-means-v-united-states-conference-catholic-bishops-complaint. Accessed September 26, 2016.

Anderson, Ryan T. "First Amendment Defense Act Protects Freedom and Pluralism after Marriage Redefinition." Heritage Foundation, November 25, 2015. http://www.heritage.org/research/reports/2015/11/first-amendment-defense-act-protects-freedom-and-pluralism-after-marriage-redefinition.

Anderson, Ryan T. "New Obamacare Transgender Regulations Threaten Freedom of Physicians." *Daily Signal*, May 13, 2016. http://dailysignal.com/2016/05/13/new-obamacare-transgender-regulations-threaten-freedom-of-physicians/.

Anderson, Ryan T. "Obama Unilaterally Rewrites Law, Imposes Transgender Policy on Nation's Schools." *Daily Signal*, May 13, 2016. http://dailysignal.com/2016/05/13/obama-unilaterally-rewrites-law-imposes-transgender-policy-on-nations-schools/.

Anderson, Ryan T. "Sexual Orientation and Gender Identity (SOGI) Laws Threaten Freedom." Heritage Foundation, November 30, 2015. http://www.heritage.org/research/reports/2015/11/sexual-orientation-and-gender-identity-sogi-laws-threaten-freedom.

Anderson, Ryan T. *Truth Overruled: The Future of Marriage and Religious Freedom*. Washington, DC: Regnery, 2015.

Anderson, Ryan T. "We Don't Need Kim Davis to Be in Jail." *New York Times*, September 7, 2015. http://www.nytimes.com/2015/09/07/opinion/we-dont-need-kim-davis-to-be-in-jail.html?_r=1.

Anti-Violence Project. "2015 Report on Lesbian, Gay, Bisexual, Transgender, Queer, and HIV-Affected Hate Violence." http://www.avp.org/resources/avp-resources/520. Accessed September 19, 2016.

Aristotle. *Ethics*. In *The Complete Works of Aristotle*, ed. Jonathan Barnes (1836), vol. 2, rev. trans. Oxford: Oxford University Press, 1984.

Atwood, Thomas C. "Foster Care: Safety Net or Trap Door?" Heritage Foundation *Backgrounder*, no. 2535, March 25, 2011, 12. http://www.heritage.org/research/reports/2011/03/foster-care-safety-net-or-trap-door.

Atwood, Thomas C. "Standard Time Zones In U.S. Mark 100 Years." *New York Times*, November 20, 1983. http://www.nytimes.com/1983/11/20/us/standard-time-zones-in-us-mark-100-years.html.

Bader, Hans. "Employment Non-discrimination Act Makes as Little Sense as Chemotherapy for a Cold." Competitive Enterprise Institute, June 13, 2012. https://cei.org/blog/employment-non-discrimination-act-makes-little-sense-chemotherapy-cold.

Bagenstos, Samuel R. "The Unrelenting Libertarian Challenge to Public Accommodations Law." *Stanford Law Review* 66, no. 6 (2014): 1205–40.

Bailey, David, and Ben Klayman. "Kim Davis' Attorney Says Marriage Licenses Issued on Friday Are Invalid." *Huffington Post*, September 4, 2015. http://www.huffingtonpost.com/entry/kim-davis-attorney-says-marriage-licenses-issued-on-friday-are-invalid_us_55e9f00ce4b002d5c076007b. Accessed September 19, 2016.

Baldas, Tresa. "Pediatrician Wouldn't Care for Baby with 2 Moms." *Detroit Free Press*, February 19, 2015. http://www.freep.com/ story/news/local/michigan/macomb/2015/02/18/discrimination-birth/23640315/.

Balkin, J. M. "The Constitution of Status." *Yale Law Journal* 106 (1997): 2313.

Beam, Adam. "Jailed Clerk's Attorney: Marriage Licenses for Gays Are Void." *Yahoo News*, September 4, 2015. http://news.yahoo. com/gay-couples-try-wed-defiant-clerk-sits-jail-082850785.html.

Beckwith, Francis. "Interracial Marriage and Same-Sex Marriage." *Public Discourse*, May 21, 2010. http://www.thepublicdiscourse. com/2010/05/1324/.

Berg, Thomas C. "Religious Accommodation and the Welfare State." *Harvard Journal of Law & Gender* 38 (2015): 103–151.

Berg, Thomas, et al. "Statement of Law Professors on Religious Liberty Implications of Proposed Hawaii Marriage Equality Act of 2013." Blogentry.MirrorofJustice,2013.http://mirrorofjustice.blogs.com/ files/hawaii-gaffney-et-al-testimony-full-final-28oct13-1.pdf.

Berman, Harold J. *Law and Revolution: The Formation of the Western Legal Tradition*. Cambridge, MA: Harvard University Press, 1983.

Bernstein, David E. "Context Matters: A Better Libertarian Approach to Antidiscrimination Law." *Cato Unbound*, June 16, 2010. http:// www.cato-unbound.org/2010/06/16/david-e-bernstein/context-matters-better-libertarian-approach-antidiscrimination-law. Accessed July 12, 2016.

Blackstone, William. *The Commentaries of Sir William Blackstone, Knight, on the Laws and Constitution of England*. Washington, DC: American Bar Association, 2009.

Blinder, Alan, and Richard Pérez-Peña. "Kentucky Clerk Denies Same-Sex Marriage Licenses, Defying Court." *New York Times*, September 1, 2015. http://www.nytimes.com/2015/09/02/us/ same-sex-marriage-kentucky-kim-davis.html.

"Bob Jones University Apologizes for Its Racist Past." *Journal of Blacks in Higher Education* 62 (2008): 22–23.

Bob Jones University. "Statement about Race at BJU." http://www. bju.edu/about/what-we-believe/race-statement.php. Accessed July 11, 2016.

Brachear, Manya A. "3 Dioceses Drop Foster Care Lawsuit." *Chicago Tribune*, November 15, 2011. http://articles.chicagotribune.com/

2011-11-15/news/ct-met-catholic-charities-foster-care-20111115_1_civil-unions-act-catholic-charities-religious-freedom-protection.

Buckley, Madeline. "Threats Tied to RFRA Prompt Indiana Pizzeria to Close Its Doors." *IndyStar*, April 3, 2015. http://www.indystar.com/story/news/2015/04/02/threats-tied-rfra-prompt-indiana-pizzeria-close-doors/70847230/.

Carmon, Irin. "Birth Control, the Supreme Court and Me." MSNBC, November 25, 2013. http://www.msnbc.com/msnbc/birth-control-the-supreme-court-and-me.

Case, Mary Anne. "Why Live-and-Let-Live Is Not a Viable Solution to the Difficult Problems of Religious Accommodation in the Age of Sexual Civil Rights." *Southern California Law Review* 88 (2015): 463–92.

Catholic Church. *Catechism of the Catholic Church: Revised in Accordance with the Official Latin Text Promulgated by Pope John Paul II*. Vatican City: Libreria Editrice Vaticana, 1997.

Centers for Disease Control and Prevention. "LGBT Youth: Lesbian, Gay, Bisexual, and Transgender Health." November 12, 2014. http://www.cdc.gov/lgbthealth/youth.htm. Accessed September 19, 2016.

Corbin, Caroline Mala. "Above the Law? The Constitutionality of the Ministerial Exemption from Antidiscrimination Law." *Fordham Law Review* 75, no. 4 (2007): 1965–2038.

Corner, Dan. "John 6:53 and the Catholic Holy Eucharist." Evangelical Outreach. http://www.evangelicaloutreach.org/communio.htm. Accessed January 12, 2016.

Corvino, John. "'Bake Me a Cake': Three Paths for Balancing Liberty and Equality." Blog entry. What's Wrong?, October 15, 2015. https://whatswrongcvsp.com/2015/10/15/guest-post-from-john-corvino-bake-me-a-cake-three-paths-for-balancing-liberty-and-equality/.

Corvino, John. "It's Time to Remove Kentucky Clerk Kim Davis." *Detroit Free Press*, September 1, 2015. http://www.freep.com/story/opinion/contributors/2015/09/01/s-time-remove-kentucky-clerk-kim-davis/71505026/. Accessed March 9, 2016.

Corvino, John. *John Corvino—What's Morally Wrong with Homosexuality?* Full DVD video. 2013. https://www.youtube.com/watch?v=5iXA_0MED98&lc=z12ysvwqhrmfyzv1x22ou1pynwb5wd23k.

Corvino, John. "Rejoinder to Dan Johnson: A Plea for Distinctions." Partially Examined Life Philosophy Podcast, October 13, 2015. https://www.partiallyexaminedlife.com/2015/10/13/rejoinder-to-dan-johnson-a-plea-for-distinctions/.

Corvino, John. "What Marriage Can Be." In *Justice through Diversity: A Philosophical and Theological Debate,* ed. Michael J. Sweeney. Lanham, MD: Rowman and Littlefield, 2016, 285–307.

Corvino, John. "What's Wrong with Gay Marriage?" *Philosopher's Magazine,* January 25, 2015. http://www.philosophersmag.com/index.php/tpm-mag-articles/11-essays/12-what-s-wrong-with-gay-marriage. Accessed October 2, 2016.

Corvino, John. *What's Wrong with Homosexuality?* Oxford: Oxford University Press, 2013.

Corvino, John, and Maggie Gallagher. *Debating Same-Sex Marriage.* New York: Oxford University Press, 2012.

Cott, Nancy F. *Public Vows: A History of Marriage and the Nation.* Kindle ed. Cambridge, MA: Harvard University Press, 2000.

Crews, Clyde Wayne. "New Data: Code of Federal Regulations Expanding, Faster Pace under Obama." Competitive Enterprise Institute, March 17, 2014. https://cei.org/blog/new-data-code-federal-regulations-expanding-faster-pace-under-obama. Accessed September 30, 2016.

DeSanctis, Alexandra. "In Michigan, a Small but Meaningful Victory for Conscience Rights." *National Review Online,* September 14, 2016. http://www.nationalreview.com/corner/440038/aclu-michigan-lawsuit-dismissed-religious-conscience-rights-win-huge-victory. Accessed September 29, 2016.

Damai Disabled Person Association Malaysia. "Hindu Temples Deny Disabled People Entry." February 7, 2012. http://damai.org.my/hindu-temples-deny-disabled-people-entry/.

Eich, Brendan. "Inclusiveness at Mozilla." *Brendan Eich,* March 24, 2014. https://brendaneich.com/2014/03/inclusiveness-at-mozilla/.

Eidelson, Benjamin. *Discrimination and Disrespect.* 1st ed. Oxford: Oxford University Press, 2016.

Eisgruber, Christopher L., and Lawrence G. Sager. *Religious Freedom and the Constitution.* Cambridge, MA: Harvard University Press, 2007.

Epstein, Richard A. "Religious Liberty under Siege in Mississippi." *Defining Ideas: A Hoover Institution Journal,* July 18, 2016.

http://www.hoover.org/research/religious-liberty-under-siege-mississippi. Accessed September 29, 2016.

Finnis, John. *Natural Law and Natural Rights.* Oxford: Oxford University Press, 2011.

Fisher, Robin, Geof Gee, and Adam Looney. "Joint Filing by Same-Sex Couples after Windsor: Characteristics of Married Tax Filers in 2013 and 2014." Department of the Treasury Office of Tax Analysis working paper 108. August 2016. https://www.treasury.gov/resource-center/tax-policy/tax-analysis/Documents/WP-108.pdf. Accessed September 30, 2016.

Ford, Worthington Chauncey, Gaillard Hunt, John Clement Fitzpatrick, Roscoe R. Hill, Kenneth E. Harris, and Steven D. Tilley. *Journals of the Continental Congress, 1774–1789.* Vol. 5. Washington, DC: U.S. Government Printing Office, 1906.

Galen, Luke W. "Does Religious Belief Promote Prosociality? A Critical Examination." *Psychological Bulletin* 138, no. 5 (September 2012): 876–906. PsycARTICLES, EBSCOhost. Accessed September 3, 2016.

Gallup. "Gay and Lesbian Rights." December 30, 2015. http://www.gallup.com/poll/1651/Gay-Lesbian-Rights.aspx.

Gallup. "In U.S., 87% Approve of Black-White Marriage, vs. 4% in 1958." July 25, 2013. http://www.gallup.com/poll/163697/approve-marriage-blacks-whites.aspx.

Garicano, Luis, Claire LeLarge, and John Van Reenen. "Firm Size Distortions and the Productivity Distribution: Evidence from France." National Bureau of Economic Research working paper no. 18841. February 2013. http://ideas.repec.org/p/nbr/nberwo/18841.html. Accessed November 13, 2015.

Garnett, Richard W. "Confusion about Discrimination." *Public Discourse,* April 5, 2012. http://www.thepublicdiscourse.com/2012/04/5151/.

George, Robert P. *Making Men Moral.* Oxford: Clarendon Press, 1993.

George, Robert P., et al. "After Obergefell: A First Things Symposium." *First Things.* https://www.firstthings.com/web-exclusives/2015/06/after-obergefell-a-first-things-symposium. Accessed October 1, 2016.

Gilabert, Pablo. "Human Rights, Human Dignity, and Power." In *Philosophical Foundations of Human Rights,* ed. Rowan Cruft, Matthew Liao, and Massimo Renzo. Oxford: Oxford University Press, 2015, 196–213.

Girgis, Sherif, Ryan T. Anderson, and Robert P. George. *What Is Marriage? Man and Woman: A Defense*. New York: Encounter Books, 2012.

Glatz, Kyle. "Why Are Sikhs Upset over New Motorcycle Helmet Law?" *World Religion News*, September 4, 2014. http://www.worldreligionnews.com/culture/sikhs-upset-new-motorcycle-helmet-law.

Gleason, Hillary A., Nicholas A. Livingston, Marianne M. Peters, Kathryn M. Oost, Evan Reely, and Bryan N. Cochran. "Effects of State Nondiscrimination Laws on Transgender and Gender-Nonconforming Individuals' Perceived Community Stigma and Mental Health." *Journal of Gay & Lesbian Mental Health* 20, no. 4 (October 1, 2016): 350–62. doi:10.1080/19359705.2016.1207582.

Goodstein, Laurie. "Battles around Nation over Proposed Mosques." *New York Times*, August 7, 2010, sec. U.S. http://www.nytimes.com/2010/08/08/us/08mosque.html.

Gordon, Sarah Barringer. *The Mormon Question: Polygamy and Constitutional Conflict in Nineteenth-Century America*. 1st new ed. Chapel Hill: University of North Carolina Press, 2002.

Graff, E. J. *What Is Marriage For? The Strange Social History of Our Most Intimate Institution*. Boston: Beacon Press, 1999.

Grim, Brian J., and Roger Finke. *The Price of Freedom Denied: Religious Persecution and Conflict in the 21st Century*. New York: Cambridge University Press, 2011, 205.

Grisez, Germain. *God? A Philosophical Preface to Faith*. South Bend, IN: St. Augustine's Press, 2005.

Grossman, Cathy Lynn. "What's Abortifacient? Disputes over Birth Control Fuel Obamacare Fight." *Washington Post*, January 28, 2014. https://perma-archives.org/warc/P767-8SPN/http://www.washingtonpost.com/national/religion/whats-abortifacient-disputes-over-birth-control-fuel-obamacare-fight/2014/01/28/61f080be-886a-11e3-a760-a86415d0944d_story.html. Accessed July 10, 2016.

Gunn, Phillip, et al. H.B. 1523 Protecting Freedom of Conscience from Government Discrimination Act. 2016. https://legiscan.com/MS/text/HB1523/id/1382645.

Gunther, Gerald. The Supreme Court, 1971 Term—Foreword: In Search of Evolving Doctrine on a Changing Court: A Model for a Newer Equal Protection. *Harvard Law Review* 86, no. 1 (1972): 1–48.

Gutting, Gary. "How Religion Can Lead to Violence." *New York Times*, August 1, 2016. http://www.nytimes.com/2016/08/01/opinion/how-religion-can-lead-to-violence.html. Accessed September 19, 2016.

Hall, Mark David. "Religious Accommodations and the Common Good." Heritage Foundation, October 26, 2015. http://www.heritage.org/research/reports/2015/10/religious-accommodations-and-the-common-good. Accessed September 3, 2016.

Hamilton, Marci A. "The Case for Evidence-Based Free Exercise Accommodation: Why the Religious Freedom Restoration Act Is Bad Public Policy." *Harvard Law & Policy Review* 9, no. 13 (2015): 129–160.

Handwerk, Brian. "Time to Move On? The Case against Daylight Saving Time." *National Geographic News*, November 1, 2013. http://news.nationalgeographic.com/news/2013/11/131101-when-does-daylight-savings-time-end-november-3-science/.

Harsanyi, David. "How a Cakemaker Became an Enemy of the State. *Federalist*, September 6, 2016. http://thefederalist.com/2016/09/06/how-a-cakemaker-became-an-enemy-of-the-state/. Accessed September 29, 2016.

Hearings before the Subcommittee on Civil and Constitutional Rights of the Committee on the Judiciary, House of Representatives. Washington, DC: U.S. Government Printing Office, 1993. https://www.justice.gov/sites/default/files/jmd/legacy/2014/07/13/hear-99-1992.pdf. Accessed October 4, 2016.

Henry, Leslie Meltzer. "The Jurisprudence of Dignity." *University of Pennsylvania Law Review* 160, no. 1 (2011): 189–190.

Hobby Lobby. "Our Story." Hobby Lobby.com. http://www.hobbylobby.com/about-us/our-story. Accessed July 10, 2016.

"Hobby Lobby Stores on the Forbes America's Largest Private Companies List." *Forbes*, 2015. http://www.forbes.com/companies/hobby-lobby-stores/.

Houston City Council. Ordinance No. 2014-530. May 28, 2014. Exhibit A, pp. 2–3, http://www.scribd.com/doc/228533432/Equal-Rights-Ordinance Accessed November 13, 2015.

Howell, Kellan. "Florida 'Muslim-Free' Gun Shop Owner Wins Discrimination Suit." *Washington Times*, November 28, 2015. http://www.washingtontimes.com/news/2015/nov/28/florida-muslim-free-gun-shop-owner-wins-discrimina/. Accessed July 11, 2016.

Human Rights Campaign. "Beyond Marriage Equality." http://www.hrc.org/campaigns/beyond-marriage-equality-a-blueprint-for-federal-non-discrimination-protect. Accessed November 12, 2015.

Human Rights Campaign. "LGBT Equality at the Fortune 500." http://www.hrc.org/resources/entry/lgbt-equality-at-the-fortune-500. Accessed November 13, 2015.

Human Rights Campaign. "Maps of State Laws and Policies." http://www.hrc.org/state_maps. Accessed September 28, 2016.

Human Rights Campaign. "New HRC Poll Finds Vast Majority of Voters Support Employment Anti-discrimination Laws." December 13, 2011. http://www.hrc.org/press/new-hrc-poll-finds-vast-majority-of-voters-support-employment-anti-discrimi/.

Human Rights Campaign. "Violence against the Transgender Community in 2016." http://www.hrc.org/resources/violence-against-the-transgender-community-in-2016/. Accessed September 19, 2016.

Human Rights Campaign Staff. "With Sweeping New Ruling, Marriage Equality Must Begin in All 50 States." http://www.hrc.org/blog/with-sweeping-new-ruling-marriage-equality-must-begin-in-all-50-states/. Accessed September 3, 2016.

Ignatiev, Noel. *How the Irish Became White.* 1st ed. New York: Routledge, 2008.

"Interracial Couple Denied Marriage License in Tangipahoa Parish." Associated Press. NOLA.com, October 16, 2009. http://www.nola.com/crime/index.ssf/2009/10/interracial_couple_denied_marr.html. Accessed July 11, 2016.

Jerde, Sarah. "Anti-gay Pastor: If My Son Married a Man, I'd Spread Manure 'All over My Body.'" Video. *TPM*, November 09, 2015. http://talkingpointsmemo.com/livewire/tea-party-pastor-same-sex-marriage. Accessed July 12, 2016.

Joe.My.God. "Ohio Bakery: No Birthday Cakes for Gay Couples." Blog entry. Joe.My.God., July 07, 2016. http://www.joemygod.com/2016/07/07/ohio-bakery-no-birthday-cakes-for-gay-couples/. Accessed July 12, 2016.

Jones, Bob. "Is Segregation Scriptural?" Sermons of Bob Jones: A Digital History Project, November 12, 2014. https://bob-jonessermons.wordpress.com/sermons/is-segregation-scriptural/.

"Kim Davis Denied Marriage Licenses for Her Friends." *ABC News*, September 23, 2015. http://abcnews.go.com/US/

kentucky-clerk-kim-davis-denied-marriage-licenses-friends/ story?id=33939041.

Koppelman, Andrew. "A Free Speech Response to the Gay Rights/ Religious Liberty Conflict." (June 7, 2016). 110 *Northwestern University Law Review* 1125 (2016); Northwestern Public Law Research Paper No. 16-14. https://ssrn.com/abstract=2791641.

Koppelman, Andrew. *Antidiscrimination Law and Social Equality.* Rev. ed. New Haven, CT: Yale University Press, 1998.

Koppelman, Andrew. "Gay Rights, Religious Accommodations, and the Purposes of Antidiscrimination Law" (February 16, 2014). *Southern California Law Review* 88 (2015): 619–59; Northwestern Public Law research paper no. 15-11; Northwestern Law & Economics research paper no. 15-06. http://ssrn.com/abstract=2571058.

Koppelman, Andrew M. "Why Discrimination against Lesbians and Gay Men Is Sex Discrimination." *New York University Law Review* 69 (1994): 197.

Koppelman, Andrew M. "A Zombie in the Supreme Court: The Elane Photography Cert Denial." *Alabama Civil Rights & Civil Liberties Law Review* 7 (2015): 77.

Koppelman, Andrew, and Frederick M. Gedicks. "Is Hobby Lobby Worse for Religious Liberty Than Smith?" *University of St. Thomas Journal of Law and Public Policy* (Minnesota) 9 (2015): 223–47.

Lambert, Bruce. "Rockettes and Race: Barrier Slips." *New York Times*, December 26, 1987, sec. N.Y./Region. http://www.nytimes.com/1987/12/26/nyregion/rockettes-and-race-barrier-slips.html. Accessed September 19, 2016.

LaReau, Jamie. "The Battle over Sunday Sales." *Automotive News*, November 22, 2015. http://www.autonews.com/article/20150503/RETAIL07/304279869/the-battle-over-sunday-sales.

Laycock, Douglas. Afterword to Douglas Laycock, Anthony R. Picarello, Jr., and Robin Fretwell Wilson, *Same-Sex Marriage and Religious Liberty: Emerging Conflicts* Lanham, MD: Rowman and Littlefield, 2008, 198.

Laycock, Douglas. "Freedom of Speech That Is Both Religious and Political." Symposium. *U.C. Davis Law Review* 29 (1996): 801–3.

Laycock, Douglas. "The Religious Freedom Restoration Act." *Brigham Young University Law Review* (1993): 221, 229–30.

Laycock, Douglas. "Religious Liberty and the Culture Wars." *University of Illinois Law Review* 2014 (2014): 839–80, 869.

Laycock, Douglas. "Religious Liberty as Liberty." *Journal of Contemporary Legal Issues* 7, no. 2 (1996): 313.

Laycock, Douglas. "The Religious Exemption Debate." *Rutgers Journal of Law and Religion* 11 (2009): 139, 171.

Lee, Tony. "Mike Huckabee: We Must Stand with Kim Davis against 'Criminalization of Christianity.'" *Breitbart*, September 07, 2015. http://www.breitbart.com/big-government/2015/09/07/mike-huckabee-we-must-stand-with-kim-davis-against-criminalization-of-christianity/. Accessed July 10, 2016.

Leiter, Brian. *Why Tolerate Religion?* Princeton: Princeton University Press, 2013.

Leiter, Brian. "Why Tolerate Religion, Again? A Reply to Michael McConnell." SSRN scholarly paper. Rochester, NY: Social Science Research Network, May 8, 2016. http://papers.ssrn.com/abstract=2777208.

Leland, John. "Tension in a Michigan City over Muslims' Call to Prayer." *New York Times*, May 5, 2004. http://www.nytimes.com/2004/05/05/us/tension-in-a-michigan-city-over-muslims-call-to-prayer.html.

Levy, Brian L., and Denise L. Levy. "When Love Meets Hate: The Relationship between State Policies on Gay and Lesbian Rights and Hate Crime Incidence." *Social Science Research*. doi:10.1016/j.ssresearch.2016.06.008. Accessed September 28, 2016.

Liptak, Adam. "Supreme Court Says Kentucky Clerk Must Let Gay Couples Marry." *New York Times*, August 31, 2015. http://www.nytimes.com/2015/09/01/us/supreme-court-says-kentucky-clerk-must-let-gay-couples-marry.html.

Lithwick, Dahlia, Sonja West, and Aisha Harris. "Quick Change Justice." *Slate*, July 4, 2014. http://www.slate.com/articles/news_and_politics/jurisprudence/2014/07/wheaton_college_injunction_the_supreme_court_just_sneakily_reversed_itself.html.

Little Sisters of the Poor. "Understanding Who Is Exempted from the HHS Mandate." littlesistersofthepoor.com. http://thelittlesistersofthepoor.com/who-is-exempt-from/. Accessed September 30, 2016.

Loller, Travis. "Kentucky Clerk Case Divides Religious Liberty Advocates." *Chicago Tribune*, September 14, 2015. http://www.chicagotribune.com/news/nationworld/sns-ap-us-rel--gay-marriage-kentucky-20150913-story.html.

Long, Heather. "The Sunday Blues: Some U.S. States Don't Seem to Realize Prohibition Is Over." *Guardian*, March 03, 2013.

http://www.theguardian.com/commentisfree/2013/mar/03/
no-sunday-alcohol-sales-states-prohibition.

Lowder, J. Bryan. "Is Brendan Eich as Bigoted as Donald Sterling?" *Slate*, May 1, 2014. http://www.slate.com/blogs/outward/2014/05/
01/is_brendan_eich_as_bigoted_as_donald_sterling.html.

Lowder, J. Bryan. "No, It's Not Too Soon to Condemn Public Figures for Being Anti-gay." *Slate*, April 7, 2014. http://www.slate.com/
blogs/outward/2014/04/07/brenden_eich_s_mozilla_resigna-
tion_proves_gay_rights_are_no_longer_up_for.htm.

Lund, Christopher C. "Religion Is Special Enough." *Virginia Law Review,* forthcoming.

Lupu, Ira C. "*Hobby Lobby* and the Dubious Enterprise of Religious Exemptions." *Harvard Women's Law Journal* 38 (2015): 35–101.

Lupu, Ira C., and Robert W. Tuttle. *Secular Government, Religious People.* Grand Rapids, MI: Eerdmans, 2014.

MacKinnon, J. B. "America's Last Ban on Sunday Shopping." *New Yorker*, February 07, 2015. http://www.newyorker.com/busi-
ness/currency/americas-last-ban-sunday-shopping.

Madison, James. "A Memorial and Remonstrance." Letter to Honorable the General Assembly of the Commonwealth of Virginia, c. June 20, 1785. Founders Online, National Archives. http://founders.archives.gov/documents/Madison/01-08-02-
0163. Accessed October 4, 2016.

Mallory, Christy, and Brad Sears. "Evidence of Discrimination in Public Accommodations Based on Sexual Orientation and Gender Identity: An Analysis of Complaints Filed with State Enforcement Agencies, 2008–2014." *Williams Institute*, February 16, 2016. http://williamsinstitute.law.ucla.edu/research/workplace/
evidence-of-discrimination-in-public-accommodations-based-
on-sexual-orientation-and-gender-identity-an-analysis-of-
complaints-filed-with-state-enforcement-agencies-2008-2014/.

Mallory, Christy, and Brad Sears. "Evidence of Employment Discrimi-
nation Based on Sexual Orientation and Gender Identity: An Analysis of Complaints Filed with State Enforcement Agencies." *Williams Institute*, October 22, 2015. http://williamsinstitute.law.ucla.edu/
research/workplace/evidence-of-employment-discrimination-
based-on-sexual-orientation-and-gender-identity-an-analysis-
of-complaints-filed-with-state-enforcement-agencies/.

Mallory, Christy, and Brad Sears. "Evidence of Housing Discrimination Based on Sexual Orientation and Gender Identity: An Analysis of Complaints Filed with State Enforcement Agencies, 2008–2014." *Williams Institute*, February 9, 2016. http://williamsinstitute.law.ucla.edu/research/workplace/evidence-of-housing-discrimination-based-on-sexual-orientation-and-gender-identity-an-analysis-of-complaints-filed-with-state-enforcement-agencies-2008-2014/.

Mantyla, Kyle. "If Kevin Swanson's Son Got Gay Married, 'I'd Sit in Cow Manure and I'd Spread It All over My Body.'" *Right Wing Watch,* November 6, 2015. http://www.rightwingwatch.org/content/if-kevin-swansons-son-got-gay-married-id-sit-cow-manure-and-id-spread-it-all-over-my-body.

Markey, Maureen E. "The Price of Landlord's 'Free' Exercise of Religion: Tenant's Right to Discrimination-Free Housing and Privacy." *Fordham Urban Law Journal* 699 (1995): 810.

Marks, Noah. "Least Restrictive Means: Burwell v. Hobby Lobby." *Harvard Law Policy Review Online* 9 (2015): 19.

Marriage Anti-Defamation Alliance. "Schulz, Craigen, Montague." YouTube video. Posted by NationForMarriage, December 15, 2011. http://marriageada.org/schulz-craigen-montague/.

Marshall, William P. "Bad Statutes Make Bad Law: Burwell v Hobby Lobby." *Supreme Court Review* 2014, no. 1 (2014): 71, 118.

Mason, Jamie. "What an Abortifacient Is—and What It Isn't." *National Catholic Reporter,* February 20, 2012. https://www.ncronline.org/blogs/grace-margins/what-abortifacient-and-what-it-isnt. Accessed July 10, 2016.

Mavrodes, George. "Religion and the Queerness of Morality." In *Rationality, Religious Belief, and Moral Commitment: New Essays in the Philosophy of Religion,* ed. Robert Audi and William Wainwright. Ithaca: Cornell University Press, 1986.

May, Simon Căbulea, "Exemptions for Conscience." In *Religion in Liberal Political Philosophy,* ed. A. Bardon and C. Laborde (Oxford University Press, 2017), pp. 191–203.

McConnell, Michael W. "Why Is Religious Liberty the 'First Freedom'?" *Cardozo Law Review* 21, no. 4 (February 2000): 1243–66.

McConnell, Michael W. "Why Protect Religious Freedom?" Review of *Why Tolerate Religion?* by Brian Leiter. *Yale Law Journal*

123, no. 3 (December 2013): 770–811. http://www.yalelawjournal.org/review/why-protect-religious-freedom. Accessed July 11, 2016.

McHugh, Paul, and Gerard V. Bradley. "Sexual Orientation, Gender Identity, and Employment Law." *Public Discourse*, July 25, 2013. http://www.thepublicdiscourse.com/2013/07/10636/.

Merkley, Jeff, Tammy Baldwin, and Corey Booker. "The Equality Act." Fact sheet. U.S. Senate, 2015. https://assets.documentcloud.org/documents/2170089/senate-equality-act-fact-sheet.pdf. Accessed November 13, 2015.

Miller, Dale. "Reluctant Florists, Same-Sex Weddings, and Mill's Doctrine of Liberty.'" *Public Affairs Quarterly* 30, no. 4 (2016): 287–311.

Mitchell Baker, "Brendan Eich Steps Down as Mozilla CEO." Blog entry. *Mozilla Blog,* April 3, 2014. https://blog.mozilla.org/blog/2014/04/03/brendan-eich-steps-down-as-mozilla-ceo/.

Moffi, Alberto. *Family and Property Law.* In *Cambridge Companion to Ancient Greek Law,* ed. Michael Gagarin and David Cohen. New York: Cambridge University Press, 2005.

Montgomery, Amy. "Same-Sex Couple Denied a Birthday Cake by Local Bakery." *13ABC*, July 7, 2016. http://www.13abc.com/content/news/Same-sex-couple-denied-a-birthday-cake-by-local-bakery-385783221.html. Accessed July 12, 2016.

Moore, Russell. "Is Divorce Equivalent to Homosexuality?" RussellMoore.com, September 25, 2016. http://www.russellmoore.com/2014/09/24/is-divorce-equivalent-to-homosexuality/. Accessed September 29, 2016.

Murdoch, Joyce, and Deb Price. *Courting Justice: Gay Men and Lesbians v. The Supreme Court.* New York: Basic Books, 2001.

NeJaime, Douglas. "Marriage Inequality: Same-Sex Relationships, Religious Exemptions, and the Production of Sexual Orientation Discrimination." *California Law Review* 100, no. 5 (2012): 1169–238.

NeJaime, Douglas, and Reva B. Siegel. "Conscience Wars: Complicity-Based Conscience Claims in Religion and Politics." *Yale Law Journal* 124 (2015): 2516–91.

Nielsen, Kai. "Ethics without Religion." *Ohio University Review* 6 (1964): 48–62.

Novak, Michael. "Aquinas and the Heretics." *First Things*, December, 1995. https://www.firstthings.com/article/1995/12/003-aquinas-and-the-heretics. Accessed September 19, 2016.

Nussbaum, Martha C. *From Disgust to Humanity: Sexual Orientation and Constitutional Law*. New York: Oxford University Press, 2010.

Nussbaum, Martha C. *Liberty of Conscience: In Defense of America's Tradition of Religious Equality*. New York: Basic Books, 2010.

Ohlheiser, Abby. "This Colorado Baker Refused to Put an Anti-gay Message on Cakes. Now She Is Facing a Civil Rights Complaint." *Washington Post*, January 28, 2015. https://www.washingtonpost.com/news/post-nation/wp/2015/01/22/this-colorado-baker-refused-to-put-an-anti-gay-message-on-cakes-now-she-is-facing-a-civil-rights-complaint/?utm_term=.7e8c24f6fd12.

Olson, Walter. "Gay Marriage and Religious Rights: Say Nada to FADA." *Newsweek*, September 10, 2015. http://www.newsweek.com/gay-marriage-and-religious-rights-say-nada-fada-370860.

Olson, Walter. "Religious Agencies and Adoption: A Case for Pluralism." Cato at Liberty, July 2, 2015. http://www.cato.org/blog/religious-adoption-agencies-case-pluralism.

Pappas, Stephanie. "Fact Check: Yes, Pregnancy Can Kill." *Live Science*. Last modified October 2012. http://www.livescience.com/24127-fact-check-walsh-pregnancy-can-kill.html. Accessed July 10, 2016.

Paul VI. Declaration on the Relation of the Church to Non-Christian Religions. *Nostra Aetate*, October 29, 1965. http://www.vatican.va/archive/hist_councils/ii_vatican_council/documents/vat-ii_decl_19651028_nostra-aetate_en.html.

Pew Research Center. "Tensions between Rights of Conscience and Civil Rights." Interview. Pew Forum. June 3, 2010. http://www.pewforum.org/2010/06/03/tensions-between-rights-of-conscience-and-civil-rights/. Accessed October 19, 2015.

"Plan B One-Step Drug Label." FDA.gov. Reference ID: 3329183. http://www.accessdata.fda.gov/drugsatfda_docs/label/2013/021998Orig1s003lbl.pdf. Accessed September 30, 2016.

Plutarch. *Plutarch: Moralia, Volume IX, Table-Talk, Books 7–9. Dialogue on Love*. Translated by Edwin L. Minar, Jr., F. H. Sandbach, and W. C. Helmbold. Cambridge, MA: Harvard University Press, 1961.

Plutarch. *Plutarch Lives, I, Theseus and Romulus. Lycurgus and Numa. Solon and Publicola.* Translated by Bernadotte Perrin. Cambridge, MA: Harvard University Press, 1914.

Prudential. "The LGBT Financial Experience." http://www.prudential.com/lgbt. Accessed April 2015.

Ramsey, William M. "Bigotry and Religious Belief." *Pacific Philosophical Quarterly* 94, no. 2 (June 19, 2013): 128.

Reid, Nick. "Signs for Jesus case against town of Pembroke to head to federal trial," *Concord Monitor*, February 16, 2016, http://www.concordmonitor.com/Archive/2016/02/signs4jesus-cm-021616.

Reisner, Sari L., Jaclyn M. White Hughto, Emilia E. Dunham, Katherine J. Heflin, Jesse Blue Glass Begenyi, Julia Coffey-Esquivel, and Sean Cahill. "Legal Protections in Public Accommodations Settings: A Critical Public Health Issue for Transgender and Gender-Nonconforming People." *Milbank Quarterly* 93, no. 3 (September 1, 2015): 484–515. doi:10.1111/1468-0009.12127.

Remizowski, Leigh. "Teacher Who Was Fired after Fertility Treatments Sues Diocese." *CNN*, last updated April 26, 2012. http://www.cnn.com/2012/04/26/us/indiana-in-vitro-lawsuit/index.html. Accessed July 11, 2016.

Robertson, Campbell. "Roy Moore, Alabama Chief Justice, Suspended over Gay Marriage Order." *New York Times*, October 1, 2016. http://www.nytimes.com/2016/10/01/us/roy-moore-alabama-chief-justice.html?_r=0.

Robertson, Gary D. "Judge Dismisses Challenge to N. Carolina Gay-Marriage Law." *Washington Post,* September 21, 2016. https://www.washingtonpost.com/national/judge-dismisses-challenge-to-n-carolina-gay-marriage-law/2016/09/21/0f23ab58-8016-11e6-ad0e-ab0d12c779b1_story.html. Accessed September 29, 2016.

Romero, McKenzie. "Salt Lake Police Officer Says He Was 'Uncomfortable' with Parade Assignment." *Deseret News*, June 9, 2014. http://www.deseretnews.com/article/865604835/Salt-Lake-police-officer-says-he-was-uncomfortable-with-parade-assignment.html.

Rousseau, Jean-Jacques. *The Social Contract* (1762). Trans. Maurice Cranston. London: Penguin, 1968.

Rubin, Alissa J. "French 'Burkini' Bans Provoke Backlash as Armed Police Confront Beachgoers." *New York Times,* August 24, 2016. http://www.nytimes.com/2016/08/25/world/europe/france-burkini.html?_r=0. Accessed October 3, 2016.

Rufus, Musonius. *Discourses XIIIA.* In *Musonius Rufus "The Roman Socrates."* Yale Classical Studies, trans. Cora E. Lutz. 1947. https://sites.google.com/site/thestoiclife/the_teachers/musonius-rufus/lectures/13-0.

"Same-Sex Couple Denied a Birthday Cake by Local Bakery." *13ABC.* http://www.13abc.com/content/news/Same-sex-couple-denied-a-birthday-cake-by-local-bakery-385783221.html. Accessed July 12, 2016.

Sandstrom, Aleksandra. "Nearly All States Allow Religious Exemptions for Vaccinations." Pew Research Center, July 2015. http://www.pewresearch.org/fact-tank/2015/07/16/nearly-all-states-allow-religious-exemptions-for-vaccinations/.

Savulescu, Julian, and Udo Schuklenk. "Doctors Have No Right to Refuse Medical Assistance in Dying, Abortion or Contraception." *Bioethics,* September 1, 2016. Accessed October 4, 2016. http://onlinelibrary.wiley.com/doi/10.1111/bioe.12288/full.

Sepinwall, Amy J. "Conscience and Complicity: Assessing Pleas for Religious Exemptions in 'Hobby Lobby's' Wake." *University of Chicago Law Review* 82, no. 4 (2015): 1897–1980.

Severino, Roger. "Gov. Bryant Stands Up to Liberal Bullying, Signs Mississippi Religious Freedom Bill." *Daily Signal,* April 5, 2016. http://dailysignal.com/2016/04/05/gov-bryant-stands-up-to-liberal-bullying-and-enacts-mississippi-religious-freedom-bill/.

"Sexting Case Highlights Quandary over Child Porn Laws." *Chicago Tribune,* September 24, 2015. http://www.chicagotribune.com/news/nationworld/ct-sexting-teens-child-porn-laws-20150924-story.html.

Spegele, Brian. "China's Banned Churches Defy Regime." *Wall Street Journal,* July 28, 2011. www.wsj.com/articles/SB10001424052702304567604576451913744126214. Accessed October 4, 2016.

"Statement Calling for Constitutional Resistance to Obergefell v. Hodges." American Principles Project, October 8, 2015. https://americanprinciplesproject.org/founding-principles/statement-calling-for-constitutional-resistance-to-obergefell-v-hodges%e2%80%af/.

Steinfels, Peter. "Clinton Signs Law Protecting Religious Practices." *New York Times*, November 17, 1993, sec. U.S. http://www.nytimes.com/1993/11/17/us/clinton-signs-law-protecting-religious-practices.html.

Steinhauer, Jennifer; Martin, Jonathan, and David M. Herszenhorn. "Paul Ryan Calls Donald Trump's Attack on Judge 'Racist,' but Still Backs Him." *New York Times*, June 7, 2016. http://www.nytimes.com/2016/06/08/us/politics/paul-ryan-donald-trump-gonzalo-curiel.html.

Stern, Mark Joseph. "Federal Judge: Religious Liberty Includes a Right to Fire LGBTQ Employees." *Slate,* August 18, 2016. http://www.slate.com/blogs/outward/2016/08/18/federal_judge_uses_religious_liberty_to_legalize_anti_lgbtq_discrimination.html.

Stewart, Katherine. "Ted Cruz and the Anti-gay Pastor." *New York Times*, November 16, 2015. http://www.nytimes.com/2015/11/16/opinion/campaign-stops/ted-cruz-and-the-anti-gay-pastor.html.

Strunk, Kamden. "LGBT Bias and Discrimination: Occurrence, Outcomes, and the Impact of Policy Change." ResearchGate, August 1, 2014. https://www.researchgate.net/publication/269277415_LGBT_bias_and_discrimination_Occurrence_outcomes_and_the_impact_of_policy_change.

Stutzman, Barronelle. "Why a Friend Is Suing Me: The Arlene's Flowers Story." *Seattle Times*, November 9, 2015. http://www.seattletimes.com/opinion/why-a-good-friend-is-suing-me-the-arlenes-flowers-story/. Accessed January 22, 2016.

Tererro, Nina. "Store Refused to Sell Dress to Lesbian Bride." *ABC News*, August 19, 2011. http://abcnews.go.com/US/nj-bridal-shop-refused-sell-wedding-dress-lesbian/story?id=14342333.

Tomasi, John. *Free Market Fairness* (Princeton: Princeton University Press, 2012).

Torre, Sarah. "Charities Become Collateral Damage in the Debate over Marriage." *Daily Signal*, July 14, 2011. http://dailysignal.com/2011/07/14/charities-become-collateral-damage-in-the-debate-over-marriage/.

Torre, Sarah. "Civil Union Law Forces Catholic Charities to Drop Adoption Service." *Daily Signal*, June 1, 2011. http://dailysignal.com/2011/06/01/civil-union-law-forces-catholic-charities-to-drop-adoption-serviceTribuneWireReports.

Torre, Sarah, and Ryan T. Anderson. "Adoption, Foster Care, and Conscience Protections." Heritage Foundation *Backgrounder* no. 2869, last updated January 15, 2014. http:// www.heritage.org/research/ reports/2014/01/adoption-foster-care-and-conscience-protection.

Tragen, Irving G. "Statutory Prohibitions against Interracial Marriage." *California Law Review* 32, no. 3 (September 1944). http://scholarship.law.berkeley.edu/californialawreview/vol32/ iss3/3. Accessed October 4, 2016.

United States Conference of Catholic Bishops. *Ethical and Religious Directives for Catholic Health Care Services.* 5th ed. Washington, DC: United States Conference of Catholic Bishops, 2001. http:// www.usccb.org/issues-and-action/human-life-and-dignity/ health-care/upload/Ethical-Religious-Directives-Catholic-Health-Care-Services-fifth-edition-2009.pdf. Accessed October 4, 2016.

"Unnatural Law." *New Republic,* March 27, 2003. https://newrepub-lic.com/article/64542/unnatural-law.

U.S. Commission on Civil Rights. *Peaceful Coexistence: Reconciling Nondiscrimination Principles with Civil Liberties.* Washington, DC: September 2016. http://www.usccr.gov/pubs/Peaceful-Coexistence-09-07-16.pdf. Accessed September 30, 2016.

U.S. Department of Health and Human Services. "Clergy as Mandatory Reporters of Child Abuse and Neglect." Children's Bureau, 2015. Child Welfare Information Gateway. https://www.childwelfare. gov/pubPDFs/clergymandated.pdf. Accessed July 10, 2016.

U.S. Department of Health and Human Services. Administration for Children and Families. "National Foster Care & Adoption Directory Search." Child Welfare Information Gateway. https:// www.childwelfare.gov/nfcad/.

U.S. Equal Employment Opportunity Commission. "Questions and Answers about Religious Discrimination in the Workplace." January 11, 2011. http://www.eeoc.gov/policy/docs/qanda_religion.html.

Vazquez, Richard A. "The Practice of Polygamy: Legitimate Free Exercise of Religion or Legitimate Public Menace—Revisiting Reynolds in Light of Modern Constitutional Jurisprudence Note." *New York University Journal of Legislation and Public Policy* 5 (2002): 225–54.

Volokh, Eugene. "Claims by Transgender Schoolteacher (Who Wants to Be Called 'They') Yield $60,000 Settlement, Agreement to Create Disciplinary Rules Regulating 'Pronoun Usage.'" *Washington Post,*

May 25, 2016. https://www.washingtonpost.com/news/volokh-conspiracy/wp/2016/05/25/claims-by-transgender-schoolteacher-who-wants-to-be-called-they-yield-60000-settlement-agreement-to-create-disciplinary-rules-regulating-pronoun-usage/?postshare=8191464189711420&tid=ss_tw.

Volokh, Eugene. "A Common-Law Model for Religious Exemptions." *UCLA Law Review* 46 (1999): 1465–566.

Volokh, Eugene. "Freedom of Speech, Permissible Tailoring and Transcending Strict Scrutiny." *University of Pennsylvania Law Review* 144 (1997): 2417.

Volokh, Eugene. "No, the Oregon Bakers Weren't Fined for Publishing the Complainant's Home Address, or for Otherwise Publicizing the Complaint against Them." *Volokh Conspiracy*, July 10, 2015. https://www.washingtonpost.com/news/volokh-conspiracy/wp/2015/07/10/no-the-oregon-bakers-werent-fined-for-publishing-the-complainants-home-address-or-for-otherwise-publicizing-the-complaint-against-them/.

Volokh, Eugene. "When Does Your Religion Legally Excuse You from Doing Part of Your Job?" *Washington Post*, September 4, 2015. https://www.washingtonpost.com/news/volokh-conspiracy/wp/2015/09/04/when-does-your-religion-legally-excuse-you-from-doing-part-of-your-job/?utm_term=.027ee99f3822.

Volokh, Eugene. "You Can Be Fined for Not Calling People 'Ze' or 'Hir,' If That's the Pronoun They Demand That You Use." *Washington Post*, May 17, 2016. https://www.washingtonpost.com/news/volokh-conspiracy/wp/2016/05/17/you-can-be-fined-for-not-calling-people-ze-or-hir-if-thats-the-pronoun-they-demand-that-you-use/.

Washington, George. "Letter to the Hebrew Congregation of Newport, R.I.," August 21, 1790. Teaching American History. http://teachingamericanhistory.org/library/document/letter-to-the-hebrew-congregation-at-newport/.

Weinberg, Steven. "A Designer Universe?" PhysLink.com. http://www.physlink.com/Education/essay_weinberg.cfm. Accessed July 11, 2016.

White, Ken. "Lawsplainer: So Are Those Christian Cake-Bakers in Oregon Unconstitutionally Gagged, or Not?" Popehat, July 8, 2015. https://popehat.com/2015/07/08/lawsplainer-so-are-those-christian-cake-bakers-in-oregon-unconstitutionally-gagged-or-not/. Accessed October 2, 2016.

White, Mercedes. "Muslim Students Struggle to Practice Faith in U.S. Schools, Seek Accommodation for Religion." *DeseretNews.com*, February 24, 2012. http://www.deseretnews.com/article/765554027/Muslim-students-struggle-to-practice-faith-in-US-schools-seek-accommodation-for-religion.html?pg=all.

Wolf, Susan. "Moral Saints." *Journal of Philosophy* 79, no. 8. (August 1982): 419–39.

Wolfson, Evan. "What's Next in the Fight for Gay Equality?" *New York Times*, June 26, 2015. http://www.nytimes.com/2015/06/27/opinion/evan-wolfson-whats-next-in-the-fight-for-gay-equality.html?_r=1.

Zucchino, David. "At Duke, Many Criticize Decision Not to Broadcast Muslim Prayer Call." *Latimes.com*, January 16, 2015. http://www.latimes.com/nation/la-na-duke-muslim-prayer-controversy-20150116-story.html.

Case Law

Alice Lindstrom; Robert Davis, Plaintiffs-Appellees, v. Postmaster General, 781 F.2d 772 (1986).

Barber v. Bryant, No. 16-CV-417-CWR-LRA, 16-CV-442-CWR-LRA (S.D. Miss. June 30, 2016).

Bob Jones Univ. v. United States, 461 U.S. 574, 580–81 (1983).

Boy Scouts of America v. Dale, 530 U.S. 640, 647–48 (2000).

Bowen v. Roy, 476 U.S. 693, 703 (1986).

Bowers v. Hardwick, 478 U.S. 186, 196–97 (1986).

Braunfeld v. Brown, 366 U.S. 599 (1961).

Brownfield v. Daniel Freeman Marina Hosp., 208 Cal. App. 3d. 405, 409 (1989).

Burwell v. Hobby Lobby Stores, Inc., 134 S. Ct. 2751 (2014).

Cannata v. Catholic Diocese of Austin, 700 F. 3d 169 (Court of Appeals, 5th Circuit 2012).

Church of Lukumi Babalu Aye v. Hialeah, 508 U.S. 520 (1993).

City of Boerne v. Flores, 521 U.S. 507 (1997).

Cohen v. California, 403 U.S. 15 (1971).

Dias v. Archdiocese of Cincinnati, No. 1: 11-CV-00251 (S.D. Ohio Mar. 29, 2012).

Elane Photography, LLC v. Willock, 309 P. 3d 53, 59 (N.M. 2013).

Employment Div., Dept. of Human Resources of Ore. v. Smith, 494 U.S. 872 (1990).

Engel v. Vitale, 370 U.S. 421 (1962) and Abington School Dist. v. Schempp, 374 U.S. 203 (1962).

Everson v. Board of Ed. of Ewing, 330 U.S. 1, 16 (1947).

Gonzales v. O Centro Espírita Beneficente União do Vegetal, 546 U.S. 418 (2005).

Henry v. Red Hill Evangelical Lutheran Church of Tustin, 201 Cal. App. 4th 1041 (Court of Appeal, 4th Appellate Dist., 3rd Div. 2011).

Hosanna-Tabor Evangelical v. EEOC, 132 S. Ct. 694 (2011).

Klein, Melissa and Aaron dba Sweetcakes by Melissa, 34 BOLI 102 (2015). https://www.oregon.gov/boli/SiteAssets/pages/press/Sweet%20Cakes%20FO.pdf.

Lawrence v. Texas, 539 U.S. 558 (2003).

Locke v. Davey, 540 U.S. 712 (2003).

Loving v. Virginia, 388 U.S. 1 (1967).

McDaniel v. Paty, 435 U.S. 618 (1978).

McGowan v. Maryland, 366 U.S. 420, 572–73 (1961).

Means v. United States Conference of Catholic Bishops, unpublished, No. 15-1779 (6th Cir. 2016).

Obergefell v. Hodges, 135 S. Ct. 2071 (2015).

Obergefell v. Hodges, 135 S. Ct. 2584 (2015).

Paul Byrne Haring, Plaintiff, v. W. Michael Blumenthal, Defendant, 471 F.Supp. 1172 (1979).

Pierce v. Society of Sisters, 268 U.S. 510 (1925).

Reynolds v. United States, 98 U.S. 145 (1879).

Roberts v. U.S. Jaycees, 468 U.S. 609, 619 (1984).

SAS v. France, no. 43835/11, dec. 01/07/2014, 36 BHRC 617.

Sherbert v. Verner, 374 U.S. 398 (1963).

The Jesus Center v. Farmington Hills Zoning Board of Appeals, 544 N. W. 2d 698 (Mich. Ct. App. 1996).

Thomas v. Review Bd. of Indiana Employment Security Div., 450 U.S. 707, 718 (1981).

Tony and Susan Alamo Foundation v. Secretary of Labor, 471 U.S. 290 (1985).

Torcaso v. Watkins, 367 U.S. 488 (1961).

United States v. Lee, 455 U.S. 252, 257–258 (1982).

United States v. Seeger, 380 U.S. 163, 166 (1965).
Welsh v. United States, 398 U.S. 333, 340 (1970).
West Virginia State Bd. of Ed. v. Barnette, 319 U.S. 624 (1943).
Wheaton College v. Burwell, 134 S. Ct. 2806, 2808 (2014), 134.
Whole Woman's Health v. Hellerstedt, 579 US (2016).
Wisconsin v. Yoder, 406 U.S. 205 (1972).

Statutes

42 U.S.C. § 18001 et seq. (2010).
42 U.S.C. § 2000cc et seq. (2000).
Harkin, Thomas. "S. Rept. 113-105—The Employment Non-discrimination Act of 2013." Webpage. U.S. Senate, September 12, 2013. https://www.congress.gov/113/crpt/srpt105/CRPT-113srpt105.pdf.
"Code of the Borough of Paramus, NJ." https://law.resource.org/pub/us/code/city/nj/Paramus.html#8544536. Accessed July 10, 2016.
Oregon Revised Statutes, 475.752(4).
Religious Liberty and H.R. 2802, the First Amendment Defense Act (FADA), Hearing on H.R. 2802, Committee on Oversight and Government Reform, 114th U.S. Congress, House of Representatives, July 12, 2016 (testimony of Professor Katherine Franke). https://oversight.house.gov/wp-content/uploads/2016/07/2016-07-12-Franke-Columbia-Law-Testimony.pdf.

ABOUT THE AUTHORS

Ryan T. Anderson, Ph.D., is William E. Simon Senior Research Fellow at the Heritage Foundation. He is author of *Truth Overruled: The Future of Marriage and Religious Freedom,* coauthor of *What Is Marriage? Man and Woman: A Defense,* and coeditor of *A Liberalism Safe for Catholicism.* He has written for the *New York Times,* the *Washington Post,* the *Wall Street Journal,* the *Harvard Journal of Law and Public Policy,* and the *Harvard Health Policy Review.* He has been cited by two U.S. Supreme Court justices in two Supreme Court cases. Anderson has made appearances on ABC, CNN, CNBC, MSNBC, and Fox News. A Phi Beta Kappa, magna cum laude graduate of Princeton University, Anderson received his doctorate from the University of Notre Dame.

John Corvino, Ph.D., is Professor and Chair of the Philosophy Department at Wayne State University in Detroit, Michigan. He is author of *What's Wrong with Homosexuality?* and coauthor (with Maggie Gallagher) of *Debating Same-Sex Marriage,* both from Oxford University Press. His writing has appeared in the *New York Times,* the *Detroit Free Press,* the *Los Angeles Times,* the *Advocate,* the *Huffington Post, the New Republic,* and *Commonweal,* as well as in various academic anthologies and journals. An award-winning teacher, Corvino has spoken at over two hundred campuses on issues of sexuality, ethics, and marriage. His YouTube videos have received over 1.5 million views. Read more at www.johncorvino.com.

Sherif Girgis, J.D., is a Ph.D. candidate in philosophy at Princeton University and a graduate of Yale Law School, where he was an editor of the *Yale Law Journal.* Lead coauthor of *What Is Marriage? Man and Woman: A Defense,* he has written on moral and legal issues in academic and popular venues, including *Public Discourse, National Review, Commonweal,* the *American Journal of Jurisprudence,* the *New York Times,* the *Yale Law Journal,* the *Harvard Journal of Law and Public Policy,* and the *Wall Street Journal,* as well as several academic anthologies. A 2008 Phi Beta Kappa and summa cum laude graduate of Princeton, he earned a B.Phil. (M.Phil.) in moral, political, and legal philosophy from the University of Oxford as a Rhodes Scholar.

INDEX

of Pilgrims, 6–7
privilege of, 217, 219
Church, Frank, 122
Church of England, 7
Church of Jesus Christ of Latter-
day Saints, 20. *See also*
Mormons
*Church of the Lukumi Babalu Aye
v. City of Hialeah* (1993), 10
Cicero, 262
City of Boerne v. Flores
(1997), 16, 39
civil liberties, 111, 116, 147–49
basic goods and, 137–38
of corporations, 157–59
in First Amendment, 150
in state, 128, 134
Civil Rights Act (1964), 247
as antidiscrimination law, 177
for dignitary harms, 191
discrimination and, 184–85
as federal, 254
SOGI laws and, 199–200
Title VII of, 47, 120
civil society
religion in, 130, 144, 171
religious conscience in, 109
state and, 144–45
Clinton, Bill, 16, 122
Coats-Snowe Amendment, 122
common good, 127–29, 148–49
compelling interest
for exemptions, 153
in RFRA, 38–39, 104
complicity, 89
conscience in, 41–43, 252–53
in culture wars, 170–71, 214, 227
of Kleins, 88–90
RFRA and, 161
Conestoga Wood, 159
Congress, U.S., 11, 16, 28, 151

Church Amendment of, 122
First Amendment of, 8
free exercise clause and, 56
Patient Protection and
Affordable Care Act of, 37–38
on RFRA, 153
conscience, 202. *See also* religious
conscience
in abortion, 132–33
of adoption agencies, 114
antidiscrimination law and,
167–68, 227
complicity in, 252–53
dignitary harms and, 172
discrimination and, 165
in FADAs, 122–23
integrity of, 138–39, 141–42
material harms and, 198
medical care and, 115
obligations of, 133–36, 143
as problematic, 62
in religious liberty, 137, 142, 146,
167–68, 171, 227, 252–53
of secular citizens, 65–66, 208,
217, 219, 237
of wedding professionals, 118–19
conscientious objection, 3, 53, 59
conscription, 11, 53
conservatism, 217, 288n212
in Christianity, 105–7
Jim Crow laws and, 191–92
Koppelman on, 198
toward same-sex marriage, 190,
197–98, 219, 224–25
Constitution, U.S., 11, 150, 241
establishment clause of, 8–9, 26
First Amendment of, 7–8
free exercise clause of, 9–10,
45–46, 159
religious liberty in, 7–8
strict scrutiny test for, 153

FADAs and, 33–36, 238–39
government employees and,
119–21, 234
in history, 195–96
invidious discrimination
and, 221
Kleins opposing, 86–90
in *Obergefell v. Hodges*, 2–3, 18,
33–34, 73, 112, 121, 213, 222,
236, 298n9
Proposition 8 and, 97–99
religious liberty and,
118–19, 249–51
Stutzman and, 93–94, 118,
194, 254
Supreme Court on, 21
Scalia, Antonin, 14, 216–18
on religious exemptions, 47,
50, 241
on *Reynolds*, 15, 31
on RFRA, 153
Scientology, 57
sectarianism, 143
secular citizens
conscience of, 65–66, 208, 217,
219, 237
RFRA and, 231–32
Selective Draft Act (1917), 11
self-determination, 134–35
separation of powers, 8
services, refusal of, 202–4, 283n174,
283n175. *See also* LGBT
citizens
for abortion, 191
in culture wars, 169
as discrimination, 220–21
exemptions and, 167–68
by Kleins, 79, 93, 251–53
moral stigma and, 169
Seventh Day Adventists, 28–29
Severino, Roger, 123

sex reassignment surgery
discrimination and, 114–15
HHS on, 199
sexual orientation, as
relational, 221
sexual orientation and gender
identity (SOGI), 4. *See also*
LGBT citizens; SOGI laws
compared to race, 99–101, 102–3,
195–96, 247–48
compared to religion, 102–3
as legally protected traits,
110–11, 176
Obergefell and, 176
social meaning and, 190
wedding professionals
and, 187
Sherbert, Adell, 28–30, 54, 56
Sherbert test
First Amendment and, 12–13
RFRA and, 15–16, 39, 44
Sherbert v. Verner (1963), 12–14, 58
Brennan on, 15, 29
free exercise clause and, 29
on Sabbath, 28–30
in South Carolina, 29–30
Shultz, John, 114
Siegel, Reva, 43, 168
Sikhs, 55
slavery, 73, 195
small business, 82
Smith. See *Employment Division
v. Smith* (1990)
Smith, Alfred, 14, 30–31
social condition, dignitary harm
and, 73–74
social harm, 226
antidiscrimination law and, 163,
177–79, 182–83
contempt as, 179–81
SOGI laws and, 189–91, 198, 222

Torcaso v. Watkins (1961),
26, 270n21
traditionalism. *See* conservatism
traits, legally protected
discrimination and, 74–75, 175–76
SOGI as, 75, 110–11, 176
transgender people, 219, 299n19
Trump, Donald, 95

United States v. Lee (1982), 13, 44
United States v. Seeger (1965), 59
Utah Compromise, 231, 255–56

Volokh, Eugene, 153, 200, 269n11,
284n178

Waite, Morrison, 11, 20–21
Ward, Julea, 119, 209
Warren, Earl, 15
wedding professionals. *See also*
Klein, Aaron and Melissa;
Stutzman, Baronelle

conscience of, 118–19
in culture wars, 71, 75
SOGI laws and, 186–87
weddings. *See* same-sex marriage
Weinberg, Steven, 63
Wellesley College, 185
Welsh v. United States
(1970), 59–60
*What Is Marriage? Man and
Woman: A Defense* (Anderson,
Girgis and George), 2, 23
Wheaton College, 41–42
Why Tolerate Religion?
(Leiter), 49
Williams, Roger, 6
Wilson, Robin F., 82, 120
Winthrop, John, 6

Yoder v. Wisconsin (1972),
12–15, 30

Zubik v. Burwell (2016), 42